A FULL LIFE

The author and Maxie

A FULL LIFE

By

LIEUT.-GENERAL

SIR BRIAN HORROCKS

K.C.B., K.B.E., D.S.O., M.C., LL.D. (HON.)

LEO COOPER

LONDON

1974

First published in Great Britain, 1960
by William Collins Sons & Co Ltd
First published in this revised and extended edition, 1974
by Leo Cooper Ltd
196 Shaftesbury Avenue, London WC2H 8LJ

ISBN 0 85052 144 0

Printed in Great Britain by
Hollen Street Press Limited at Slough, Bucks.

TO NANCY

ACKNOWLEDGMENT

I wish to express my deepest thanks to C. D. Hamilton, Editorial Director of Thomson Newspapers, for his continuous encouragement and help. I could never possibly have written this book without his unfailing support. I am also most grateful to James McDowall of Thomson Newspapers for the trouble he has taken to check the original chapters. Finally I am very indebted to my secretary Miss Weyman for all her selfless work over many many months ; and last but by no means least to Messrs. Collins, who have proved themselves to be the most understanding and considerate of Publishers.

CONTENTS

ILLUSTRATIONS

ILLUSTRATIONS

MAPS

FOREWORD

EARLY DAYS

UNLIKE, AS it would seem, many children of to-day, I had an extremely happy childhood. My father was Lancashire born and after taking his B.Sc. at the age of nineteen he became a doctor, joined the Royal Army Medical Corps, and was sent to India. It was here that he met my mother who had all the gaiety and charm of the Irish. Her ancestors, like a lot of those old Northern Ireland families, had all been Presbyterian ministers and doctors. They were married in 1894 and I was born a year later at Ranniket—a hill station in India. We now led the usual wandering service life, and I have particularly happy memories of the four years spent at Gibraltar when my father was working on the causes of Malta fever—as time went on he concentrated more and more on research.

I used to travel out by P. & O. every holidays from my preparatory school in Durham and the Gibraltar of those days was a small boy's paradise, much more so than to-day, as we had free access to Spain. Life consisted of bathing, hunting with the Calpe hounds, cricket matches, race meetings and children's parties—all great fun. In 1909 my father was posted home to the War Office and subsequently I moved from my preparatory school to Uppingham where I gravitated automatically into the army class. There was never any question of my entering a profession other than the army. My school reports of those days referred to "impetuosity—too prone to answer without thinking—inclined to rush things without making sure of what he is doing." There was, I am afraid, no mention anywhere of an aptitude for work which was hardly surprising as my whole life was devoted to sport. In October, 1912, I passed into the Royal Military College, Sandhurst, bottom but one.

It was a most undistinguished start to a military career. Apart from the games side I achieved nothing at all and remained a gentleman cadet (the equivalent of a private soldier) throughout my time at the college. Let me be quite honest about it: I was idle, careless about my turnout—in army parlance, scruffy—and, due to the fact that I am inclined to roll when I walk, very unsmart on parade. Throughout my military career I have always been allotted a position on ceremonial parades where I was least likely to be seen. To make matters worse I got into trouble with the railway officials during a return journey from Gatwick races. We had gone there with such an absolute certainty for the third race that I had refrained from buying a return ticket in order to have more to invest on the horse. I did not even buy a race card so certain was I of a lavish win. As might be expected the certainty did not materialise and the railway company took strong exception to my return journey ticketless and penniless. The result was three months' restrictions which meant that I was unable to leave the premises during my last term at the Royal Military College and spent the time doing additional fatigues and parades. I was lucky not to be rusticated.

Up to now my life had been typical of that led by many young men with average or slightly below average intelligence who entered the British Army in those days. I was a games addict, did as little work as possible and seemed all set for a normal, somewhat humdrum, military career, but the First World War altered all that.

When war was declared in August, 1914, I was waiting with considerable anxiety to hear the result of the passing-out exam from Sandhurst. My immediate reactions were, first of all, irritation that it should have come in the middle of the tennis-tournament at Littlehampton where we were spending our summer holiday, and secondly, anxiety about my father's reception of the news that I had pawned the revolver which he had lent me and, worse still, lost the pawn ticket. He was certain to want it back because in August, 1914, revolvers were very scarce.

CHAPTER I

ACTIVE SERVICE 1914

THE MOBILISATION arrangements for the B.E.F. in 1914 must have been very efficient, because only four days later I reported for duty with a militia battalion of the Middlesex Regiment at Fort Darland, Chatham. Within fourteen days and still only eighteen years of age I was marching down to the railway station at the head of ninety-five reservists who comprised the first reinforcement for the 1st Battalion the Middlesex Regiment then in France with the British Expeditionary Force. This was, I should think, the last time there was any romance and glory attached to war. It is impossible now after the bitter experience of two world wars to recapture the spirit of this country in August, 1914. As I marched through those cheering crowds I felt like a king among men. It was all going to be over by Christmas and our one anxiety was whether we would get over there in time. And all ranks felt the same. I arrived at Southampton with ninety-eight men, as three more had hidden themselves on the way down in order to get to the war.

I was the officer in charge of the draft, but as all of them were old soldiers it was really they who conducted me to the front. Looting was strictly forbidden and when our troop train through France halted, as it frequently did, we officers leant from the window to ensure that the wayside crops, carrots for instance, were left untouched. Not a soldier was ever to be seen yet the extraordinary thing was that carrots would be certain to figure prominently in the stew which the cooks provided for us that evening. My first lesson on active service was the astonishing capacity of the old soldier to look after himself and be as comfortable as possible under the most adverse conditions. Those famous wagons bearing the words

"Hommes 32-40; Chevaux 8" could not be described as comfortable.

We joined the battalion during the retreat from Mons and everybody was much too busy and tired to bother about us. I was left in charge of my ninety-eight reservists, my first independent command in fact; and I was still in command during the battle of the Aisne. We were not destined to play a particularly important part in this battle, but it was a thrill to come under shell-fire for the first time. We were lining a bank on the top of a hill and when I heard the sound of horses' hoofs behind me I looked down into the valley and saw the Horse Artillery galloping into action. It was a magnificent sight and just what I had always imagined war would be like. Shortly afterwards I was joined by an impressive-looking gunner observation officer who, pointing to a mass of cavalry in the distance asked me whether they were French or German. As a knowledge of foreign uniforms had not been included in my military education I said I had no idea. "Anyhow," he replied, "it is too good a target to miss."

Very soon shells were bursting over the target area and the cavalry scattered. Whether they were our allies or enemies I never discovered. Shortly after the battle my ninety-eight men were allocated to their companies and I found myself a platoon commander. I was lucky, because my two chief mentors, Captain Gibbons, the company commander, and Sergeant Whinney, my platoon sergeant, were both first class at their jobs.

My chief memory of those days, and the memory retained by all platoon commanders, was of marching—endless and exhausting marches. I had never realised before that it was possible to go to sleep while the legs continued automatically to function. It was during these hard, comfortless days that I first met that priceless Cockney sense of humour. A small private soldier in the rank in front of me looked up at his neighbour, who was blessed with a long lugubrious face, and said, "Why don't you give your face a holiday, chum? Try a smile."

Gibbons held me completely responsible for the welfare of the men in my platoon. Woe betide me if I attempted to have my own meal without first reporting to him, " All ranks in number sixteen platoon fed, sir." Once we arrived in pouring rain to find that a muddy field which had previously been rather over-populated by cows had been allocated as our bivouac area for the night. It was a depressing thought, but my spirits rose when the adjutant appeared and said that the officers could sleep in a house nearby where battalion H.Q. was billeted.

Gibbons was furious. " If the men sleep out, we sleep out." My heart sank but I knew instinctively that he was right. But Gibbons's influence did not last long, as on 21st October, 1914, at the beginning of the battle of Ypres, my platoon was surrounded by the enemy and I was wounded and taken prisoner. The war for me was over and my active military career had stopped for four years.

Yet, odd though this may sound, I now realise that being a prisoner-of-war was probably the best apprenticeship for the difficult business of command in war. The lessons were there for the learning, and unquestionably the most important was self-reliance. There was no longer a C.O., adjutant, company commander or kindly platoon sergeant to keep me straight. I was alone, and surrounded by a hostile population.

I was taken to a German military hospital on the outskirts of Lille, where I was placed in a bed beside a private soldier from a Highland regiment who had lost a leg. As I had been shot through the lower stomach, neither of us was very mobile. At that time the Germans were accusing the Allies of using dum-dum bullets, i.e., twisting the sharp nose off the .303 bullet so that instead of a comparatively small hole it caused a ghastly wound.

I had never even heard of dum-dum bullets, but periodically Germans used to collect round my bed, give me a British rifle and shout—I have associated Germans with shouting ever since those days—" Now, you British swine, show us how you make dum-dum bullets."

It was a nasty hospital. The whole time I was there, which was nearly a month, neither our shirts nor our blankets were changed, and we were still wearing the blood-soaked garments in which we had been wounded. As our wounds were suppurating we soon became unpleasant objects.

The most degrading thing of all, however, was the fact that, as a refinement in beastliness, we were not allowed to use bed-pans or bottles, but were forced to heave ourselves out of bed and crawl, because neither of us could walk, along the floor to the lavatory which lay at the end of a stone passage. The sight of our bare anatomy as we crawled laboriously along always excited loud jeers from the rest of the ward.

My Jock companion, a cooper by trade, had managed to save the bowl of his cutty pipe and it was a big day if either of us could retrieve from the floor the stub end of a cigar discarded by one of the German doctors. There was just sufficient stem for him to smoke if he drew his lips right back, but the look of ineffable bliss on his old, weather-beaten face was worth all the indignity of searching for the cast-off stubs.

It was a lonely life, and to add to my misery something seemed to have gone wrong with one of my legs, which had become very swollen. Nevertheless, although I could hardly walk, I was judged fit to be sent back to a prisoner-of-war camp in Germany. My escort turned out to be a *Feldwebel* of the Imperial Guard who had been at the front since the beginning of the war, and was now on his way back to Germany to do some course or other; he spoke a little English, and had once been to London to take part in a swimming race.

At the station I was leaning out of the carriage window when a German Red Cross girl passed along the platform carrying a large bowl of soup with an appetising smell. She stopped, and then, seeing that I was an Englishman, spat into the soup and threw it on the platform. There was a bellow of rage from my escort. He made me sit well down in the carriage while he leant out and collected food from all who passed, every bit of which was passed back to me.

On another occasion we went to the station-master's office to find out about trains. As there was no one in the room, my *Feldwebel* pushed forward a chair for me to sit on. Suddenly the door burst open and in came a typical fat, German railway official.

"Why is this English swine seated in my office?" he shouted "Get up!"

The *Feldwebel* walked slowly over to him, bent down towards the little turkey-cock and said: "This is a British officer who was wounded fighting, which you are never likely to be. He will remain seated."

And I did.

Afterwards he apologised for his fellow countryman, saying: "All front-line troops have a respect for each other, but the farther from the front you get, the more bellicose and beastly the people become."

How right he was. I have always regarded the forward area of the battlefield as the most exclusive club in the world, inhabited by the cream of the nation's manhood—the men who actually do the fighting. Comparatively few in number, they have little feeling of hatred for the enemy—rather the reverse.

Dating from this train journey I have had a great respect for the German front-line soldier. In spite of many stories to the contrary it has been my experience that he fights cleanly. He must not, of course, be confused with the S.S. or Gestapo types of the last war, who were capable of any beastliness.

The British soldier's astonishing sense of humour when in adversity came to the surface again after only a few hours of this journey. A German general, complete with attendant, glittering, staff officers, came to our platform to say good-bye to a German troop train which was setting off for the front. There were all the familiar signs of an official departure—band, weeping women-folk and so on—when suddenly on the other side of the platform there pulled in a long train packed with British prisoners-of-war. Dirty, unkempt, many of them wounded, their morale should have been at its lowest. But when the German general walked across to have a look, there was a cry down the train of: "All tickets, please!"

The more I saw of British soldiers during those difficult days, the more I came to like and respect them. Their morale and sense of humour remained high throughout. The Germans held them in considerable respect, and in one camp inhabited by warrant officers, N.C.O.s and men from all the Allied nations, I saw a notice which said: " German sentries will refrain from striking British prisoners-of-war, because they are all mad." British, mind you. No mention of the other nationalities. The reason was that their madness took the simple form of always hitting back.

This was the second lesson I learned and my affection for the British soldier has increased steadily throughout my thirty-five years' service. I always tell young officers: " There will be moments when your soldiers will drive you almost mad, but never forget this—that we are privileged to command the nicest men in the world."

By the end of the journey the *Feldwebel* and I had become great friends and I was sorry to get a letter from his father some years later to say that he had been killed in the second year of the war.

After some months in the hospital of an officers' prisoner-of-war camp, where I was cared for by a most able Canadian medical officer, my leg was reduced to its normal size, and I emerged into the camp itself, where I found myself living with several hundred British, French, Russian and Belgian officers.

Life in a prison-camp was a severe test of character. The deadly monotony of it all, the same routine day after day, nothing to look forward to and always the sight of that eternal barbed-wire, with the German sentries marching round outside to remind us of our degradation. There was no getting away from it. At the back of everyone's mind was a lurking sense of shame at being a prisoner-of-war at all.

Life was hardest for the older officers, many of whom were worrying about their families. Others realised that their military careers were finished. The great opportunity of rising to the top of their profession had slipped from their fingers and almost daily younger officers were being promoted over their heads. Some emerged triumphantly from the test, but all too many sank into despondency, and deteriorated physically and mentally. Therein lay the danger of prison-camp life. I am not certain which was the greater test of character, the sheer endurance demanded by the harsh treatment and the brain-washing handed out to unfortunate prisoners in the last war, particularly in Japanese camps, or this softer treatment.

Luckily I was young, and most of all this passed me by. As I grew fitter, my whole life became devoted to one thing—to outwit the Germans and escape. In every camp there was a small minority of escapees, mostly younger officers—though a few senior officers, to their great credit, also joined in. Three things were involved. First to get out of the camp, usually the most difficult part of all; then the long trek across country to the frontier, and finally to cross the frontier into neutral territory, usually Holland or Switzerland, from where one would be sent home to rejoin one's regiment.

Escaping, unfortunately, was unpopular, because the commandant usually " strafed " the camp after some successful attempt, curtailing for a period such small privileges as the right to go for walks, or use a certain part of the camp for recreation.

I suffered from one rather bad example of this. After the war had lasted for some time arrangements were made between the British and German Governments for an equal number of their prisoners-of-war, who had been in captivity longest, to be sent to Holland, where they would live comparatively freely but on parole. It was a tempting thought to get away once and for all from the hated barbed-wire and live a normal life again.

But giving parole meant that we relinquished all chance of getting back to our regiments and fighting again. This offer arrived at a time when I was doing a period at the famous Fort Zorndorf, Custrin, a sort of penal-camp to which habitual escapees were sent to cure them of their evil ways. Apart from the fact that it was cramped for space, and we lived in the dark galleries underground with a moat all round, life there was not as bad as it sounded. Nobody was ever sent to Fort Zorndorf unless they had actually attempted to escape, so everyone was of the same kidney.

Many of the prisoners were very clever with their fingers and every week a market was held at which escaping kit was auctioned; boxes with double sides and bottoms, maps, compasses, odd pieces of civilian clothing which had been acquired somehow and even rubber dies cut to resemble the German official stamps. All could be purchased.

The commandant at Custrin was an unusual type for a German because he seemed to enter into the spirit of this escaping business. On one occasion a German search party discovered that the bars in a particular window had been sawn through and were only held in place by putty. Instead of laying a trap outside so as to catch the culprit emerging from the window the commandant merely hung a large notice on the bars carrying in German the word " Useless."

What he did not realise was that we had duplicate keys to his own office and next morning he found the same notice hanging over his table. This, of course, was a stupid thing to do because all the locks were immediately changed but we simply could not resist the temptation to pull his leg. He was renowned for the detailed searches of the camp which were carried out under his orders. So, a specially-drawn map was hidden in a place where it was almost certain to be found. Sure enough a few days later it was borne off in triumph by the N.C.O. in charge of the search party. A little later the British officers who inhabited that room were sent for by the commandant, who complained that he could not understand this map. He was invited to inspect it more closely, and then realised that all the roads pointed to a central lunatic asylum in Berlin.

Having been captured in October, 1914, I was among those designated for repatriation, but to the commandant's fury I refused to go.

" You will be sent down under escort to a camp near Holland and you will be put over the frontier whether you like it or not," he said. " What is more, we shall be very glad to see the last of you."

I repeated that I had no intention of going to Holland and giving my parole. " If I am sent I shall escape."

" We shall see," he replied.

It was soon obvious that no escape would be possible during the road and rail journey to the final camp. I was paid the compliment of being given an escort of a senior N.C.O. and two soldiers, who sat all round me and never let me out of their sight for one moment, even when I went to the lavatory. By the time I arrived at the camp I was getting desperate, but once there my hopes rose rapidly.

Although it was surrounded by barbed-wire and guarded by sentries, this protective screen had obviously not been laid out by an expert, and by this time I was very experienced at getting out of camps. There was one very weak spot which could not be observed by the adjoining sentries. At dusk I climbed over the wire and, hiding in a shed beyond, turned my British-warm inside out. It had a neutral-coloured lining which, in the evening light, effectively covered up my uniform. I had a small compass which, in spite of a rigorous search, the Germans had failed to find, and I set off towards the north.

The streets of Aachen (Aix la Chapelle) seemed endless, and every moment I expected a hand to descend on my shoulder, but nobody took any notice of me at all, and eventually I got out into the open country beyond. I then turned west and headed for the Dutch frontier, which was quite close, with the intention of crossing into Holland that night. This was a mistake, because the frontier in the neighbourhood of the big towns was always more strongly guarded than elsewhere, not because of escaping prisoners-of-war but rather to catch smugglers and, above all, German deserters.

After walking for a couple of hours I came to a railway embankment lighted by arc lamps. I decided to take a small secondary road, almost a lane, which passed under the railway through a tunnel. As I emerged on the far side two figures jumped out of the shadows and a bayonet pointed at my tummy. My bid for freedom was over. Next day I was escorted back into the town and placed in solitary confinement in Aachen civilian jail.

I found myself a popular figure with my fellow prisoners, mostly German deserters, pick-pockets, and petty criminals. Small files and pieces of map of the frontier were slipped surreptitiously into my cell, and I acquired a lot of useful information about the precautions the Germans took to guard the frontier, and the best places at which to cross. When I eventually returned to Fort Zorndorf I was able to pass this information to another habitual escapee, who had also refused repatriation to Holland. I am glad to say that when his turn came he also escaped, and was successful in getting to England and back into the war again.

I hadn't been long in my civilian cell when I was visited by two very angry officers, the German commandant of the camp from which I had escaped, and the senior British officer, a lieutenant-colonel whom I do not propose to name. He said that as a result of my attempt at escape the repatriation scheme might be stopped. He then had the effrontery to say that on reaching Holland he would report me to the War Office for having broken my parole.

He went on insisting on this, in spite of the fact that the German commandant, although equally angry, chipped in to say, " No, I do not accuse this officer of breaking his parole, but of not behaving like a gentleman." Luckily for me, Cartwright of my regiment, who subsequently escaped to England, explained my side of the question to the authorities and later I received a message to say that I was exonerated from all blame.

After the departure of the two furious senior officers I was consoled by the sympathy of my fellow-criminals, all Germans. And I came to the conclusion that life was very odd.

CHAPTER II

PRISONER OF WAR

THIS BUSINESS of escaping was all-absorbing; it was a battle of wits between the prisoners and the Germans. So at the age of eighteen I was already learning another important lesson—to put myself in the mind of the enemy in order to be just one jump ahead. It also demanded extreme physical fitness. Very often the camps were situated many miles from the frontier, involving long journeys on foot, subsisting almost entirely on the rations which could be carried in a pack on one's back.

Escaping was a profession in itself and like all professions the more one worked at it the more proficient one became. One of the most ingenious escapes of the war centred round a distinguished Russian general who died in captivity. The German commandant agreed to his body being placed in a coffin and returned to Russia via Sweden. This particular camp consisted of huts with a space between the floor and the ground level. Some Russian officers cut through the floor of their room and crawled along until they were under the room where the coffin rested. They then cut another hole in this floor and a live captain climbed into the room and took the place of the dead general just before the coffin was due to start on its journey. Two days later the German commandant received a message from Sweden, " In place of one dead general, one live captain has arrived." The poor old general was subsequently retrieved from underneath the floor and buried locally by the angry German authorities.

My first efforts at escaping were very clumsy, and I had the indignity of being caught sometimes even before I got out of the camp at all. But I built up experience, and was quite confident that if the war went on long enough I would eventually succeed. That is why I had refused to go to Holland.

The trouble was time. The usual punishment for each escape was at least a month's solitary confinement followed by a period of some months in a fortress, like Fort Zorndorf, Custrin, from which it was practically impossible to escape. So after each failure there was a longish period before the next escape could be planned. Escapees naturally gravitated towards one another, and moved round together. Unfortunately, as we were sent from fortress to camp, our records, which from the German point of view were very black indeed, preceded us and we were never regarded by the different German commandants as a healthy addition to their flock.

Our reception at Holzminden, a comparatively new camp under the command of that notorious German, Commandant Niemeyer, usually known as " Milwaukee Bill," was far from friendly. He spoke a curious sort of English slang with a strong American accent, and was a very irascible character. On our first arrival he paid us the compliment of parading his whole command, British prisoners on one side, German staff, composed mainly of the sentries who guarded us, on the other. We, the new arrivals, were placed in between. Niemeyer then addressed the assembled throng.

Turning to the Germans he said: " Look well at these criminals and mark them down. If I see any German speaking to them he will immediately be sent to the front." This was the worst punishment with which any German could be threatened at the time. Then turning to the British, he said: " These are not officers and gentlemen, they are criminals, and I hope you will treat them accordingly."

But the dramatic scene was entirely spoilt by his final gesture. Shaking his fist under our noses, he bawled, " You are very clever? Yes? Well, I make a special study of this escaping. You will not escape from here. You think, I, the commandant, know nothing. You are wrong. I know damn all!"

The subsequent roar of laughter from the officers sent the unfortunate Niemeyer stumping off parade scarlet in the face.

The amusing thing was that within three weeks eighteen officers had escaped from his camp and he had no idea at all how we were getting out. He went nearly mad. The sentries were doubled, then trebled. They were ordered to shoot at sight. But still every morning there were two or three officers missing at roll-call. Poor Niemeyer must have had the most frightful visions of being sent to the front himself; yet it was perfectly simple. We just walked out of the main gate at dusk when the guard was being changed.

I was in the first party to go. Our living quarters adjoined the barracks where the German sentries lived. We discovered an uninhabited attic in the top and cut a small hole through the wooden partition which enabled us to get from our part to theirs. We managed to construct a "mock-up" of the German soldier's fatigue dress—a red stripe down grey flannel trousers, a pyjama jacket dyed in coffee and so on. It was good enough to pass muster in the dusk. Carrying our food in a sack slung over our shoulders, which made us look like Germans who had been on some working party, we walked down through the building, across the yard and choosing the time when all eyes were on the guard-mounting ceremony, we strolled through the gate out past the sentry. No one paid any attention to us.

I can still remember the thrill of it; that wonderful moment when, from outside the wire, we could look back at the camp with its sentries, its arc lamps, its barbed-wire. We were free. We were out, with several hours' start, because our absence was most unlikely to be noticed until roll-call next morning. We had, of course, taken the elementary precaution of placing most realistic dummies in our beds.

Unfortunately on this occasion the weather was against us. It was bitterly cold and never stopped raining. After eight days' hard walking, when we were still some fifty kilometres from the Dutch frontier, we were discovered lying under a heap of disused sacks at the end of a barn. Owing to the bad weather the farm-workers, instead of being out in the fields, were all sitting in the barn sorting potatoes.

It was very disappointing, but as always, I consoled myself with the thought that to-morrow is another day.

By the beginning of 1918, although I had not succeeded in crossing the frontier into Holland, I was getting closer on each occasion. But in German eyes I had been branded, quite correctly, as an habitual escapee, with the result that I spent more and more time at Fort Zorndorf, Custrin. And from here, as I have already said, it was virtually impossible to escape.

Then in March, 1918, for some unaccountable reason, the German authorities decided to remove all the British officers from this fortress and send them to other camps. I was partnered with three officers of the Royal Flying Corps, who were prepared to adopt any plan to escape, however hazardous it might be. They were Macintosh, now Sir Robert Macintosh who holds the chair of anæsthetics at Oxford, Robinson, V.C., who had shot down the first Zeppelin over this country, and Hervey, who afterwards became the chief instructor in the London Gliding Club—a most intrepid trio.

We four were destined for a camp called Clausthal, situated in the Harz Mountains, and, in spite of an extremely rigorous search on leaving, we managed to take with us quite a number of useful aids to escape. Small compasses were concealed in the handles of shaving brushes, maps inside the covers of books, German money in the double sides and double bottoms of boxes. British-warms were fitted with civilian linings.

Our arrival was somewhat marred by the fact that Macintosh had succeeded in jumping off the train and escaping *en route*. To my disgust I discovered that the commandant was yet another Niemeyer, brother of that unpleasant character whom I had met at Holzminden. From the outset he realised that the arrival of three little nigger boys instead of four did not augur well for the future good behaviour of Clausthal Camp. We were not welcome.

Clausthal, which before the war had been a hotel, had the reputation of being one of the most comfortable prison-camps in Germany. In contrast to the gloom and squalor of our late fortress, here we found pleasant rooms, a large dining-room and quite extensive grounds, which included two tennis-courts, a miniature golf course and a couple of rough squash-courts built by the prisoners.

But from our point of view there were drawbacks. The most serious was that escaping was definitely unpopular with quite a number of the other prisoners. A few days after our arrival we were had up before the senior British officer and warned that if we tried to escape we should be reported to the War Office after the war, and he would recommend us for a court-martial. He added that escaping was useless; it merely caused unpleasantness for the remainder. Several people had broken out of the camp but no one had yet succeeded in getting across the Dutch frontier, which was over 200 miles away. But two almost equally senior officers told us afterwards not to take any notice of the old fool, as it was plainly our duty to escape if we could.

Clausthal proved a most difficult place from which to get away, because, as with all camps which had been in existence for a long time, every possible loophole had been sealed. Quite a number of the officers were determined to get out if they could. Often, however, some elementary plan organised by people with no escape experience would interfere with a much more promising scheme being prepared in the same area. Eventually, as we had had far more experience than anyone else, we were elected by the hard core of escapees to take charge of all escaping activities in the camp. It was our task to vet the different plans, say if they were possible, provide the necessary assistance in the form of civilian clothes, maps, money, and advice about the best place to cross the frontier.

By this time we were very well equipped with escaping kit. By arrangement with the authorities at home, in conjunction with our families, certain food parcels, sent by some fictitious relative, would contain wire-cutters, maps, compasses, in fact everything we wanted, concealed inside tins, in the backs of brushes, in bits of soap, even in innocent-looking hams.

The Germans were very suspicious of parcels, and no prisoner was allowed to open them himself. In each camp there was a large "tin room." Every parcel was opened by the Germans in front of the officer concerned, who noted the contents, which were then placed in his particular locker. When required, the tins were opened by the German staff, and the contents cut into pieces before being handed over to the officer. According to the rigid German mentality this scheme made it impossible for any officer to receive escaping gear. It never seemed to enter their heads that, in almost every camp, we had made duplicate keys with which, after precautions had been taken, it was possible to enter the tin room at night and remove the contents of Aunt Maud's parcel.

To prevent the Germans becoming suspicious at the disappearance of tins we constantly registered bitter complaints that our tins were being stolen by the Germans, and, in consequence, the unfortunate tin room staff was always being changed. Much of the escaping kit we thus acquired was concealed under the floors of our room, which became a sort of central store. This caused us a good deal of anxiety because of the constant surprise checks and searches carried out under Niemeyer's orders. But little was found.

Though all this was satisfactory, it wasn't getting us very far, for we were still inside the camp. As the months passed, Hervey and I, who were now in close partnership, became more and more desperate. Ill-luck seemed to dog our every attempt, though somehow we managed to avoid actual detection. In one attempt, for days on end we were placed in a large sack which, when the sentries were in a certain position, could be shoved underneath the rubbish in a cart driven by an old man to a dump outside the camp.

All to no avail. The sentries were too much on the alert. An attempt to pull away some boarding, cut through the wire and make a bolt for it failed for the same reason. A tunnel we were constructing, with several others, was discovered by sheer chance.

The most hare-brained scheme of all was to run across the intervening ground at night, place ladders against the wire fence, climb up and jump over. Weeks were spent in constructing and hiding the ladders. Then, night after night, we lay in a ground-floor room waiting for the signal to go from watchers who could see the movements of the sentries from the top stories. Unfortunately, the weather was never quite bad enough to keep the sentries in their boxes, and this plan, too, had to be abandoned.

After five months of fruitless attempts, Hervey had an idea, brilliant in its simplicity. At one end of the camp, separated by a barbed-wire fence, was an enclosure inhabited by the British orderlies who worked in the camp. When orderlies wished to pass from their part to ours, or vice versa, the sentry outside the gate of the main perimeter wire came inside and opened another gate in the fence which separated the two compounds. After the orderlies had passed through, the sentry locked the gate between the two compounds, went out and resumed his normal beat outside the main perimeter wire, locking this gate also. But—and this was the point of the whole scheme—while the orderlies were passing through and he was standing beside the inside gate he usually left the outside gate open.

All we had to do was to join the orderlies returning to their camp at dusk, and as soon as we had passed through the gate into their compound turn left and dash out of the open gate in the main perimeter wire. Admittedly this meant crossing the area outside the main fence, which was brightly lit with arc lamps, and we were certain to be shot at. But the German sentries were such poor marksmen that we hardly gave this a thought. We arranged, however, to separate after passing through the gate, and to meet at a rendezvous some hundreds of yards away from the camp.

The night selected for the attempt could hardly have been better. A concert organised by the officers was being held in the main dining-hall. We slipped away during the last item, and changed into clothes which looked approximately like those worn by the orderlies, who were as usual attending the concert in force. The expert in make-up set to work and gave us each a fine moustache; this was necessary because we were fairly well known to the sentries.

After " God Save the King " we joined the crowd of orderlies walking to their enclosure. Hervey had won the toss and was to go first, so I walked a couple of paces behind him. It was an exciting moment, and I kept on murmuring to the orderlies near me, "For God's sake don't keep on looking at us."

We approached the inner gate with the sentry standing beside it. The outer gate was open. Hervey passed through, but unfortunately he turned just a fraction too soon and made for the outer gate. The sentry leapt forward, caught him by the arm and they started to struggle. Running up behind, I hit the sentry as hard as I could on the back of his neck and he rolled over on to the ground. Hervey dashed through the outer gate, with me after him. I went to the right, as we had arranged, and heard a shot, followed by another. Then I was through the lighted zone into the darkness beyond.

Very soon I came to the rendezvous, but no Hervey turned up. I waited, still no Hervey. I began to fear the worst. Perhaps he'd been shot.

I circled back towards the camp where the most infernal din was going on—sentries shouting, British cheering. Obviously everyone was being rounded up for a roll-call.

But then I heard a more sinister sound, the baying of the police dogs. As I was somewhat weighed down by a home-made body-belt with huge pockets containing the food on which I was to subsist during my 213-mile journey to the frontier I couldn't wait any longer. I was terribly worried about Hervey, who had been my constant companion for months now, and I didn't look forward to the long trek through a hostile countryside by myself, because as I knew well, search parties would be out.

Meanwhile the baying was getting closer. I had once seen one of these Alsatian dogs attack an officer and I had no wish to experience a similar fate. Luckily they were trained to run beside their keepers, who were usually middle-aged German soldiers. I had taken the precaution of rubbing solid alcohol from a Tommy's cooker on the soles of my boots, which helped to kill the scent. I also walked rapidly down a small stream for a hundred yards or so, and gradually the baying became more distant.

The normal procedure on these occasions was to walk all night and sleep by day, lying up in the thickest cover that could be found. It was advisable to go round, rather than through, villages, and this I did for the first two nights. But going across country in the dark, round village after village, proved a very slow business, and it was soon obvious that unless I made better time my food would run out long before I got to the frontier.

So, from the third night onwards, I decided to chance it and walk straight through. It was an eerie experience, for though the villagers might be sound asleep every single dog started barking. Dogs became the bane of my life. One sniffed me out in my day-light hideout and I was forced to slide straight down a steep embankment, taking the seat completely out of my trousers, and run for it. It never stopped raining, which made it difficult to sleep by day as I was always soaking wet.

Still, I was making pretty good time, and, according to my map, by the tenth night I was only five kilometres from the Dutch frontier. This was just as well, because I had finished my food twenty-four hours before, and had caught a bad cold. Very stupidly I had also removed my boots, and my feet were so swollen owing to the wet that I could not get one boot on again.

I realised that the last five kilometres would have to be treated with great respect, because the Germans used patrols, hidden sentries and police dogs to search this frontier belt.

But it was a perfect night to cross. The rain was teeming down and it was blowing half a gale; no sentry was likely to be very alert on a night like this. So, full of hope, I set off across country on a compass bearing. Hour after hour I struggled forward, but still I did not come to a small narrow-gauge railway line which, according to my map, would have been a few hundred yards on the German side of the frontier.

From this point extreme care would be required if I was to get across into Holland unobserved. I might even have to cut through a barbed-wire fence.

Then it began to get light. There was only one thing for it; to hide for the day and make my crossing the next night. Very cautiously I approached a barn on the outskirts of a farm. Stacked high with hay, it was just the sort of hiding place I was looking for. So having helped myself to some eggs, which I ate raw, I clambered up to the top, burrowed deep into the hay and settled down for the first dry day I had experienced since leaving camp.

Unfortunately I had developed a cough which the dry hay seemed to aggravate. Try as I would I simply could not control it.

Then I heard footsteps in the barn below; they moved round for some time, then went out. Some minutes later I heard a party of men returning to the barn. Then, with much shouting, bayonets were stuck into the hay and I was unearthed.

The barn was surrounded by German frontier guards, and when I emerged, there was the Dutch frontier in front of my eyes—barely 500 yards away. It was a bitter moment. To have come more than 200 miles by myself, through the most impossible weather, and then to be caught on the frontier itself was infuriating.

For the heinous offence of having struck and knocked down a German sentry I was sentenced to fourteen days solitary confinement in a dark cell. This is a rather worse punishment than it sounds, because with only a wooden shelf for a bed, and bread and water as fare, the time passes very slowly. In order to prevent one getting used to the monotony, which is easily possible, the authorities provided a bowl of hot soup and a hair mattress every third day.

In my case, however, this was all wasted because the cells adjoined a prisoner-of-war camp occupied by British soldiers, and on the very first day a note was pushed under my door telling me to go to the latrines at a certain hour every day. There, in place of the usual bucket, I would find a parcel containing chocolate, cigarettes and biscuits which had been placed there with the amazing generosity of the British soldier.

Eventually, escorted by four German soldiers in spite of the fact that I could only hobble along, I arrived back at Clausthal camp. To my joy I saw, gazing through the bars of the prison compound, the beaming face of Hervey—very much alive. He had been extremely lucky. After running through the gate he tripped over a bucket and fell heavily to the ground. While he was struggling to get to his feet, much impeded by all the food he was carrying, the sentry had jumped up, fired twice at my disappearing figure and then run up to Hervey *and pressed the trigger*. But he had forgotten to reload!

He then went on pulling the trigger and shouting for help. Several of the sentries came running up, but by then, with many eyes on them from inside the camp, it was impossible to murder

Hervey in cold blood. He was taken off for a period of solitary confinement in the cell where I later found him.

This proved to be the last escape I was to make, for a few weeks later, while we were still undergoing solitary confinement, the Armistice was signed and the war was *over*.

In spite of all our efforts the final triumph of getting over the frontier and back to England had been denied to us. Still I am certain that these four years in captivity were not wasted. I am not suggesting that life in a prison-camp is an essential prelude to high command in battle—far from it. All the same I had learned at an early age and in a hard school to stand on my own feet and make my own decisions, often in a split second. I had also acquired the useful habit of thinking things out from the enemy point of view so that I might always be one jump ahead. These were lessons which served me well later on.

So at the age of twenty-two, although lacking in conventional military experience, I was far more self-confident and sure of myself than is normal in a young regular regimental officer of that age.

The less said about my period of leave after returning to England the better. Though I did not realise it at the time, those four years as a prisoner-of-war had taken their toll. The lonely treks right across Germany with every man's hand against one, lying up by day and moving by night, the weeks of solitary confinement and, above all, the eternal barbed-wire—they had all left their mark.

I was young and physically fit, but my nerves were in rags. I was unable to lead a quiet life at home, and was far too restless even to play games. So I spent every available moment beating it up in London. I had four years of pay saved up, and I got through it all in six weeks, coming home every morning by the milk train.

This was one of those critical moments when a very light hand was required on the reins, and luckily for me it was there. The world to-day is full of so-called " mixed-up kids," often the product of uncaring families or of broken marriages. I was fortunate to have a very happy home and two parents who were devoted to each other, and to whom the mental and physical well-being of their family came first. How understanding they were in all the crises of growing up. I must have been a great anxiety to them, but it was their understanding and patience which saved me during this critical period. Not one word of protest about my outrageous behaviour was ever uttered by either parent.

I know now that my Irish uncle, an experienced neurologist, kept on insisting, " For goodness's sake, keep him *quiet*." But my wise old father merely said: " Leave the boy alone. Let him get those four years out of his system in his own way; he'll be all right."

Two doctors with diametrically opposite views, but one was my father and he was right. At the end of that period I emerged a reasonable human being, though the only concrete results visible at the time were an overdraft at the bank and an intimate knowledge of most of the night-clubs in London.

My mother told me afterwards that she got her reward in that I *did* come home by the milk train! I can see her now sitting on my bed listening to her twenty-two-year-old son with a twinkle in her eye while I told her just as much as was good for a mother to know.

In later years, dealing with the misdeeds of some young officer, I often thought of those days and tried to temper justice to give the young man another chance.

During my time in Germany I had lived for many months with one other British officer in a room with fifty Russian officers. So I had perforce to learn Russian. When, therefore, the War Office called for volunteers who knew the language to go to Russia to help the White armies in their struggle against the Bolsheviks, I immediately applied and was ordered to Siberia. Instead of returning to my regiment for some elementary instruction in military matters and for some much-needed discipline, I set off on what promised to be a far more exciting venture.

In January, 1919, with a dozen other officers also on their way to Siberia, I set sail from Liverpool in a Blue Funnel liner to travel round the world to Vladivostok. It was a wonderful trip, particularly for somebody who had been shut up behind barbed-wire for four years. As we were travelling in a cargo boat, several days were spent at every port of call, Suez, Colombo, Penang, Singapore, and so on. In each place we were almost the first officers in British uniform whom the local residents had met since the war, and their hospitality was prodigious.

We had been told by the local inhabitants in Hong Kong that it was fatal to drink the extremely potent local variation of a gin sling after dark. Two of us decided to try this out, and after dinner we drank several. I remembered nothing more until I woke up in a strange bed in a comfortable room to find a Chinese servant offering me a cup of tea and a plate of fruit. I had a terrible headache.

Suddenly the door opened and the tousled head of my comrade in crime looked through.

" Where on earth are we? " he asked. I replied that I had no idea. It emerged that we had engaged rickshaws the night before, but, as we could not explain where we wanted to go, the Chinamen had taken us, as a matter of course, to the house of a famous lady of easy virtue who, realising our condition, had us put to bed.

Hong Kong had a club famous throughout the Far East. On entering one day I found at the immense expanse of bar a solitary officer. He turned, and, with a distinct north of Ireland accent, asked me my name.

When I told him, he suddenly beamed and said: " If that's so, then I'm your Uncle Charles from Australia! " At the beginning of the 1914 war he had been out there growing vines very successfully, but at once threw it all up to enlist. As there was now nothing left of his vineyard, he also had volunteered for service in Russia, and our meeting like this was a remarkable coincidence.

On 16th April, 1919, we landed in Vladivostok and our picnic was over. We passed at once from the richness and luxury of our world cruise to the filth and degradation of this Siberian port. The place came as a great shock because it was my first introduction to the misery of the refugee problem. Vladivostok swarmed with people who had fled eastward after the Bolshevik revolution. The thing which impressed me most was the fortitude with which the women, many of them reared in luxury, were facing their hopeless future. The menfolk were much more given to self pity.

Most of these unfortunate people had been rich, with large

houses. They were now almost penniless—living in old railway trucks or in any hovel they could find. There were also Cossacks, Khirghiz, Mongolians, Chinese, Japs, with a few Americans, British and French thrown in, and the harbour was packed with ships bringing war material—most of it British—for the White armies.

It was now, for the first time, that I began to realise the size of the task which confronted us. I knew, of course, that the Allied Governments had decided to support the Whites in their struggle against the Red Bolshevik forces, but that was the sum total of my knowledge.

On arrival we were taken to the British headquarters where, sitting in front of a large map, the situation was explained to us.

The Red armies after seizing power in Moscow and Petrograd had overrun most of Siberia. During the winter of 1918-19 the Whites, under command of Admiral Koltchak, had driven them back into Russia proper. Apparently this success had been achieved mainly by the Czechs. After the revolution thousands of Czechs had come to Siberia and, realising that their only chance of survival lay in a cohesive effort, they had formed themselves into a corps under command of a Czech general called Gaida. With the exception of a few battalions formed from Russian officer cadet training units, plus one division of Poles, these Czechs were the only reliable troops at Koltchak's disposal. Now, very naturally, they wanted to go home, and it was our task to train and equip White Russian forces raised in Siberia to take their place on the front.

The British forces in the country in the spring of 1919 consisted of one first-class territorial battalion of Hampshires, a garrison battalion of my own regiment which was on its way home, and two organisations called missions. The first was a military mission with headquarters in Omsk whose task it was to hand over British equipment to the Whites and then train them in its use. The second was a railway mission sent to help the White Russians sort out the chaos on their long lines of communication. We were to join the first of these under command of General Knox. There was also a small French military mission doing similar work, though the bulk of the assistance and equipment was British.

This all sounded excellent. The missions were composed of first-class officers and N.C.O.s, most of them with considerable war experience and, at the end of the war, the Allies possessed masses of surplus equipment. In theory, therefore, we should have been able to remove the Bolshevik menace to world peace once and for all, but like so many grandiose plans it was not working well in practice because the Russians wasted the stores in the most shameless manner and refused flatly to accept advice.

The lot of the would-be benefactor is a hard one, as the Americans have found since the last war. We were warned that the White Russian officers and intelligentsia resented both our help and our presence in their country. One wise old British colonel said even in those early days, "I believe we shall rue this business for many years. It is always unwise to intervene in the domestic affairs of any country. In my opinion the Reds are bound to win and our present policy will cause bitterness between us for a long time to come."

How right he was: there are many people to-day who trace the present international impasse back to that fatal year of 1919. This was well above my head: the whole project sounded most exciting and that was all I cared about.

The Vladivostok of those days was full of graft and vice. We were advised never to go out alone after dark and always to carry a loaded stick and a revolver. There was one particularly unsavoury quarter in the brothel area known to the Allies as "The Bucket of Blood," because it averaged one murder a night. My stay was a short one, and three days later I set off with a cheerful heart on my long journey westwards along the trans-Siberian railway.

CHAPTER III

SIBERIA

We were fourteen British officers and a platoon of British soldiers on a train with twenty-seven wagons full of shells. We officers were due to report to the British military mission, but our first job was to deliver these wagons intact to the town of Omsk, just over 3,000 miles away. This was not quite so easy as it sounded. One British officer had recently arrived at his destination with only six of his original quota of wagons left. At this time railway wagons were worth a lot of money to the profiteers, and it was remarkable what excuses were produced by the local station-masters at almost every stop for detaching the odd wagon which had developed some mysterious defect.

A hot axle-box was the usual trouble. This was my particular headache, as I was acting as interpreter. The station-master was always quite desolate. " But to-day is a holiday," he would say, " No workman can possibly be induced to do any repairs." Every day seemed to be a holiday. As for replacing it with another wagon, that was out of the question. He hadn't seen an empty wagon for months and months. No, the only thing to do was to detach the wagon and go on our way one short. After all, what was one wagon more or less?

I was equally polite, but adamant. We would wait until repairs could be done—thus incidentally blocking one of his sidings.

" A delay of one, two or even three days makes little difference to us when our journey is likely to last for anything up to five weeks."

Invariably, within a matter of minutes, the station-master would return, sorrowful but still polite, with an empty wagon which by a most extraordinary chance he had overlooked in a far corner of his yard.

The fourteen of us lived in one box-car, called a *terplushka*, sleeping in double wooden bunks, and it was cold enough for us to be glad of the stove which burned continuously in the centre of the wagon. Captain Moore, my new-found Uncle Charlie, was in charge of the train, and as he was pretty good on a banjo the evenings passed cheerfully enough. The snow had almost gone but immediately after the winter this Siberian landscape is very bleak and desolate; miles and miles of bare country, small stunted trees, and no undergrowth at all.

As we rumbled steadily westwards at eight to ten miles an hour, the monotony of the journey was broken by our arrival at stations and small wayside halts. For in Siberia the station is the centre of the social life of the district. People come from miles around and there were always dozens of small, shaggy and incredibly tough Siberian ponies tethered at the back of the building, while their owners, male and female, paraded up and down the platform. The arrival of a train was the great moment in the day, and the platform very quickly developed into a small market.

Sometimes, owing to engine trouble, we were forced to stop for longer periods at the bigger stations, and I still remember the night spent at the small town of Manchuli on the frontier between Manchuria and Russia. Bored with being shut up in the train for so long, three of us who were off duty that night—we took it in turns to provide orderly officers, and guards who had always to be posted immediately we stopped anywhere—set off to explore the town.

We were directed to the local night-club though Manchuli did not seem to be the sort of place where one would expect to find a glittering night-life. But the Siberia of those days was a place of many surprises, and, sure enough, we found ourselves peering into a large, smoke-filled room, filled with Russian officers and their lady friends, listening and dancing to a first-class tzigane, or gypsy, orchestra.

As we entered, a fine-looking cavalry colonel jumped to his feet and said: " English, I do believe. Please join me at my table," which we did. It was a cheerful party. The Russians, anyhow in the old days, really knew how to enjoy themselves. Vodka flowed and the small dance floor resounded to the stamp of feet and the jingle of spurs as the dancing became more and more uproarious. The only drawback was that I happened to be the only one of our party who could speak the language, and as the Russians could speak no English I was kept busy interpreting.

Then suddenly, after several loud chords, the band broke into some special tune and everybody jumped to his feet. We of course followed suit, but our host begged us to be seated as we were his guests. So down we sat; the only people in the whole place sitting down, two gypsy girls, and three British officers. We all felt rather embarrassed, but what could we do?

Our embarrassment increased when a swarthy Cossack colonel approached our table. He was a magnificent figure in a wonderful furry cap, long coat with flared skirt girdled with a belt complete with revolver and small knives, while on his legs were the most beautiful long, black riding boots I have ever seen—with enormous spurs which jingled at each step.

" Get up," he shouted. But as his manner was extremely insolent we had no intention of doing so. Our host, the cavalry colonel, leant forward and slapped him smartly across the face saying, " These are my guests and will remain seated, you Cossack dog."

Then the fun really started and the whole place collected round our table. Our host turned to me, bowed, and said, " Will you honour me by acting as my second in a duel which I now propose to fight with this Cossack?"

" Delighted," I replied, though I had not the faintest idea what I was supposed to do. However, at this critical moment a posse of Russian military police, who must have been sent for by the manager, dashed in and we were all arrested and conducted into a private room where a court of inquiry was to be held—two Russian colonels, two girls and three British officers.

Feeling that the moment had come when I had better step in and try to retrieve the situation, I advanced to the centre of the room and delivered an impassioned speech in broken Russian to the effect that we had come all the way from England to help the Russians, and now, right at the start, thanks to our ignorance of their customs, we had caused this terrible quarrel to break out between two distinguished officers from the Russian cavalry and the Cossacks, both of whom were renowned throughout the world for their bravery and skill at war.

The effect was magical! I was immediately embraced by both colonels who, I strongly suspect, were by this time delighted to accept a painless solution to the quarrel. It turned out that the particular tune which had caused all the trouble was the national anthem of the local Cossack chieftain, a certain colourful Ottaman Semenov, who was all-powerful in this part of the world. He lived in a magnificent railway train with an attractive blonde whom we all called Marusia.

Anyhow, the Cossack now insisted on joining our party and, as the troops would say, " A good time was had by all "—until the early hours of the morning. Then three slightly bemused young officers returned to their train in Manchuli station, to find that there also the night had not been without incident.

Although large notices in Russian and Chinese warned the general public to keep away from our ammunition train on pain of being shot, these were not always effective. At dusk that evening the duty officer heard a shot outside. He rushed out to find a dead Chinaman lying on the ground, with a bullet hole between his eyes. He had been shot by a British sentry in bad light, at a distance of 200 yards, as he had tried to enter one of the wagons in search of loot. No one was more surprised than the sentry who, it turned out, had always been a third-class shot.

We expected trouble with the Manchurian station-master when we explained, but we had not then realised the cheapness of human life in this part of the world. " A dead Chinaman," said the station-master, shrugging his shoulders, " a pity! But there are plenty more. I will send a couple of coolies to move the body." In one way and another our short stay in Manchuli was filled with incident.

Up to now we had been passing through a comparatively peaceful region but west of Lake Baikal the country had already gone very Red and Bolshevik bands were constantly raiding the railway. So each night we spent in the sidings of some station, protected by soldiers of the White Russian Army.

We were soon involved in one of these raids. In the middle of the night we were awakened by rifle and machine-gun fire coming from all round the perimeter of our small station. I climbed pessimistically to the flat roof of our sleeping wagon which was my alarm post in an attack.

There was a great deal of noise and bullets were flying overhead, but most of the shooting seemed to be wild. Suddenly I spotted the dark shape of a figure in the branches of a tree a couple of hundred yards away, outlined by the arc lights which surrounded the station. I fired fifteen carefully-aimed shots, but, to my disgust, without any apparent result.

Then all at once the firing died down as suddenly as it had started, and we returned to bed. Next morning I discovered that my fifteen rounds had been fired at a large disused lamp, but even this, I must admit, showed no ill effects from my marksmanship.

In spite of these incidents, on the 20th May we pulled proudly into Omsk station, and handed over our twenty-seven ammunition trucks intact to the British authorities. It had taken us just over a month to complete the three thousand miles journey. Not bad going in the circumstances!

But my final destination was Ekaterinburg, now called Sverdlovsk, some 800 miles farther west, a charming place complete with gardens and a lake—very different from the normal, dusty unattractive Siberian town. It was here that the Tsar and his family were murdered and I used to pass the house every day on my way to work.

In Ekaterinburg I got to know the Russian soldier, for I was second in command of an N.C.O.s training school attached to the Anglo-Russian brigade. It was planned to form a brigade of four battalions, each of which had about seven British officers and twenty senior British N.C.O.s while all the rest were Russian. When this scheme had originally been put forward it had received the enthusiastic approval of the Russian authorities from Admiral Koltchak downwards, but, as we soon came to realise, there is all the difference in the world between approval in theory and practical help. In fact, every conceivable difficulty was put in our way.

When the first batch of recruits, some 2,500 strong, shambled into the barracks we could hardly believe our eyes. In front came the extremely-smart band and drums of the Hampshire regiment followed by the filthiest and most unkempt mass of humanity I have ever seen in my life. Many of them were without boots or hats and nearly all were carrying the most dreadful-looking bundles which contained their worldly possessions. It was soon obvious that we had been allocated the dregs from all the call-up depots in Siberia; thirty per cent were subsequently discarded on medical grounds alone.

The main trouble was lack of interpreters, as only fourteen were available in the whole brigade. General Gaida had promised a large contingent of Czechs who spoke the language perfectly but they did not appear. As very few of the British officers or N.C.O.s spoke any Russian at all there was great difficult in sorting out and training this mass of ignorant Siberian peasants.

Nor was this all we had to contend with. At first we thought that the unhelpful attitude of the civilian authorities in Ekaterinburg was due to the normal Russian inefficiency but we then began to realise that it was deliberate. We had to fight for everything we wanted; water, food, transport. They even declined to remove the refuse from the barracks until they were made to do so by force of arms.

In spite of all these difficulties somehow or other, due almost entirely to the very hard work of the British officers and N.C.O.s, the four battalions began to take shape.

My task in the school was, of course, much easier because our students were all picked men. Moreover Captain Ulhman, my boss, spoke excellent Russian and I could make myself understood fluently but ungrammatically.

It was an interesting experiment which, surprisingly, worked reasonably well. I became quite attached to the Russian N.C.O.s in our school. They were practically all illiterate; just simple, decent chaps, who combined a great sense of humour with considerable peasant cunning. As soon as they realised that we were doing our best to look after them, to see that their food was properly cooked, that they really got their tobacco ration, and that they were paid regularly, they became very devoted.

I know this was so because on two separate occasions later on, after we had been captured, a soldier pushed his way through the Red guards and wrung me by the hand saying: "Oh, Gospodin Kapitan, do you not remember me, Nicolai Vacilevitch? What times we had together in that brigade in Ekaterinburg."

And, looking back, I think they were good times. Those Russian soldiers were tough; they could march for miles and miles, singing the whole time most beautifully. They formed their own choir which was always in the middle of the column. In our innocence, we started off by holding foot inspection on return to barracks, which caused great amusement. They had never heard of such a thing before. But we soon realised that we were wasting our time, because whether or not their boots fitted properly made not the slightest difference to the lumps of hide which they called feet.

A large collection of women and children seemed to belong to our N.C.O.s. Whether they were married or not I had no idea. To our British eyes it seemed very wrong that the barrack room should swarm with women every night, but this was apparently a Russian custom. When we shut the gates they merely climbed in through the windows, so after a couple of days we decided to acknowledge defeat. We insisted, however, that all the women should be out of the place in the morning by the time we arrived for our day's work.

The sad thing was that the better our brigade became the more the Russian officers came to hate us. To start with they used to halt our men in the streets, find fault with them for saluting in the British fashion and then upbraid them for serving under British officers. They then descended to acts of personal violence and hardly a day passed without some member of the Anglo-Russian brigade being beaten up by these Russian officers. The officer standard in Koltchak's armies was, of course, abysmally low. Very few of the old regular Tsarist officers still remained. They, with all their faults, had at least shown courage and knew how to behave but these interlopers who now strutted about in officers' uniform had no intention of fighting at all if they could help it. In fact the rear areas were full of them.

Because of the deterioration in the situation General Knox thought that it would be madness to send the Anglo-Russian brigade into the fighting line where it would be dependent on Russian co-operation which would almost certainly not have been given.

So we never went into battle with our brigade. Orders were received from the United Kingdom that the experiment was to cease and the British officers were to return home.

Many of us were so upset at having to desert the men whom we had been training that we went to the senior British officer and offered to resign our commissions if we could stay on. Luckily for us he was a sensible man and pointed out that, had we gone to the front, we should have been sacrificed needlessly. He was quite right but the departure of the British officers from Ekaterinburg provided a wonderful opportunity for the White officers to twist the lion's tail.

The full brunt of this was felt by George Hayes—who subsequently commanded the 3rd division—and myself, as we had been left behind to act as liaison officers with the 1st Siberian Army. We were constantly accosted by people in the street who said with charming smiles: "What, two British officers still left? Surely the Reds are getting rather close? Hasn't the time come for you to clear out like the rest of the British?" It was most unpleasant.

In our new job Hayes and I owned a small railway train of our own, consisting of three wagons. We lived in one, our Chinese servants and Russian groom in the other, and in the third we kept our horses. If we wanted to go anywhere, all we had to do was to ring up for an engine.

Our main task was to keep in touch with the situation on the front which was worsening rapidly, and report back daily to the chief of the British military mission, General Knox, at his headquarters in Omsk, 700 miles farther east.

As the only way to visit units was on horseback, I used to ride off with my Russian groom, and was often away for up to a week at a time, spending each night in some small Russian village many miles north of the railway line.

In some of these I must have been the first foreigner the villagers had ever seen. When I asked one old peasant if he knew where I came from, he shook his head: "You are not a Russian, that I know from your accent, but where you come from I could not know." "*Ya ne mogy znat.*" This is the stock answer of the Russian peasant to almost all questions.

"Could I be a Japanese?" I asked him. "Of course, Barin, how stupid of me! Japanese, of course." Now, I don't look in the least like a Japanese, but the Japs were apparently the only foreigners whom these peasants had ever heard of.

As soon as we rode into a village, the headman always advanced bowing and offered us the hospitality of his home. Every hut I stayed in was built on exactly the same pattern: two large rooms, in one of which lived the animals, and in the other the people. In this living-room the two grandparents and the babies slept on top of the immense stove, which always occupied at least one-third of the available space, while the remainder, the man, his wife, usually many children, my groom and myself shared the floor.

At meal times a huge wooden bowl of thick soup was placed on the table. We were each given a wooden spoon, and then it was a question of the survival of the fittest. I never took very kindly to this communal feeding, for as a result of long practice they were so much better at it than I could ever hope to be that I usually fared rather badly. Nevertheless, they were kindly, hospitable folk, passionately attached to their small piece of land. How they must have hated the collective farms!

During this time I made friends with the chieftain of a Khirghiz tribe. The Khirghiz are a nomadic people who breed horses, move where the grazing is best, and live in small felt tents called yurta. Whenever I could manage it I used to ride down before breakfast to see my friend, the chief, and having inspected the horses we repaired to his tent where, sitting cross-legged on the ground, we drank that Khirghiz speciality called koumiss—which is mare's milk fermented in casks lined with dung. Although this sounds dreadful it is a most appetising drink. It is, however, extremely intoxicating and I had to be careful on an empty stomach. It would have been most unfortunate if the only visible representative of the British had fallen off his horse on the return journey.

CHAPTER IV

PRISONER OF THE BOLSHEVIKS

THINGS WERE getting steadily worse and the Reds were advancing against very little opposition. The trouble was that as soon as a White Russian battalion arrived at the front—having been trained and equipped by us—it almost invariably deserted *en bloc* to the Red workers' paradise on the other side of the lines.

One day even the army headquarters to which I was attached was attacked by a Red battalion. I sat on the roof of my wagon watching the Reds advance, and trying to decide when was the last possible moment for me to destroy my precious cipher book—all my messages to H.Q. were sent in code—which must at all costs be prevented from falling into enemy hands. It was a difficult decision, because if I destroyed it unnecessarily, it meant going back 700 miles to get another one.

I never had a better view of any battle in my life. In front of me were lines of Red infantry advancing steadily towards us, while the White officers and cadets were hurriedly dashing into defensive positions. Luckily for me and my cipher book, the attack was beaten off within 400-500 yards of our train.

But the writing was on the wall, and we were soon heading eastwards to Omsk. I did not like the look of the situation at all. Hayes and I were a lone English rearguard some 3,000 miles from Vladivostok, our base. Most of the people inhabiting the country in between sympathised with the Reds, and were hostile to us; in fact the only troops who could really be relied upon were the Czechs and some Polish units. Both loathed the Reds and were busy withdrawing to Vladivostok themselves.

To make matters worse, it was now October, with the winter closing in, and the cold of a Siberian winter is almost unbelievable, with temperatures down to forty degress below zero. It was not a bright prospect.

We got back the 700 miles to Omsk without much difficulty, but then our troubles really started. The front disintegrated, and we were told to make our way back to Vladivostok as best as we could. Omsk itself was a seething mass of terrified people, all mad to get away from the Red terror spreading eastwards.

Civil wars are always cruel. Neither side was particularly kind to prisoners, who were often bayoneted out of hand. We were always being shown photographs of atrocities committed by the Reds. But it was six of one and half a dozen of the other, because after being captured we were shown identical photographs as examples of atrocities committed by the Whites. Certainly it was not a gentle affair, and there were sinister stories of Red soldiers hammering nails into their officers' shoulders, one for each star on their epaulettes. It was not surprising that the people were terrified.

A mass retreat is one of the saddest and most despairing sights in the world. Most of these people were quite destitute. Families became split up, and the walls of the stations were covered with pathetic little messages such as: " If Maria Ivanovna should see this, her parents passed here on 10th October, making for Irkutsk." There were only two ways of escaping from the Red tide which rolled inexorably eastward; by train, or by sleigh along the tracks which ran parallel to the two railway lines.

On arrival in Omsk, we were lucky enough to join up with Major Vining and a dozen other British officers and other ranks, who belonged to the British railway mission which had been helping the Russians to run their railways. We were fifteen all told. They were now frantically trying to deal with the chaos in the station-yard, and to get trains moving east.

Vining had secured a couple of wagons on which he had painted the Union Jack. These immediately became the rallying points for all sorts of people who claimed British nationality—Persians, Russians with English names who could not speak a word of English, Indians, and goodness knows who else. We came to realise how very wide-flung was the British Empire. Unfortunately there were a number of women among them. This was the sort of situation where we would have gladly done without the female sex because the journey in front of us was likely to be tough and not the sort of thing for women at all. But we had no alternative and they were all packed in somehow.

On 13th November we pulled out of Omsk in one of the last trains to leave. The Red Army was approaching rapidly. We were attached to a train full of Polish soldiers, and we travelled on the right-hand track which was usually reserved for up-trains. To start with we made good progress, passing a ribbon of stationary trains on the left, or down-track. In fact, we arrived in Novosibirsk, 550 miles away, only one week later.

But from now on things became very difficult. Both lines were blocked with trains standing nose to tail, moving on perhaps a few miles at a time, then remaining stationary for hours. There was no water for the engines, so at frequent intervals we turned out and formed a human chain passing baskets of snow up to the engine. Not much fun this in the bitter cold of a Siberian night, but unless we kept up steam our chances of escape were nil.

The people were now getting desperate. At Tiaga, 150 miles farther east, Czechs, Poles and Russians were fighting for engines and the station echoed to the continuous rattle of machine-gun fire. I managed to wriggle my way into the station-master's office where I was handed a message from Vladivostok. It read: "If the situation seems to warrant it, do not hesitate to take complete control."

Could anything have been better? At this particular moment, it would have taken at least a division of well-trained British troops to have sorted out the situation. But the message did serve a useful purpose: it caused great amusement.

We managed to keep fairly cheerful in spite of the endless tragedies which were going on. Always that steady stream of sleighs pulled by Siberian ponies, with their pathetic burdens, old and young, women and children, some starving, many of them ill, but somehow clinging on desperately to the top of the few possessions which they had managed to save. The sick just fell down and died in the snow—there was nothing anybody could do about it.

Things were going from bad to worse. The Reds were now only thirty miles away and our engine was finished. We managed to get the women and children into one wagon on another train manned by the Russian railway battalion, which we knew had a better chance of getting through than any other. Having seen them depart, the men of the party decided to take to the sleighs.

It was the night of 15th December. We had been retreating for nearly a month, and we had had practically no sleep for seventy-two hours. It was almost dark when I heaved myself wearily on to the top of the loaded sleigh which had been allocated to me. The cold was frightful and the going terrible. Every now and then I was flung off into the snow and had to run to catch up again. But we were forced to walk and run pretty often, because of the intense cold. I was lucky enough to own a pair of Russian felt boots called *pymwy*. They are the only possible footwear in Siberia in winter.

And so the journey went on, riding, walking, falling off, running, hour after hour and day after day. The only time we were really warm was at night which we usually spent all packed together into one room in some village. Eighteen of us in a room which measured twelve feet by ten feet—you could have cut the air into slabs and thrown them outside.

After five days on the sleighs we crossed the railway line again at a small station. The Polish commandant here told us that the line to the east was much clearer now, and then we suddenly saw, standing in the yard, the wagon containing our women and children—a most remarkable coincidence. They felt rather lonely and begged us to rejoin them. So we all crowded in, some forty-two people in a wagon meant for sixteen. However, it was warmer than on the sleighs.

Finally, we came to a longer stop than usual, some eight miles west of the Siberian town of Krasnoyarsk. Then, all around us, we saw officers and men throwing away their arms. It appeared that the Red Army had done a wide encircling movement and had captured Krasnoyarsk four days before. The date was 7th January. We had now been retreating for six weeks and had covered nearly

1,000 miles, but this was the end. It was infuriating to think that all our efforts had been in vain. Here we were, cluttered up with women and children, almost exactly in the middle of Siberia in the depth of winter. We saw no Reds, there was no shooting—nothing. So, working on the principle " When in doubt, feed," we decided to have supper.

Then into our carriage came a soldier with a huge red cockade in his fur cap. He was followed shortly afterwards by a couple of officers, one of whom said he was the Red battalion commander. We were now their prisoners but, having discovered that we were British, they beamed with delight and asked us whether they might join us for supper—a truly Gilbertian situation.

It was difficult to see what the future held in store for us. Hayes and I made an elaborate plan to buy a sleigh and a couple of ponies with a view to escaping over the Mongolian frontier 500 miles to the south-east. Major Vining, who, as the senior officer, was in charge of the party, was perfectly prepared to let us go. In fact he was very understanding about it, but he pointed out that I was the only officer who could talk Russian. So we concluded that it would not be right to desert the rest of the party. I am very glad now that we never attempted this extremely hazardous journey, which would have been difficult enough in summer, let alone in mid-winter.

As a first step we managed to get our mixed party of some forty-two people out of the railway train into a couple of rooms in the town of Krasnoyarsk; this was no mean achievement, because this small Siberian town was bursting its seams with people—Red Army soldiers, refugees, Poles, Czechs, and thousands of White Russian prisoners-of-war.

I spent my day going round trying to get some food or money with which to buy food, because the Omsk roubles we possessed had been declared illegal by the Reds. We were, therefore, penniless. It was not pleasant standing for hours in queues in the bitter cold waiting to see these commissars. Eventually we were issued with bread-tickets, which was something, but even then, like everybody else, we were always hungry. We tried every possible way of getting money and food. I got a job teaching English in a girls' school, for which I received the princely salary of 250 roubles—the equivalent of ten shillings a week—but, what was far more important, I was given some thick soup for lunch. Another man played a piano in a café; in fact everyone did his best to contribute in some way.

One young Canadian officer had the important task of taking our clothes to the market and swopping them for food with the peasants who came in daily from the surrounding country. He was not always very successful, and I can remember how angry I was when in exchange for my last shirt all he obtained was a pair of skates and a bag of nuts.

Obviously this sort of existence could not continue for long, so Vining, Hayes and I decided to pay a visit to the head commissar of all. Our first attempt failed as we found a long queue, which hardly moved at all, stretching right down the street outside the house where he worked. The only thing to do was to bluff our way in.

So, next day, having polished up the remnants of our uniform in order to look as smart as possible, we walked straight to the head of the queue, brushed the sentry on one side and said haughtily: "An English delegation to see the commandant." Everyone was suitably impressed and very soon we found ourselves in the holy of holies—the commandant's office.

On entering we saluted: he jumped up from the table and returned our salute. First blood to us, we felt, because in the early days of the Red revolution saluting was strictly forbidden as it smacked too much of the old régime. "We hold you personally responsible to the British Government for our safety," I said. "Of course," he replied most politely, "but I did not know that there were any British in the town. What do you want?" "First of all, food," I replied, "and secondly to go back to the U.K."

The whole interview was conducted most courteously and he gave us food cards which enabled us to feed not only ourselves but quite a number of starving White Russians as well, but there seemed little prospect of getting home in the immediate future, for, as he pointed out, between Krasnoyarsk and Vladivostok there was a war going on between the Red Army and the Japanese. The railways had broken down, the horses were all being eaten by the starving people and it was mid-winter. "I will try and send you to Vladivostok as soon as possible," he said, "but in the meantime you must remain here." And remain we did.

After a month of this sort of existence, the headquarters of the 5th Red Army moved into the town and as a soldier I was interested to see how the Bolshevik or Communist Army really worked. I was sorry for the officers, most of whom had served in the Imperial Russian Army. The only reason they were now fighting for the Reds was because their families were held as hostages. One mistake and their wives and children would be thrown into prison and they themselves would be executed.

The real power in the army headquarters lay in the hands of the three political commissars who sat in a room together and vetted every order before it was sent out. The army itself was a very happy-go-lucky affair, with little discipline, run entirely on the friend or *tovarish* principle. No officer was allowed to wear the hated epaulettes which belonged to the bad old days of the Tsar's army.

The whole thing was, of course, extremely inefficient from the point of view of actual war, and the only reason the Reds were victorious was because they did have the backing of the people, and the Whites were even more inefficient. What a contrast to the Russian army of to-day, with its rigid discipline in which privates have to salute even corporals. The Russian officer caste has now become far more exclusive than it was even in the Tsar's army. Epaulettes are worn proudly again and a Russian major-general receives more pay than his counterpart in the American army.

The head political commissar of the 5th Army was a fanatical Bolshevik and a difficult customer to tackle. From the outset his attitude was quite clear, for he said: "If you will now carry out the same work for the Red army that you have been doing with the White armies you will be given plenty of food, money, and good quarters. If not there is always the prisoner-of-war camp on the outskirts of the town."

This was no idle threat. Our present existence, packed like sardines into two rooms and short of food, might not be ideal, but it was heaven compared with life in the ghastly P.O.W. camp where 40,000 White Russians were dying at the rate of 200 a day. Nevertheless, we were British officers and N.C.O.s and there could be no question of our working for the Reds. Vining made this quite clear to the commissar, and he never wavered in this attitude during the whole time we were in Russia, in spite of repeated threats from the Bolshevik authorities.

Suddenly, orders were received that we were to go home; though whether via Vladivostok or back through Moscow was not clear. Little did we care, as with light hearts we moved down to a fourth-class railway carriage in the station and made the acquaintance of the Red soldiers who were to be our guards.

But of course nothing happened. It never did in Russia. We merely sat in the wagon for days on end in a siding at Krasnoyarsk station.

Then the worst happened. I began to feel very ill, a high temperature, constant sickness, and a burning thirst. This was the blackest moment of my life, for in the anxious eyes of the others I could read one word—typhus, that dread disease which was sweeping through Russia, carried from person to person by lice. It was almost impossible to free ourselves from these filthy vermin. There were reputed to be 30,000 cases of typhus in Krasnoyarsk alone. Luckily by this time we were inured to death because we had been living for so long literally surrounded by dead. Naked corpses were stacked on the platforms, and sleighs packed with frozen bodies were such a common sight in the streets that no one even glanced at them. It was not the thought of death which worried me, but the fear of a Russian hospital. All the so-called hospitals were crammed, and I knew only too well what they were like. In one which I had visited, the patients were lying unwashed in their clothes in serried ranks on the floor. The corridors had been used as lavatories. The stench was so overpowering that I had been sick before I could get outside. It seemed a cruel fate that this should have happened to me just when we were about to go home, because if I had typhus there could be no question of my remaining in the crowded railway wagon.

Next day a doctor arrived to examine me. One look at his face was enough; I had got it all right.

By this time I was delirious, I have only vague memories of a sleigh journey, and then being laid on a bed—not on the floor as I had expected. Among the features of this disease are the extremely high temperature, deliriousness and appalling nightmares. To this day I can remember these dreams in which I went through all the tortures that the most diseased imagination could produce. I was a traitor to my country. I had sold my dearest relations to the Reds, and so on.

When I regained consciousness some six days later I was tied down to my bed with ropes, my arms were bandaged and my lips so swollen I could only swallow water a drop at a time. I could not make out where I was but I was too weak to care. Then beside my bed I saw the friendly figure of George Hayes. We had been together the whole time in Russia, and when I was taken to hospital he had moved out of the train into a room so as to be near me, and every day he paid a visit to the hospital. He was a brave man because even though he wore a raincoat buttoned up to the neck and had covered himself with anti-louse powder he ran a very big risk of being infected.

Gradually the picture became clearer to my mind. Thanks to the efforts of Vining and Hayes I had been moved into the best hospital in the town, which actually possessed beds. It had originally been a school. There was one heroine of a Russian nurse, and half a dozen orderlies to look after 125 patients. Most of the doctors had become casualties themselves and one exhausted young man used to visit our hospital for one hour a day, if we were lucky.

But the chief problem was food. A typhus patient after he has passed the crisis needs building up with good food, but all that was available here was black bread and thin soup. Somehow or other Hayes managed to get me some milk and white bread, and this undoubtedly saved my life. According to the nurse I had been a most obstreperous patient, had broken the ropes which tied me to the bed, and had smashed the window with my fists trying to get out. Hence the wounds on my arms.

One of the most interesting things about that hospital was the bed psychology. There were not enough beds to go round, so with the exception of one single bed in a corner we were three people on two beds. Not a very happy position if the next-door patient happens to be a hairy great Cossack in the delirious stage of this beastly disease. The burning ambition of everyone in the room was to get moved to that single bed. I had occupied it until my crisis had passed, when I was moved away and my place was taken by another bad case. We became dreadfully callous and discussed endlessly whether the occupant of the bed was likely to die in the near future and which of us might be lucky enough to take his place.

In spite of everything I now made rapid progress, and was delighted to hear that the remainder of our party, instead of having departed as they had hoped, were still sitting in the same old siding.

On 18th March, after nine adventurous weeks in Krasnoyarsk, we finally left for Irkutsk 600 miles to the east, the first stage, we hoped, in our journey home via Vladivostok. But we remained there for the next two months. It was in Irkutsk that I met my first woman commissar. She was an awesome sight, tougher than any man I have ever seen. Her hair cut short, a cigarette in the corner of her mouth, a skirt which hung round her like a sack and a large revolver fastened to her belt. I would rather have tackled six men commissars any day.

It was interesting to see the effect we seemed to produce on the Red soldiers who were sent to us as guards. To start with they were very strict and regimental, but after a few days we always became great friends and they invariably wept when they were relieved.

We were destined not to return home by Vladivostok at all. On 12th June we set off to the west and for the next six weeks, with many stops and starts, we trundled steadily along the railway line until we arrived in Moscow, 3,500 miles away. At last we felt that we were really going home, but by now we should have known better.

Instead of home we found ourselves for the first time in a proper prison-camp, inside the walls of what had previously been the Ivanoffsky Monastery. Here were 457 prisoners of whom forty-five were women; generals, admirals, politicians, common or garden thieves, counter revolutionaries, speculators, ex-ladies-in-waiting from the Tsar's court, and prostitutes, all mixed up together. It was the most pathetic place I have ever seen, because all these people were without hope of any sort. Some indeed had gone mad.

One distinguished elderly Russian general was in charge of the lavatories where he worked without ceasing all day. The trouble was that he strongly resented anyone entering his domain. The only method of doing so was to click your heels, salute and shout out in a loud voice, "Your most Highest. May I have the privilege of using your lavatories to-day?"

He would then return the salute most punctiliously and shout permission in an equally stentorian voice. Honour was thus satisfied and all was now plain sailing.

The prison fare was slow starvation. Three-quarters of a pound of black bread in the morning, some boiled grain at midday and in the evening some watery soup made from highly-flavoured fish, or meat which was often horse flesh. The only thing that kept the prisoners alive was the food their friends and relations brought them in. Fortunately for us there was a French organisation in Moscow run by a Madame Charpentier and her two daughters which was helping to feed destitute foreigners. If it had not been for these very gallant women we should unquestionably have starved. Twice a week, at great personal risk, they brought us in extra bread, potatoes and sometimes even a small quantity of eggs and sugar. Even so I always used to eat my bread over a piece of paper—so that not a single crumb would be wasted.

A constant battle was waged between ourselves and the Bolshevik authorities over the question of work but in spite of repeated threats we continued to refuse to do anything which would in any way benefit the Reds. How we got away with this I do not know but we did.

From time to time someone would depart from the camp "without baggage." Those were sinister words—we all knew what that meant. None of them was ever seen again. After a month we were moved to another prison in the former Andronoffsky Monastery where life was much the same.

Then one day the unbelievable happened; we were visited by an official from the Red Foreign Office, a fat little man in riding breeches who brought us some of the best news I have ever heard in my life. In accordance with an exchange scheme arranged between our two governments we were to return to the U.K. at once. Our departure next day to Petrograd was entirely spoilt, for me at any rate, by the sad, white faces of our fellow prisoners looking out from the monastery windows. They, poor devils, had no kindly government to look after their interests and their fate was all too certain.

During this last period in Russia we all received offers of marriage from Russian women. " If only you will marry us so that we can get over the frontier out of Russia," they would say, " we will promise never to worry you again." It was a difficult situation for we felt very sorry for these unfortunate women and would gladly have helped them to escape from the country. But we all realised that we could not possible just abandon them on the other side of the frontier. So after much discussion and soul searching we had to say " No."

On 29th October—eighteen months after I had entered the country on the other side—Vladivostok—we crossed the frontier into Finland and freedom. I turned and shook Vining by the hand. Thanks to him our morale had always been high and discipline in our strangely assorted party had withstood the strain of all these months of captivity. On his shoulders had rested the ultimate responsibility and now he had brought the whole party safely out of the darkness of Bolshevik Russia into the light of the free world again. It was a great moment.

We came home via Finland and Denmark, and the first part of the journey from Helsinki to Copenhagen was made in almost regal state—or so it seemed to us—on board the British cruiser H.M.S. *Delhi*. What the Royal Navy must have thought about us I cannot imagine for it was a most peculiar-looking military party, dressed in all sorts of odd garments, which climbed up the gangway into their beautiful ship. But the hospitality of the senior service did not fail. We couldn't have been more kindly treated. The captain even went so far as to move into his sea-cabin by the bridge in order to put his quarters in the stern at my disposal.

In Copenhagen we were met by English-speaking Danes who looked after us during our stay in their capital. After the squalor of Russia it was wonderful to experience the comfort of the Hotel Angleterre and to dine in Wievells Restaurant. I shall never forget the kindness of those hospitable Danes.

It wasn't until I met my parents on our arrival in London that I realised what they must have suffered on my account, for I had disappeared into Russia and literally passed out of their lives for over a year.

So ended my extremely unorthodox preparation for higher command. I cannot pretend that my military education had benefited to the slightest degree from my sojourn in Russia. My only claim to distinction at this period of my career, and I was now twenty-six years old, was an intimate knowledge of prison life both in Germany and Russia. These seemed not the slightest chance of a successful career for me in the army.

Yet I wonder whether the varied experiences of those years were not an excellent preparation for the stresses and strains of command in war. I had learned to live rough and depend on nobody but myself and, having experienced the seamy side of life to the full, I was unlikely to be taken by surprise, however unexpected the crisis might be. Orthodox military life in those days was not calculated to develop the qualities of robust initiative so necessary in a commander on the battlefield. The inevitable economies which afflict all military forces between wars made regimental soldiering in the United Kingdom a frustrating business. The British Army at home had been reduced largely to a flag basis. On exercises lance-corporals carried boards round their necks bearing the words "This represents a section." When they wanted to carry out a reconnaissance they hung the board on a tree and went forward as a scout themselves.

We have all been amused by the story of the young officer who, at the start of the last war, on receiving his first orders to move out into the desert to fight the Italian Army, had asked his commander whether the Italians understood that a green flag represented an anti-tank gun. That was the depth to which we sank between the wars.

CHAPTER V

BETWEEN TWO WARS

When I returned to my regiment as a captain I was lucky, for the 1st Battalion The Middlesex Regiment then formed part of the British Army of the Rhine. For us in the occupation forces life in Cologne was very pleasant, because, owing to the chronic inflation of the German mark, we always had plenty of money, a most unusual experience for me.

It was all too easy. I opened an account for £10 sterling in a German bank and as each day the pound become worth more in German currency all I had to do was to call and draw out the extra marks. Towards the end of this period we used to get the weekly pay for our companies in sacks. But the Germans suffered terribly. Here were all the horrors of galloping inflation. The more expensive bars were filled with fat profiteers and their hard-faced, brassy mistresses who drove round in huge cars and seemed to batten on the wretched, starving, professional classes.

I was horrified to meet a distinguished German professor and his family who never saw meat at all and could only afford potatoes for their one main meal of the day. Prices in the shop windows were altered four or five times a day, but owing to protests from the British garrison, the N.A.A.F.I. canteen promised to keep their prices stable for a week. By the end of the second day some wonderful bargains were available because the mark had continued to fall.

The result was fantastic. The whole garrison descended on the N.A.A.F.I. like a crowd of vultures. There were lorries and cars blocking all the streets round their premises, and women were diving for the counters and seizing anything they could lay their hands on, golf balls, bottles of whisky, fruit, it didn't matter, it was a bargain. I don't think anybody who has not witnessed at first hand the real horrors of inflation can understand what it means. I came away convinced that any sacrifice was worth while in order to avoid this economic cancer.

The next few years were occupied by many and varied activities. In April, 1921, the battalion returned to the United Kingdom for duty in connection with the coal strike. Then came Ireland during "the troubles" where our life consisted of searches for hidden arms, patrols, keeping a lookout for road-blocks and dealing with ambushes organised by the Sinn Feiners—a most unpleasant sort of warfare and not unlike what has been going on in Cyprus recently.

This was followed by a trip to Silesia in order to maintain law and order during a plebiscite which was being held there to decide on the frontiers between Poland and Germany. Tempers among the local inhabitants ran high and it required considerable tact to prevent an ugly situation developing among the thousands of Polish miners who came out on strike as a protest against our presence in their district. These cold war activities, as they would be called to-day, ended in October, 1923, when we returned to orthodox peace-time soldiering as part of the 1st Guards Brigade in Aldershot. Owing to the shortage of men, which made training very difficult, life centred more and more round games and in 1924 as an added sporting interest I became involved in the modern pentathlon.

There is something romantic about this event which has its origin in the ancient Greek Olympic games. In those days the pentathlon, a contest of five events—in all of which each competitor had to take part—was considered to be of such importance that the winner was acclaimed "Victor of the games." The modern pentathlon, as reconstituted in 1912, is based on the conception of a courier carrying dispatches through a hostile country. He starts by riding a horse across country, but if he becomes dismounted he must then be able to continue his journey on foot—by running. As the bridges may be guarded he should be prepared to swim across any river encountered during his journey and he must be capable of defending his dispatches both with sword and pistol. So there are the five events in which we had to compete, riding, swimming, running, fencing and revolver shooting.

I was fortunate enough to win the championships in this country and so was selected with three others to represent Great Britain in the Olympic games which were held in Paris that year. For four months we were struck off all duties in order to train and at the end of this period I was superbly fit but the standard of performance in Paris was so high that I finished well down in the order of merit.

Unlike certain other international contests this particular event seems to spread a spirit of friendship and co-operation among the competitors—a very important factor in this shrinking world of to-day.

At the conclusion of these 1924 Olympic games an international party was taken round Paris by one of the young French competitors in the modern pentathlon. He kept on looking at us anxiously and saying: "Tell me—what really interests you, gentlemen?" As we had been in strict training for six months it was difficult to decide what forbidden fruit to sample first. Anyhow, it was a truly memorable night which resulted, I am afraid, in my running dead last in the final of the army mile a week later—much to the disgust of my regiment.

At this stage of my life a disproportionate part of my time was devoted to games, particularly during the early days at Aldershot. I was now unquestionably in danger of ruining any chances of success which I might have had by allowing sport to fill my life to the exclusion of everything else. But fortunately for me Aldershot was quite close to my parents' house at Hersham in Surrey, and I went home frequently. This gave my father a chance to bring his influence to bear on his work-shy, sport-loving son. Nothing would satisfy him but that I must work hard in order to get into the Staff College, Camberley, where regimental officers did a two-year course to study the wider aspects of their profession. There was, however, fierce competition to get there because, unless an officer bore the magic letters P.S.C. (Passed Staff College) after his name, he was unlikely to reach the higher ranks of the army. So, driven on by his constant urging, I at last started to work hard at my profession and at languages.

In January, 1927, when I was preparing to take the entrance

examination to Camberley, my battalion was ordered to form part of a division earmarked for China, where trouble was expected as a result of the Chinese civil war. The instructions, however, said that any officers working for the Staff College were to stay behind in this country. This venture in China sounded most exciting, just the sort of thing to appeal to young men like us, and it was automatically assumed by all my brother officers that I would chuck up the Staff College and not leave the battalion at that particular moment.

When I told my father that I proposed to go to China he listened quietly as always. Then he said just as quietly but with great firmness, " China will be a picnic, that's all. There is only one thing that matters to you now—to get into the Staff College." As might be imagined I was not very popular with the regiment when they heard that I was staying in England. But as usual, my father was right. China was, in fact, a picnic and I eventually got into the Staff College. That was the turning point in my life as a soldier.

The departure of the 1st Bn. the Middlesex Regiment, my military home, for China left me a sad and lonely man, but I was soon up to my eyes in a new job with the Territorial Army which appealed to me immensely. In January, 1927, I became adjutant of the 9th Battalion the Middlesex Regiment with headquarters at Pound Lane, Willesden, and outlying companies in the Hendon and Wealdstone districts. And so I made my first contact with those truly remarkable people, the British territorials.

It has always seemed to me a curious phenomenon that in this, the most non-military of countries, where, ever since the days of Oliver Cromwell the army has been regarded with extreme suspicion, there should exist in their thousands these enthusiastic people who after a hard day's work are prepared to desert their families in the evening to travel, in many cases, long distances to some bleak, dreary drill-hall (now called T.A. centres) for military training.

Yet this happens almost every night in the week all over the country, and the curious thing is that the more difficult the authorities make it for these dedicated people, the more the T.A. seems to flourish. There was before the war, and to some extent, still is to-day a chronic shortage of cash, accommodation and men, but if the Territorial Army was called upon to-morrow it would render the same first-class service to this country that it did in the last two world wars. I was particularly glad when I was commanding an infantry division during the last war to be able to recommend a T.A. officer aged thirty-two to command one of the only two regular battalions in the division.

Up to now I had never met any territorials and indeed knew practically nothing whatever about the civilian world which existed outside the narrow confines of life in the Regular Army. I found it a most invigorating experience and a vital step in my military education because, after all, these are the people who in the final analysis win or lose our major wars. Moreover as a Territorial adjutant I had to be a jack-of-all-trades, organise training, set week-end tactical exercises, run boxing shows, dances, tattoos, have an intimate knowledge of the many regulations which governed the Territorial Army, and act as a sort of father confessor to the officers and men about their civilian occupations.

The time I spent with the 9th Middlesex was not only valuable from the point of view of my military education, it was also a very happy and momentous three years.

I became engaged to be married at an odd place, outside Wormwood Scrubs Prison, on my way to a dance at Pound Lane drill-hall, and was married a few months later, at the Savoy Chapel, to Nancy Kitchin. This story is mainly concerned with my military life and I have the strongest objection to baring my family life in public so I will only say that up till then my eyes had been completely closed to beauty of any sort. It never even struck me that the army barracks in which I lived were supremely ugly buildings. Old furniture, old houses, meant nothing to me at all and I don't remember ever entering a picture gallery of any sort. My wife is an artist or, as she would prefer to call it, "puts paint on canvas," and thanks entirely to her, my life is now much fuller and my appreciation of beauty is increasing steadily.

My daughter was born in the following year and like so many other military families we started the merry-go-round of military stations and lived in some twenty-six different houses in our first twenty years of married life.

Being married was an added incentive to work for the Staff College. Moreover my father kept on insisting that I should take special courses and study even harder with this one end in view.

At the time my prospects of a successful career in the army were far from bright. In addition to my inauspicious start as a prisoner-of-war in Germany and Russia I had now spent fifteen years as a captain, and owing to the block in promotion I was most unlikely even to get command of my own regiment. Nevertheless he persisted, and finally at the fifth and last attempt I secured a nomination to that seat of all military knowledge, the Staff College, Camberley, where I joined for the two-year course in 1931.

In the entrance hall to the Staff College there are racks where letters and papers for the students are placed, and it is here that the senior and junior divisions congregate before going to their lecture halls. When I gazed round on that first morning I looked upon some 120 officers, almost all of whom in due course were to play a prominent part in the 1939-45 war. In the senior division were two captains; Captain M. C. Dempsey, M.C., of the Berkshire regiment who subsequently commanded the 2nd British Army throughout the fighting in north-west Europe, and Captain W. H. E. Gott, M.C., of the K.R.R.C., one of the best-known corps commanders in the desert. Both were very keen horsemen and Dempsey was a first-class cricketer. Those were their chief claims to fame at this time.

We think that our course which joined in 1931 contained more students who later rose to command divisions and corps than any other. Moreover Nicholson (Adjutant-General), Brownjohn (Quartermaster-General) and Kirkman (Quartermaster-General), all eventually became members of the Army Council, while Simpson (Lieut.-General Sir Frank E. W. Simpson) proved a most successful Vice-Chief of the General Staff during the war. It was the practice for a naval officer to join the course for the final year, and our sailor turned out to be that remarkable all-rounder Warburton-Lee who won the V.C. at Narvik.

In those years before the war Camberley provided probably the best military education in the world and I have no doubt at all that the high standard of staff work in the army during the last war was due to this instruction.

I say this deliberately after studying the systems in the staff colleges of other countries.

We were also fortunate in our commandant, General Sir John Dill, a brilliant soldier, who, after commanding the 1 Corps in the British Expeditionary Force in 1939, became C.I.G.S. He was a man of the highest integrity, great charm and with a first-class brain. It is only recently that he has received credit for the magnificent work which he did as the senior British representative in the U.S.A. during the last war.

General Marshall liked, and trusted him completely, which made all the difference to Anglo-U.S. co-operation at the highest military level. He died on 4th November, 1944, and was buried in Arlington Cemetery in the U.S.A., the highest honour the Americans can bestow on a foreigner.

He was also a man with a sense of humour. One of my brother officers on the course had won several decorations for gallantry during the 1914-18 war but did not show much promise as a staff officer. At his final interview with the commandant, Dill is reported to have said: " You would be a wonderful man to have by my side in a tight corner on the battlefield. But, if you were on my staff and I found myself in such a predicament, I should have no doubt at all about who had been responsible for getting me into it."

The system of instruction by which officers studied and worked out military problems in syndicates could not have been better. In fact in this direction the army was in advance of the civilian world. It is an interesting fact that most of the staff colleges now run by civilian firms are based mainly on the Camberley pattern.

When at the end of our two-year course I heard that my first staff appointment was to be a staff captain in the Military Secretary's branch of the War Office I was bitterly disappointed because I loathed the idea of serving in Whitehall. I was quite wrong.

As soon as I arrived it became apparent that the work carried out by this particular department was extremely interesting. Under the guidance of the Military Secretary and Deputy Military Secretary, my sub-branch, called M.S.2, was responsible for the promotion of all regimental officers from 2nd lieutenant to lieutenant-colonel, and we had access to the confidential reports which were rendered annually on each officer in the army. I took over from Dempsey who in his turn had succeeded MacMillan, later on a distinguished corps commander who ended his service as General Sir Gordon MacMillan of MacMillan, Governor-General of Gibraltar—so M.S.2 must have been a breeding ground for generals.

The work was completely strange to me and to start with I made many mistakes. It was with considerable trepidation that on one occasion I reported to my chief that I had inadvertently written to offer accelerated promotion to an officer who was dead. The annual reports on officers are made probably by as many as three senior officers who are serving over him. All these reports are kept in a book and everything good is underlined in blue, bad in red. This book very soon provides a most comprehensive commentary on an officer's character and it is extraordinarily interesting to see how, over the years, the same characteristics tend to appear, although the reports are rendered by different people.

I soon found that few secrets were hidden from M.S.2. The shortest and most damning report I have ever read was compiled by a distinguished cavalry commander who merely wrote, "I would hesitate to breed from this officer."

After two years as a staff captain I was delighted to learn that I had been appointed brigade major of the 5th Infantry Brigade in the 2nd Infantry Division at Aldershot. Once again I was to take over from Dempsey. It is the ambition of every young staff officer to become a brigade major and as this particular brigade formed part of the embryo expeditionary force I couldn't have been more fortunate. As chief staff officer responsible to my brigadier for three regular infantry battalions, I was now able to put into practice the results of my two years' training at Camberley.

During the next two years the 2nd Division was commanded by two fine soldiers, Wavell and Wilson. "Jumbo" Wilson was a shrewd tactician who invariably put his finger on the weak spot in any exercise, and from him I learned a lot, but the man who had a profound influence on my whole military career was Wavell, who, in my opinion, had probably the most brilliant brain of any general I have ever met. From him I learned the value of really imaginative training.

Exercises organised by Wavell were always a challenge and a joy, never a bore. There was one, for instance, in which our 5th Brigade was sent to protect the Golden Fleece—of all things! As a matter of fact we lost it but not for want of trying by everyone from the brigadier down to the newest-joined recruit. What an astonishing contrast he was. This brilliant, imaginative brain lay behind the most expressionless, poker face I have ever come across. Wavell wrote brilliantly, but never spoke at all if he could help it. On arrival young officers were warned that if they met a man who looked like a gamekeeper and said nothing, he was certain to be the divisional commander.

One night when dining in the Wavell house at Aldershot, I found myself with the wife of an up-and-coming young staff officer sitting between the divisional commander and myself. With a gleam in her eye and considerable skill she subjected her host to a sparkling account of her husband's prowess as a soldier. I listened with some amusement, because all Wavell said was "I see," repeated at intervals. Unfortunately for her he did see, only too well. Eventually in desperation she turned to me and said, "For goodness' sake, tell me something he is interested in!" I very nearly replied, "It's no good, better women than you have tried and failed," but having, I hope, a kindly nature, I refrained.

We who knew Wavell admired him immensely, but owing to his almost pathological taciturnity he was completely unknown to the bulk of the officers and men under his command. He was quite incapable of going round inspiring the troops as was done so

With my sister Jean at Gibraltar, 1904

Attending a levee at Buckingham Palace after promotion to major

At the British Modern Pentathlon Championship of 1924 which was won by the author (second from left in the front row)

With my wife, daughter and batman-groom Hodder at the Staff College, Camberley in 1938

successfully by Lord Mountbatten and Slim in Burma, and by Montgomery in the Middle East and before D-Day. Yet later on during the war as C.-in-C. Middle East he had the strength of character to stand up to some severe buffeting from the United Kingdom. This is what the Middle East official history has to say on the subject:

> The main operations in East Africa had, therefore, succeeded beyond all expectations, and had ended just in time. This was largely due to the steadiness of purpose of General Wavell and Air Chief Marshal Longmore, who had to achieve a workable and appropriate balance of forces while doing their best to comply with a rapid succession of instructions and suggestions, such as to part with forces from Kenya, to capture Kismayu quickly, to capture Eritrea quickly, to deter the Japanese by "liquidating Italian East Africa," to treat as a "first duty" the air defence of Malta, to be prepared to send ten squadrons to Turkey, to regard the capture of Rhodes as "of first importance," and to "let their first thoughts be for Greece."

Yet through it all Wavell, outwardly at any rate, remained steadfast and unmoved. In 1941 he was conducting simultaneously five different campaigns at a time when supplies of all sorts were very short indeed. By the time later commanders arrived on the scene, the material of war was beginning to roll off the assembly lines, but it required genius to run all those operations on a shoe-string.

By the end of my two years at Aldershot I could claim to be an efficient craftsman in the art of war but nothing more. So what was my surprise when I was selected to become an instructor at the Staff College, Camberley; this was an appointment usually reserved for brilliant young officers who were destined to rise to the highest ranks in the service and I did not think that I fitted into this category at all. I therefore entered into my new and rather frightening life with considerable apprehension. I thought I had worked hard when a student at the Staff College but I soon found that this was child's play compared with what was expected from me as an instructor.

I made matters still worse by setting and correcting military exams in order to make a little extra money.

By the middle of 1938 it became clear to most of us that war against Hitler was almost inevitable and this added an edge to our labours. Nearly all my fellow instructors subsequently rose to command divisions and corps and in 1939 our commandant was General Sir Bernard Paget, subsequently Commander-in-Chief Home Forces in the U.K. He had a very strong character, and was one of the most honourable men I have ever met. His attention to detail was fantastic and he could read through a massive military paper without missing the smallest mistake. Towards the end of my period there I acted as his chief staff officer, so I came to know him well and the better I knew him the more I admired his sterling qualities.

No account of life at the Staff College would be complete, however, without my mentioning someone who is known affectionately to British officers all over the world, Miss McGlinchy, who ran a typing agency just outside the gates of the Staff College. She knew the official abbreviations better than did most of the officers themselves, and many a time she was routed out of bed in the early hours of the morning by some desperate young officer clutching an ill-written sheaf of papers which had to be handed in to the directing staff by 9 a.m. next morning.

Sure enough it would be ready, so beautifully typed and legible that the officer himself would hardly recognise his own work. On one occasion a student who had handed her an essay on Napoleon found next morning a somewhat bulky package in his rack. Inside was a covering letter from Miss McGlinchy which said, "I enclose your essay on Napoleon but as all the other gentlemen have written essays about Wellington I enclose one on him too." She had the reputation of never letting anyone down.

With the outbreak of war all our regular officers departed to take up staff appointments in the rapidly expanding army and we were ordered to organise short war courses for regular and T.A. officers. By this time we were used to dealing with the mind of the regular soldier; now we were faced with an entirely different problem. Most of the officers selected to attend No. 1 war staff course were successful young barristers, businessmen, schoolmasters, dons, and there were five M.P.s including Captain J. S. B. Lloyd (better known as the Rt. Hon. Selwyn Lloyd, our Foreign Secretary) and a Second Lieutenant D. C. Walker-Smith, afterwards Minister of Health. They were a brilliant collection of young men and instead of the usual shop to which we had become hardened the ante-room now resounded to fierce arguments ranging over every possible topic in the world. We thoroughly enjoyed trying to teach them the art of war, and it was encouraging to learn that they in their turn were quite impressed with our standard and method of instruction.

CHAPTER VI

DUNKIRK

MAY 10, 1940, was the turning point in my life; the day my lucky break came. At 7 a.m. the telephone rang in my room at Camberley, where I was acting as chief instructor at the Staff College, and the operator said: " I thought you might like to know, sir, that Hitler has invaded Holland." I sat up with a jerk. So the phony war was over at last.

At this time I was a major (brevet lt.-colonel), but I had been told verbally that I was to go to France in a fortnight's time to take command of the 2nd Battalion the Middlesex Regiment as the present C.O., Lt.-Colonel Haydon, had been promoted to command a brigade. My successor at the Staff College had arrived a couple of days previously and I was in the process of handing over to him. But this news altered everything. I must get out there as quickly as I possibly could. I rang up the commandant, who was most understanding, and offered me the loan of his car.

Within two hours, complete with valise, I was on the road to Southampton. In the hurry of departure I had forgotten to bring any money, but I managed to borrow two pounds from the A.T.S. driver which was repaid faithfully by my wife the next day. The trouble was that I had no written orders of any sort. I was working entirely on a telephone message received a few days earlier from the War Office. Luckily I ran into Brigadier " Bubbles " Barker, who was returning to his brigade after a short leave, and he took me under his wing.

Barker was, as usual, very cheerful, and brimming over with energy. He didn't look a day older when, in the autumn of 1944, we went round my front together just after he had been promoted lieutenant-general to command 8 Corps. It was the same Barker.

full of drive and enthusiasm, who led the final advance of 21st Army Group from the Rhine to the Baltic.

I spent my first night in France at his headquarters. Though I didn't realise it at the time, we were the last boatload to get up to the front; all those who came across subsequently were kept in the base area and not allowed forward into Belgium. So my luck was in—by a matter of hours.

We at the Staff College had of course been studying the plan for the B.E.F. and I knew not only that our army was now streaming up to Belgium to take up positions on the River Dyle, but also by which routes they were moving. So all I had to do was to sit on my valise beside the road while the lorries streamed past in an endless procession, and wait for a halt. As luck would have it the vehicle which pulled up nearest to me was a dental truck, and I slipped into a vacant seat in the back. I thought as we drove along that commanders had entered battle in many different ways—on horseback clad in armour, on foot, later on in cars, tanks or aircraft—but I was almost certainly the first commander to enter battle in a dental truck.

We drove through the waving, welcoming crowds in Brussels and on 13th May I took over command of my battalion at Louvain, an attractive Belgian university town, where the 3rd Division, commanded by General Montgomery, alongside other divisions of the B.E.F., was taking up a position to halt the German thrust into Belgium.

I don't think I made a very good first impression on the men of the battalion because I roundly abused them for being unshaven. I could almost see them saying to themselves "Another of these awful spit-and-polish blimps." Nevertheless, I insisted and this is not quite so stupid as it sounds. The one thing which is always in short supply in battle is sleep, and the refreshing effect of a shave is worth at least two hours' sleep. Moreover, if a man keeps himself clean he will almost certainly keep his weapons clean, and this is vital. In my experience of two wars I have always found that the clean soldier fights better than the dirty one, however tough the latter may look with his unshaven chin.

The 2nd Middlesex was a machine-gun battalion and as such came directly under divisional H.Q. I hadn't been there two hours when I was told that the divisional commander, General Montgomery, was in his car on the road and wanted to see me. Monty had obviously come up at once to cast an eye over his new divisional machine-gun commander. This was my first meeting with him, apart from once in Egypt. I saw a small, alert figure with piercing eyes sitting in the back of his car—the man under whom I was to fight all my battles during the war, and who was to have more influence on my life than anyone before or since.

I knew him well by reputation. He was probably the most discussed general in the British Army before the war, and—except with those who had served under him—not a popular figure. Regular armies in all countries tend to produce a standard type of officer, but Monty, somehow or other, didn't fit into the British pattern. His methods of training and command were unorthodox, always a deadly crime in military circles. He was known to be ruthlessly efficient, but somewhat of a showman. I had been told sympathetically that I wouldn't last long under his command, and, to be honest, I would rather have served under any other divisional commander.

Anyhow, if my battalion was any example, there could be no question about the efficiency of his division—the period of the phony war had obviously been used for some hard, intensive training. I doubt whether this country has ever been represented at the outset of a war by a more efficient army than this B.E.F. of 1940.

It is always an exciting moment when one first meets the enemy. This came the next day, on 14th May, when the Germans launched an attack which made a slight penetration into our position, but they were at once driven out again by a counter-attack. Here I learned my first lesson in practical command—from Lieutenant-Colonel Knox of the Ulster Rifles. Some three or four of his men came running back through the town of Louvain towards the rear. He stopped them.

Their position had been heavily shelled and the Germans had got round behind them, they said. After a few words from their

C.O. they turned and started to trot back to the front, looking rather ashamed of themselves. "Wait a minute," he said, "let's have a cigarette." In spite of some fairly heavy shelling he made them finish their smoke. He then said: "Now *walk* back to your positions"—and they went.

The 15th saw more German attacks, and another penetration—but again they were thrown back by counter-attacks, and there was no doubt we were solid on our front. As the divisional machine-gun officer I had ready access to divisional headquarters and was able to study the operational and intelligence maps. From these I used to construct a rough situation map, and as I went round my platoons I collected the men together and explained what was happening on the whole front.

This was a practice I tried to keep up through the war. The modern soldier is more highly educated, more imaginative and more intelligent than his father who fought in 1914-18. He is capable of rising to greater heights, but he can also sink to greater depths. He will give of his best only if he understands the reason for what he is doing. As a rule the front-line soldier has no idea at all about what is going on elsewhere, even on the front of another company in his own battalion. His view of the war is restricted to the field and hedgerow in his immediate foreground. To pierce this fog of ignorance requires forethought and much hard work, but it is well worth the effort, as I have proved over and over again.

But the situation on the 3rd Division maps began to look disquieting. The German panzer divisions had driven a sharp wedge through the French forces on our flank in the Ardennes, and every time I visited the map the panzer thrust seemed to have pierced deeper into the French positions. But I wasn't unduly worried. I had been brought up to believe that the French generals were the best strategists in Europe, and here was a wonderful opportunity for a strong counter-attack by their armoured divisions. There were, however, persistent rumours of confusion and indecision in the ranks of our allies, and there was no sign of mobile reserves moving to the danger spot.

Then on 16th May, to our disgust, orders were received to withdraw from our strong position back to the line of the River Seine. Though we didn't realise it then, this was the beginning of the retreat to Dunkirk, and a withdrawal in face of the enemy is about the most difficult military operation. A sycophantic friend once said to the famous Von Moltke " You are one of the greatest captains of war." He replied " No, because I have never commanded a withdrawal, and that is the most difficult military manœuvre."

I realise now that we got out just in time. There were several occasions during the next fourteen days when most people would have laid very long odds against the B.E.F. ever escaping at all. The man for whom I felt most sorry was our commander-in-chief, Lord Gort. The French seemed to have gone to pieces on his right, yet he was under their command, and the orders he received didn't make sense. At the same time he was responsible to the British Government for the safety of the British troops. And then, as a final blow, the Belgian Army on his left was forced to capitulate.

Gort was neither a great strategist nor a deep military thinker. He couldn't stand up at a conference and deliver a brilliant military appreciation. Even when C.-in-C. he remained essentially a front-line regimental officer who was always more interested in the details of battle than in the strategical picture. Yet, where a more brilliant soldier might have lost his nerve, Gort remained staunch to the end, and thus showed the one essential quality required in times of adversity by all commanders—mental toughness. I have always felt that he never received the credit which was his due.

But the more I have studied this campaign the clearer it becomes that the man who really saved the B.E.F. was our own corps commander, Lt.-General A. F. Brooke (now Viscount Alanbrooke). I felt vaguely at the time that this alert, seemingly iron, man without a nerve in his body, whom I met from time to time at 3rd Division headquarters and who gave out his orders in short, clipped sentences, was a great soldier, but it is only now that I realise fully just how great he was. We regarded him as a highly efficient military machine. It is only since I have read his diaries that I appreciate what a consummate actor he must have been. Behind the confident mask was the sensitive nature of a man who hated war, the family man-cum-bird-watcher, in fact. Yet he never gave us the slightest indication of those moments of utter despair when it seemed to him almost impossible that any of us would ever escape.

If you ask anybody what they remember most clearly about the retreat to Dunkirk they will all mention two things—*shame and exhaustion.* Shame—as we went back through those white-faced, silent crowds of Belgians, the people who had cheered us and waved to us as we came through their country only four days before, people who had vivid memories of a previous German occupation and whom we were now handing over to yet another. I felt very ashamed. We had driven up so jauntily and now, liked whipped dogs, we were scurrying back with our tails between our legs. But the infuriating part was that we hadn't been whipped. It was no fault of ours. All I could do as I passed these groups of miserable people was to mutter " Don't worry—we will come back." Over and over again I said it. And I was one of the last British most of them were to see for four long years.

I have always claimed that I was the last man out of Belgium. I had been given command of a small composite force consisting of two machine-gun battalions, an anti-tank battery and a carrier platoon which acted as a flank guard-cum-rearguard. We arrived in the dark on the Escaut Canal to find most of the bridges blown. Eventually, however, we discovered one intact.

On the far side was a British general in a greatcoat. I still don't know who he was. As I crossed he called out, " Any more of our troops on the far side? " I said " No, I can guarantee there are none." " Right! " he said, and the next thing I knew was an ear-splitting roar as the last bridge over the Escaut went up.

There is no point in describing the retreat in detail. We usually moved by night and held positions on canals or rivers by day, where we might or might not be attacked by the German advance guards. But a high standard of training stood us in very good stead; units were so quick into and out of action.

Though generals like Brooke and Montgomery were no doubt achieving miracles at their level, in the long run it was the discipline and toughness of the regimental officers and men which pulled us through. Retreats are always nightmares of confusion, and this was no exception. The roads were packed with refugees, many of them old people and children trudging hopelessly along with all their pathetic bits and pieces piled high on hand-carts or even prams, their eyes constantly scanning the skies for the German bombers which seemed to be perpetually overhead. Mixed up with them were despondent-looking columns of French and Belgian troops with their inevitable horse transport, all moving in one direction—to the rear.

And always the rumours which eat into all armies in retreat like some deadly virus; the panzers were here, there and everywhere; such-and-such a formation had been wiped out, and so on. It would hardly have been surprising if, under these depressing circumstances, the morale of our troops had sunk to zero, and indiscipline had crept in. Not a bit of it.

Through it all our men marched seemingly indifferent to the chaos around them. I know this will sound most insular, but time after time I thanked my stars that they were British troops, in whom disaster brings out all that is best in our national character. In spite of the desperate situation there was no chaos. It was a well-ordered retreat, and, as always when things are really unpleasant, the British sense of humour was much to the fore. When I asked one of my company commanders who had just had a sharp brush with the enemy how he was getting on he replied: " Don't look round, sir, I think we're being followed."

It is this unquenchable sense of humour which makes the Britisher such a good soldier. Other nations produce men who are as brave, or who are better disciplined, but none with a keener sense of humour, which is of inestimable value when things are going wrong.

The chief menace was not the Germans but sheer exhaustion. After two days and two nights without sleep I find it very difficult to think straight, and I develop a burning feeling behind my eyes. The way I solved the problem was by making my intelligence officer, Gordon, into a sort of A.D.C. who slept whenever possible by day, and did all the map-reading when we moved by night.

I got into the car and went straight to sleep, and he woke me when we arrived at our destination. This lack of sleep affected everybody, high and low, with one exception—General Montgomery. During the whole of the withdrawal he insisted on having meals at regular hours and never missed his normal night's sleep. Consequently when we arrived at Dunkirk he was as fresh as when he started.

And he was about the only one who was.

There were many crises during the retreat, but the most critical came on the night of 27th–28th May. I happened to be at 3rd Division headquarters when the corps commander, General Brooke, called to see Montgomery. The situation he disclosed could hardly have been worse. The 5th Division, commanded by General Franklyn, was being heavily attacked and had not yet established contact with the 50th Division on its left. If the 5th Division gave way then the whole front would crumble, and General Brooke proposed to reinforce it with everything he could lay his hands on.

But there was worse to come. On the extreme left, beyond 50th division, was a wide gap into which the Germans were likely to pour at any moment. The Belgians who should have been there had ceased to exist as a fighting force. The whole Belgian Army surrendered at midnight. Beyond the gap was the French 2nd Light Mechanised Division which had been placed under General Brooke's command.

To fill this gap, and to join up with the French, Monty's 3rd Division was ordered that night to carry out one of the most difficult manœuvres in war—withdraw from the line, embus and move to the north along small roads only a few thousand yards in the rear of the 5th Division front which might break at any moment under German pressure. We machine-gunners were luckier than the rest because we moved off just before dark in order to hold the gap until the remainder of the division arrived. Luckily we were not attacked, for machine-guns are not much good on their own at night. I have never felt more naked in my life.

This would have been a difficult move at any time, but owing to the congestion on the roads it looked well-nigh impossible. Yet

Monty took it all in his stride. His orders were clear and concise and he seemed completely confident.

"Of course the 3rd Division will get there."

And they did. General Brooke must have sighed with relief next morning, for the gap was closed.

Early next morning I was with a party of sappers who were preparing a bridge for demolition, and with them was a Belgian soldier working with a will. Suddenly we heard the news. The whole Belgian Army had surrendered. The Belgian soldier might have been pole-axed. With a stricken look on his face he put on his equipment, saluted, and walked away towards the German front, saying, "*Je ne suis pas lâche, moi—comme les autres.*" It was a dramatic little scene which has remained in my memory ever since. The solitary figure of the Belgian soldier disappearing towards the enemy seemed to accentuate the shame of his country in defeat.

The trouble was that Belgium tried to mobilise too many soldiers too quickly with inadequate mobilisation arrangements. Given time this might have worked, but the Germans moved so fast that the whole country became flooded with bewildered conscripts who were an embarrassment rather than an asset. But some of the Belgians fought well. On one occasion I was alongside a Belgian division composed mainly of tough little chasseurs from the Ardennes, who seemed to be giving a good account of themselves.

On 29th May, after a fortnight's ceaseless activity, we got back behind the Furnes-Nieuport Canal which was the last-ditch position to protect the evacuation from Dunkirk. This, of course, had been going on for several days and a number of administrative units had already gone. Many people have assumed that it was largely due to luck and improvisation that the B.E.F. escaped from Dunkirk. Quite the contrary—it was due to foresight and planning on the part of two men, Vice-Admiral Sir Bertram Ramsay, Flag Officer Dover, who planned the naval side (called Operation Dynamo) and General Sir Ronald Adam, who organised the Dunkirk beach-head.

It was impossible to evacuate our heavy weapons and transport, so as soon as we got inside the bridgehead we were ordered to immobilise our vehicles and move in on foot. The drivers hated doing this because in war each driver develops a feeling of affection for his own lorry or truck. It was a horrible sight—thousands of abandoned vehicles, carriers, guns and pieces of military equipment of all sorts. It was a graveyard of gear.

We took up our position near Furnes. This was the last time that I was to command a battalion; for next day I was summoned to 3rd Div. H.Q. As I approached I saw two figures standing on the sand-dunes. I recognised our corps commander, General Brooke, and my divisional commander, General Montgomery. The former was under a considerable emotional strain. His shoulders were bowed and it looked as though he were weeping. Monty was patting him on the back. They then shook hands and General Brooke walked slowly to his car and drove away.

I remained a silent and interested spectator of this astonishing scene. Monty beckoned me over and said, " General Brooke has just received orders to hand over the 2nd corps to me and go back to England." It was part of a plan to get back into the country a nucleus of experienced officers and warrant officers who would be available to command and train new armies if the main fighting part of the B.E.F. failed to escape, as seemed very likely at that time. Even at battalion level this had happened. I had already dispatched two officers and N.C.O.s to the United Kingdom.

General Brooke hated to go. No one likes leaving his command under these circumstances; that is why he looked so depressed and miserable. But the orders were very strongly worded for this very reason, and there was no alternative.

I was sent off at once to find the 11th brigade of the 4th Division, which was somewhere on the left flank. My instructions were to tell the brigade commander, Anderson (afterwards commander of the 1st Army in North Africa) that he had been selected to command the 3rd Division and I was to take over his brigade.

My period as battalion commander had lasted precisely seventeen days, and for almost the entire time we had been in action against the enemy; never once had I seen the whole battalion concentrated. I must pay a sincere tribute to the C.O. who had preceded me, Bill Haydon, who was subsequently killed when in command of a brigade of the 50th Division in the desert. He had trained the battalion so well that my task was comparatively easy. Even at the end there was no dent visible in either the morale or the sense of humour of our Cockneys.

A divisional machine-gun officer is a general dog's-body who gets all sorts of jobs thrust on his shoulders. I was detailed to carry out reconnaissances, act as commander of flank guards, rearguards, and often had to slip off with my battalion to build up the defensive framework of the next position before the arrival of the division.

Orders for all these tasks were given me by Monty himself so I was in a unique position to watch him at work during this testing period. It was a remarkable performance. I remember once sitting packed into a room lit by only a few candles, and with a most inadequate map at my disposal—during the final stages of the withdrawal the supply of maps, down to battalion level, at any rate, completely failed, and at one stage I had to rely on a fly-blown railway map which I had removed from the wall of a small wayside station.

Monty was about to issue orders, and I wondered desperately how on earth I could possibly grasp the complicated role which had been allotted to my battalion. I needn't have worried. With the minimum of words he made the whole plan clear to us all. And this, of course, is one of his greatest attributes—his capacity to reduce the most complicated situation to its simple, basic essentials. I saw him every day, sometimes several times a day, and he was always the same; confident, almost cocky you might say, cheerful and apparently quite fresh. He was convinced that he was the best divisional commander in the British Army and that we were the best division. By the time we had reached Dunkirk I had come to the same conclusion!

I eventually discovered Brigadier Anderson eating bully-beef in a small room in La Panne. He indicated the positions of his three battalions, the 5th Northamptons, 1st East Surreys and 2nd Lancashire Fusiliers, all in action on the left flank, and then departed. I doubt whether any brigade commander has ever made less impact on his brigade than I did on the 11th. I managed to find their battalion H.Q.s and to visit one or two of their companies—that was all. For next day we were ordered to withdraw to the beach at La Panne from which the whole 4th Division was to embark and sail for the United Kingdom.

I established a control point at Coxyde, and to start with it all seemed to be going according to plan. The different units passed through steadily on their way down to the beach. Unfortunately we had to thin out gradually; platoons and companies at a time. So no battalion came through my control point complete.

This could not be helped, but it caused confusion later on. Once the troops got on to the beach they came under the orders of an embarkation staff, whose job it was to get them on to the ships and away. By ten o'clock my last unit had passed through, so I decided to follow them down to La Panne, where the 4th Division H.Q. was established. The town itself was being steadily shelled and occasionally bombed, and some houses were on fire.

I expected that most of the troops would by now be on their way to England. I was horrified when I found the beach covered with men. As far as I could see no one had been evacuated at all. Ramps had been constructed out to sea from the shore, but the tide was right out and no boats, not even rowing boats, could get anywhere near the ramps. I could see in the distance some ships, but they were a long way out.

At a rough guess I would say that there were some 6,000 troops spread along that beach. Luckily the sand seemed to absorb the splinters of the enemy shells, and the casualties were not as high as might have been expected. But it was a pretty desperate situation.

General Johnson, V.C., the commander of the 4th Division, seemed to think so too, for when I entered the room in which he had his temporary H.Q. he was standing with a telephone in his hand, and to my amazement he was speaking to someone at the War Office in London. I heard him explain that none of his division had been able to get away. He then said: " And this is not a very healthy place." He held up the receiver, and as luck would have it just at that moment a shell burst on the roof of the house with a resounding crash.

"I am now moving my division to Dunkirk," he said, "and you will arrange for their evacuation from there to-morrow morning." I felt very sorry for the staff officer in the War Office who had been at the receiving end of this conversation. It must have been frightful to sit there and not be able to do anything to help. What could he do, poor devil?

Anyhow, Johnson dispatched us to get the troops moving on the ten-mile march along the beach to Dunkirk. My job was to rout soldiers out of the cellars. By the time I had done this the beach was comparatively clear, so I set off at the tail of the column along the coast towards Dunkirk. As we came round the headland I had my first view of the little ships—small rowing-boats and motor-boats suddenly appeared out of the dark in the shallow water some fifty yards out. The trouble was that crowds of troops were wading out towards these, and in their eagerness to get on board many of the boats were overturned. This was the only sign of indiscipline I saw during the evacuation, and it was due to the fact that units were mixed up and men were separated from their officers and N.C.O.s.

The troops were, however, as always, perfectly amenable to reason. I arranged with one of my officers to stand on the beach while I waded in. When I flashed my torch shorewards he sent out twenty men to me at a time. Meanwhile I kept my torch flashing out to sea as well, and arranged for the boats to come to me. I could then ensure that the men got into the boats carefully, so that none was upset; and in this manner we got rid of quite a lot of troops.

Unfortunately, although the sea was warm, after standing for some time with the water up to my chest I suddenly got cramp and was forced to retire to dry land, which by then was once more packed with troops. That was the trouble. However many troops were got away it seemed to make no difference to the numbers packed on the beach.

So I walked back towards La Panne calling out rather forlornly "Anyone belong to the 11th Brigade?" But no one replied. It seemed that the whole of the 4th Division had passed on its way to Dunkirk. So I set off to follow them, a very wet, very tired, and very temporary brigadier with no staff and no troops.

As dawn broke the beaches presented a fearsome sight; thousands and thousands of troops, like an immense, khaki-clad, football crowd, straggling along towards Dunkirk. German aircraft soon arrived overhead, greeted by a fusilade of rifle shots which couldn't do them any harm, but no doubt helped morale. Then we saw our own R.A.F. streaking in from the sea. What a cheering sight. If it hadn't been for them I doubt very much whether many of us would have got away. The Army was in a real mess, and our sister services, the Royal Navy and R.A.F., were doing their utmost to get us out of it.

As I gazed at these masses of British troops armed only with rifles I was consumed with one great fear—those German panzer divisions. There was nothing to stop them. If the ugly snouts of the German tanks had appeared on the dunes overlooking the beach the slaughter would have been frightful, but luckily for us they never came. It was a miraculous escape, which has often been attributed to a stupid intervention by Hitler, who halted his tanks and thus enabled the B.E.F. to escape. This was a vital turning point in the war, and it is of such historical importance that I have taken considerable trouble to find out what happened.

The original order to halt the tanks had nothing to do with Hitler at all. This is one mistake for which the German generals cannot blame the Fuehrer. The German armoured divisions were, in fact, halted on 24th May by Von Rundstedt, the German armoured commander, and he did this for three reasons.

First, the German tanks had been streaming through France for over a fortnight and were scattered all over the place. He wanted to concentrate them for maintenance, as they would shortly be needed for the new offensive which the Germans were about to launch against the many French divisions in the south.

Secondly, he considered that the armoured divisions had done their job. They had cut through to the coast and isolated the British Expeditionary Force from the 1st French Army. The country which lay in front was enclosed and intersected with waterways, unsuitable for armoured action. It was now the turn of the German infantry to clean up the remainder of the British

Expeditionary Force which couldn't possibly, he thought, get away.

Thirdly, he received information that the British were sending troops from England to Calais and Boulogne, and that divisions belonging to the B.E.F. were moving down towards the south. There were also indications that the French were moving up fresh divisions from the south. He therefore expected to be counter-attacked very soon and wanted to have his tanks intact as a mobile reserve. All these were sound military reasons.

Hitler, who arrived at his headquarters eighteen hours afterwards, agreed with the action taken by Von Rundstedt and added an additional reason of his own, that if the armour closed in on the British too much it would handicap the Luftwaffe. So Hitler authorised the issue of a new order confirming Rundstedt's original halt, and he added that no further armoured advance was to be made without Rundstedt's decision.

Dunkirk has been described as a miracle, and so it was. Throughout the evacuation the sea remained as calm as a mill pond. This was clearly Divine Providence. But the evacuation was also a miracle of foresight, planning and discipline by all three services, and our French allies, who held part of the perimeter to the end. By 4th June, 338,226 men had been evacuated, in as fine a piece of combined planning and initiative as this country has ever produced. There was no panic and surprisingly little chaos.

But let me return to the lonely, wet brigadier trudging along the beach; because my final experiences were typical of what happened to thousands of others. I arrived in Dunkirk to the most appalling din from naval and army anti-aircraft guns which I have ever heard. I was too tired even to bother to look up, and I noticed that no one else did either. We were marshalled along a jetty by a lieutenant-commander who obviously hadn't slept for about three nights either. Then came the unbelievable comfort of the ward-room of a destroyer, with some hot rum and milk.

But fate hadn't finished with us yet. There was a sickening crash. We had been bombed. The ship stopped and began to heel over on one side. We scrambled out on to the sloping deck to see two other craft manœuvring into position on either side of us. I climbed on board one of these, a small Dutch cargo boat which appeared to be under the command of a cheerful young naval lieutenant. It was already bulging with troops, but they made room for a few more.

"Can anyone fire an anti-aircraft Lewis gun?" came a bellow from the bridge. So I manned the forward gun. I can say quite honestly that this was the only part of the withdrawal which I enjoyed. We were being continuously attacked by German bombers, and I fired many, many magazines without any visible effect on the enemy aircraft. But the great thing was I had no responsibility; this had passed to the naval lieutenant on the bridge, and all I had to do was to keep the gun firing. It was a wonderful relief.

All the same I wasn't looking forward to our arrival in England. We couldn't be said to have covered ourselves with glory in our first encounter with the Germans. So, I was astonished to see the waving, cheering crowds welcoming us home at Ramsgate. We might have been the heroes of some great victory instead of a beaten army returning home, having lost most of its equipment.

I could see the troops perking up all round me. In some mysterious way the letters B.E.F. began to appear in chalk on the front of the steel helmets. I couldn't help smiling. Even in moments of disaster the British soldier always has an eye to the main chance! Tired and still wet, I was shown to a train which I was told was going to Reading. This would suit me well, as my wife and daughter were still at Camberley. So with a comfortable feeling that my brigade was also in trains somewhere in the United Kingdom I dropped off to sleep.

The next thing I knew was a figure in khaki shaking me vigorously. "Sorry, sir," he said, "but you've all got to get out here."

"Are we in Reading?" I asked.

"Reading?" he repeated in astonishment, "No, Darlington." I was whisked off to a nearby camp, and while the adjutant rang up the War Office to find out where I was to report, I enjoyed my first hot bath since leaving England. He arrived very shortly with the news that I was to go at once to Lyme Regis. So I set off again. At this time the whole of England was covered with troops making similar journeys, and the War Office must have had a difficult time sorting us all out.

When I arrived there next day I found Lyme Regis looking its very best. It was a beautiful summer evening and happy family groups were wending their way up the hill from the beach. There wasn't a soldier in sight and there could have been no greater con-contrast to the Dunkirk beaches. As I was still very tired and extremely hungry I decided to spend the night peacefully, and start trying to sort things out next morning. So having booked a room in the Victoria Hotel I went straight into the dining-room. When I started ordering a gargantuan meal the manager suggested that I should leave the choice of menu to him. He produced a wonderful dinner complete with a bottle of champagne but as dish followed dish my uneasiness increased as it was obviously going to be extremely expensive.

But when I asked for my bill, the manager said: "We should like you to have your first proper meal back in England as our guest." I was very touched, and as I found out afterwards it was typical of what was going on all over the country.

The following morning I was told that all the promotions made during these last days at Dunkirk were cancelled. Monty was back with the 3rd Division, Anderson was returning to the 11th Brigade and I was to go back to my battalion once more.

CHAPTER VII

THE UNITED KINGDOM 1940-42

ON THE 17th June, 1940, I was ordered to take command of the 9th Brigade in the 3rd Division. This was wonderful news. I was back in the fold with Monty again, and the 3rd Division was being re-equipped before any other formation in the U.K. in order to return to France at once. I couldn't have wished for a better brigade. The 9th was called "The International Brigade" because it consisted of the Lincolns, K.O.S.B. and the Royal Ulster Rifles; English, Scots and Irish. Luckily for us we did not return to France.

My first task was to defend the south coast of England from Rottingdean to Shoreham—one brigade of some 3,000 men was stretched in a thin line along ten miles of densely-populated coastline. We wouldn't have stood much chance against a well-organised invasion, but even so this was probably one of the most strongly defended parts of Britain, because we were a well-trained and experienced regular division, complete with war equipment. Fortunately, few people in this country realised quite how thin was the shield protecting them from Hitler's victorious armies which were now just across the Channel.

There was a curious atmosphere along the south coast. Everyone seemed to expect an invasion at any moment, but nobody was doing very much about it, and there was still an atmosphere of the peacetime holiday resort about Brighton. We took over our responsibilities from a nondescript force which had been collected from the highways and byways, with very little equipment. I was never quite so worried about the prospects of an invasion as were some people, because having studied combined operations at the Staff College I knew that, owing to the immense amount of detailed organisation required for an operation of this sort it could not possibly be laid on in a hurry, particularly by the Germans, who were not really a sea-faring nation.

We, as a maritime power with territories all over the world, have had considerable experience in landing troops from the sea; the Germans have not. Nevertheless, given time there was little doubt that they could eventually stage a large-scale invasion of Britain, so our defence had to be organised with the utmost care to make up for our lack of numbers.

It proved a very difficult problem because an enormous town like Brighton is laid out primarily to provide holidays by the sea, not as a fortress from which to repel an invasion.

Monty used to pay constant visits. " Who lives in that house? " he would say pointing to some building which partly masked the fire from one of our machine-gun positions. " Have them out, Horrocks. Blow up the house. Defence must come first."

He was, of course, absolutely correct, but it was not always so simple as it sounded. My predecessor had, somewhat unwisely, positioned troops on the two piers without first of all allowing the civilian firms responsible for the entertainment booths to remove their possessions. I have never seen anything like the chaos which confronted me on my first visit; dolls and mementos were strewn all over the place, the slot machines of the " What the butler saw " type had all been broken open and the contents removed. We were in for trouble and we got it. Some months afterwards I received a bill for many thousands of pounds, which I hastily passed on to divisional headquarters.

One day Lieut.-Colonel Selby Lowndes, my local gunner commander, said to me in disgust, " I never thought I should live to see the day when I occupied a battery position outside the Metropole on the front at Brighton."

It was here that I first met the Prime Minister, Mr. Winston Churchill. He came down to have a look at our defences and watch the Royal Ulster Rifles carry out a small exercise. Though no one knew of his visit, he was quickly spotted and a large and enthusiastic crowd soon gathered. The complete confidence shown in him was most touching, and rather frightening to us who knew that, to all intents and purposes, the military cupboard was bare. During one of these spontaneous demonstrations of affection I found myself standing at the back beside Mrs. Churchill. There were tears in her eyes, and I heard her murmur, "Pray God we don't let them down."

It was important that the troops, who spent long hours putting up barbed-wire entanglements, constructing defensive positions and preparing demolitions, should not become static minded, so I insisted on as much mobile training being carried out as possible. Our defensive positions, however, had to be manned every night.

The most vital observation posts were at the end of the two piers from where the first warning of a sea-borne invasion would almost certainly come. They were occupied each night by some signallers under command of one experienced, reliable officer, whose orders were to communicate direct to his battalion and to my brigade headquarters both by wireless and line, as soon as he saw the invading craft, but only when he *actually* saw them with his own eyes. He was also to fire a white signal rocket.

As more and more information came in about the German preparations on the other side of the Channel, which included the collection of barges suitable for invasion, I decided that no chances could be taken. My small brigade operations room was manned throughout the twenty-four hours and I slept in the room next door. One night just as I was going to bed my brigade-major, Charles, dashed in to say that a white rocket had gone up from the end of the pier. "Shall I send the code word, sir?" This would alert the brigade group and start a chain of operations. It was a bad moment because I had never really thought that the invasion would come. Yet here it was. But was it? I wondered. Surely there must be some mistake.

"Hold hard," I told Charles, "check up with the other observation posts! And why have we had no message?" It was lucky that these second thoughts prevailed because there was no invasion at all. We discovered afterwards that a ship exactly in line with the end of the pier had fired a white rocket which to our observers on shore had looked as though it was coming from one of the vital observation posts.

It was now decided that as the 3rd Infantry division was the most powerful formation in the country it should be pulled back into reserve with a counter-attack role. This involved several moves for the 9th brigade—to Gloucester, Dorset and Somerset.

Our first night in Gloucestershire produced a battle of a very different sort. The brigade was billeted round Cirencester which up to now had been an R.A.F. leave centre as there were many airfields in the vicinity. Unfortunately our troops were convinced that the R.A.F. had let them down during the retreat to Dunkirk and subsequent evacuation. At this stage of the war unless the soldier actually saw our planes over his head he would not believe that they were operating at all. Do what we could it seemed impossible to explain to him that the R.A.F. was fighting most gallantly against heavy odds many miles away, and well out of sight. It was particularly irritating because without the R.A.F. we should never have got back from France at all.

Anyhow that was the feeling, and on that first night a battle royal between khaki and air force blue took place in Cirencester. It was entirely our fault and I spent much of the next day apologising to high level R.A.F. commanders who were justly indignant at the rough manhandling their men had suffered.

Much of our training took place with the Home Guard, particularly while we were in the Beaminster area of Dorset. The more I saw of the Home Guard the more I came to respect their keenness. Their greatest asset was local knowledge and operating against them on exercises was like hitting a cushion; we could make a dent but they always bobbed up somewhere else. It was embarrassing at the conferences which were held after each scheme to find myself addressing rows of be-medalled figures who had held high rank in the last war and were now N.C.O.s or privates in the Home Guard. Quite apart from the military value there is no doubt that service in the Home Guard was good for the morale of the country. Men, and women too, who could not be spared from their civilian occupations felt that they were playing a part in the defence of their country.

I enjoyed my time with the 9th Brigade but all things come to an end and in January, 1941, I was sent to be brigadier-general staff, Eastern Command, where I remained for the next five months, engaged mainly in organising large-scale training exercises. It was interesting work but I was delighted when on the 25th of June I was made an acting major-general and ordered to take over command of the 44th (Home Counties) Division, because I much prefer being a commander to a staff officer.

The 44th was an old-established Territorial division whose three brigades came from Surrey (The Queens—131st Bde.), Kent (The Buffs. and West Kents—132nd Bde.) and Sussex (133rd Bde.) and it occupied the south-eastern corner of England. I found myself, therefore, responsible for what was then regarded as the No. 1 German invasion area, stretching from the Isle of Thanet to Dover and on to Folkestone.

Invasion or not, it was certainly the most exciting part of England at that time. We had a grandstand view not only of the Battle of Britain, with its dog-fights over our heads, but also of the nightly naval war that went on in the Channel. This was directed by Admiral Ramsay from his operational H.Q. at Dover and whenever possible I used to slip down in the evening and listen in to these exciting high-speed operations fought out by the small ships of both sides. My pleasant host was to play a momentous part in subsequent combined operations, notably during the Sicily and Normandy landings. Bertie Ramsay was a true friend to the army and when he died on 2nd January, 1945, we all felt his loss deeply. It was a tragedy that he did not live to see the successful conclusion of the war to which he had contributed so much.

A division is probably the best command in the British Army because it is a tactical unit complete with its own gunners, sappers, supply and medical services, and as I was once more back in the Monty sphere of influence, the next few months were hectic and intensely interesting.

I had previously experienced Montgomery's training methods

when I had been a brigadier in his 3rd Division just after our return from Dunkirk, but even so I was unprepared for his astonishing activity as the G.O.C.-in-C. South Eastern Command. It was as though atomic bombs were exploding all over this rural corner of Britain. Before his arrival a distinctly peace-time atmosphere had prevailed; officers and warrant-officers were in many cases living with their families and, according to Monty, commanders and staff were spending too much time in their offices to the detriment of active training.

All this changed almost overnight, and the first bomb exploded among the wives and families, who were summarily packed off, out of the command. Monty argued that in war a soldier could not concentrate on his military training if half his mind was concerned with domestic problems, and if an invasion materialised he would be worrying about the safety of his family instead of getting on with his job as a soldier. Every conceivable effort was made to circumvent this order and the wives clung on like limpets. Monty, however, was quite ruthless, and I have even seen him send an officer on a motor-bicycle to intercept and interrogate some female who looked as though she might have a military connection.

Out they went, one and all, and this gave rise to many amusing incidents. There was one young officer in Monty's own H.Q. who explained to the landlady where he was billeted that his wife was coming to visit him for the week-end, but in view of Monty's orders she must be called Miss Smith. The landlady was all sympathy and agreed at once. The week-end proved an unqualified success. And the visitor really was Miss Smith after all.

The second explosion might be called the cross-country bomb. "Too many officers spend too much time in their offices and are becoming fat and almost permanently chair-borne. No good for war," Monty said. "Every officer in the command must carry out two cross-country runs weekly, irrespective of age or rank." His senior medical officer protested against this no-exception rule and mentioned a senior administrative staff officer. "Colonel X must not run, sir. If he runs he will probably die."

Monty replied, "Let him die. Much better to die now rather

than in the midst of battle when it might be awkward to find a replacement." Colonel X did run and Colonel X didn't die.

There were constant training exercises of every sort and by now Monty had perfected his famous conference technique, when the lessons learned during the exercise were rammed home to all concerned. It was a superbly staged performance. All the officers, and, if there was room, warrant-officers as well, were concentrated in some immense cinema. On the stage were large maps and diagrams, while the walls were covered with "No smoking" notices. Suddenly the audience would be called to attention, as the well-known figure of the army commander wearing battle-dress advanced to the centre of the stage.

"Sit down, gentlemen," he would say in a sharp, nasal voice. "Thirty seconds for coughing—then no more coughing at all." And the curious thing was that we didn't cough.

Then, perhaps for as long as two hours, he would keep us spell-bound as he described all the salient points of the exercise. I have held many similar conferences myself and have always tried to follow the Monty technique, though I have never had the face to insist on that no coughing rule, as I could never hope to acquire Monty's power of mass hypnosis.

Army commanders with many thousands of troops under their command tend to become remote God-like characters whom few know even by sight, yet in some extraordinary way Monty's influence permeated all strata of S.-E. Command, and his knowledge of the personalities under his command was uncanny. Often he would ring me up in the evening and make the most searching inquiries about some young second-lieutenant whom he had noticed on training. He would certainly have made a first-class talent spotter for any football club. The only way I could deal with these inquiries was to have a book containing details of every officer in the division handy beside the telephone. I showed it to Monty during one of his inspections and he was much amused.

I always reckon that I learned most of my practical soldiering first of all as a brigade-major at Aldershot under Wavell and secondly during the nine months which I spent in south-east England under Monty. I had hoped to go overseas with the 44th (Home Counties) Division but it was decided otherwise, and on the 20th March, 1942, I was ordered to take command of the 9th Armoured Division then in the Northampton area with H.Q. at Guilsborough. I hated having to leave this division, which I had been training for nine months, though it was some consolation to know that I was to be succeeded by Ivor Hughes, a " Queensman " himself, who had been commanding the 131st Queen's Brigade. He was the perfect choice, and he would, I knew, be very popular.

Hughes had been an outstanding staff officer, acting as brigade-major of the Dover Brigade, but in 1935 he decided to retire from the army and accompany his brigadier, Sir Charles Howard, to the House of Commons, where they became Serjeant and deputy Serjeant-at-Arms respectively. As he ended the war a Major-General, C.B., C.B.E., D.S.O., M.C., and is now a most successful Serjeant-at-Arms himself, he has had a remarkable career in two widely different spheres of activity.

It didn't take me long to realise how fortunate I was to have been given command of this particular division. It was composed of first-class cavalry regiments such as the 15th/19th Hussars, 5th Dragoon Guards (Skins), 4th/7th Dragoon Guards, the 13th/18th Hussars blended with the East Riding and Fife and Forfar Yeomanry.

For the rest of the war I always had yeomanry regiments under my command. In spite of mechanisation they have retained that independent, self-reliant outlook which was the hall-mark of their ancestors, the yeoman farmers of this country. They were largely composed of young men with a gleam in their eyes, who took to mobile armoured warfare as ducks take to water. I liked and admired them very much. I am indebted to a yeomanry regiment for my most precious souvenir of the last war. One day long after it was over I received by post a beautifully-bound book from the Sherwood Rangers Yeomanry claiming that they had fought more battles under my command than any other armoured regiment, and inside on vellum were inscribed the signatures not only of the officers but of some 500 warrant-officers, N.C.O.s and men as well. An immense amount of trouble must have been taken to produce this book, which now occupies a special position of honour in my study.

A couple of years back I was lunching in a famous Oxford restaurant, and as we were being shown to our table by the dapper, suave head-waiter I noticed that he was wearing some miniature medals, including the D.C.M. He seemed such a smooth young man that I could hardly believe my eyes, so in a somewhat doubting voice I asked him where he had won it.

With a broad smile he replied: "You ought to know, sir, because I got it while fighting in your corps." It turned out that he had served in the Sherwood Rangers Yeomanry, as a tank commander, the whole way from Alamein to Luneburg Heath. Moreover ten tanks had been "brewed up"—burned out—under him. Underneath that smart tail-coat he must have been a man of iron to have survived with his nerve unimpaired. "It only goes to show" as the troops say, that neither a man's appearance nor his civilian occupation are any indication how he will react to moments of great danger on the battlefield.

My predecessor in command of the 9th Armoured Division, General (Brocas) Burrows had insisted on the most meticulous basic training for all ranks. The gunners, signallers, drivers and technical experts, who comprise such a large part of an armoured formation, were all highly trained. The framework had been well constructed, and all I had to do now was to weld the different component parts into a fighting formation.

I came to the conclusion that they had been too long in Northamptonshire. The wives and families had of course arrived and they were all living too soft. So I moved the division to the Newmarket area where many of the units lived under canvas in winter and, most important of all, good training areas for tracked vehicles were available. I worked them very hard indeed; exercise after exercise, and the harder they worked the more they seemed to enjoy it. I think by now they had come to accept me as a necessary evil, even though I originated in a lower stratum of life—the infantry.

During this period I also learned a great deal myself about the control of armour in mobile warfare where all orders are given by wireless from a command tank, and this was to stand me in good stead later on.

When in the field all messing was done on a tank basis. Officers' and sergeants' messes and O.R.s' cook-houses disappeared. My own particular mess in the field consisted of the driver, operator-gunner, tank commander and myself. There was nothing unusual about this; it was the normal practice during operations in the Middle East, but it surprised the Press who, during one exercise, descended on my tank complete with camera men. I was highly embarrassed the following day to find large photographs in the daily papers bearing the caption "A new type of general has appeared." This took a lot of living down during the next few weeks.

I have always been a great believer in working hard, and then playing hard, so when the time came for the war-time Derby to be run at Newmarket, I gave the whole division four days' leave, and added that I hoped they would all go to the Derby as I would be there myself. I was careful to add no government petrol must be used to get there. Almost the whole division turned up, and the most assiduous questioning by a young reporter who was out for a lovely story failed to elicit one single scandal. They would probably have got there in any case. How much better, therefore, that they should do so with a clear conscience.

Suddenly orders were received that we were to move to the Northumberland/Durham area. The long drive up went very smoothly, and it seemed that the division was rapidly becoming fit for active operations.

If you were to ask any W.O., N.C.O. or man in the 9th Armoured Division to name the pleasantest billets which he occupied during the war he would unquestionably mention some small northern mining village. The Geordies and their wives invited the soldiers into their homes, threw open their clubs, and allowed them free access to the pit-head baths. They were magnificent hosts. By now I was firmly wedded to this division with its famous Panda sign and hoped that I might be privileged to command it in battle. But once more authority stepped in and it was not to be.

At 7 p.m. on 15th August, 1942, the telephone rang in my billet near Newcastle and the voice of a senior staff officer from the War Office said, " You are to travel down to London to-night, and you will be going on a journey almost immediately."

" Cold or warm ? " I asked—in those days, remember, walls had ears, or so we were constantly reminded.

" Warm," he replied, " and you will be moving ' one up.' "

This seemed to indicate that I was to be sent to the Middle East to command a corps; and so it turned out. Within thirty-six hours I took off from Lyneham in Wiltshire as the sole passenger in a Liberator on my way to Cairo, with one intermediate stop at Gibraltar.

I suppose I ought to have been jubilant. After a year's training in England I had been selected to command one of the only two corps which were actually fighting. In point of fact I was miserable. And the lonely figure sitting in that bomber was about as far removed from the popular idea of an up-and-coming young general as it was possible to be. I hated leaving the 9th Armoured, which was developing into a first-class division, for the entirely strange atmosphere of the desert about which I knew very little. I had once, years before, done a company training round the Pyramids at Mena, and that was all. It seemed a rather inadequate preparation for the impending battles with the redoubtable Rommel.

How would I shape as a corps commander, I wondered ? It was a big step up from command of the 2nd Battalion, The Middlesex Regiment during the withdrawal to Dunkirk, which was the last time I had been on active service. My subsequent promotions to brigadier and divisional commander had been made during training in the United Kingdom. I thought of all these things and I wondered whether I really had the qualities necessary for high command in battle. I was not unduly concerned about the technical military side. Even though warfare in the desert had certain peculiarities of its own, it was still warfare, in which the normal rules held good, and as an ex-instructor at the Staff College, Camberley, I ought to be able to cope with this side. No, it was the personal aspect of command I was worried about. I strongly suspected that neither Monty nor I would receive a very warm welcome from the desert veterans. How right I was!

Suddenly Gibraltar lay below us, with its rather precarious-looking runway jutting out into the sea. It is always a heart-warming sight to arrive at Gibraltar by air and see the famous Rock looming like an old lion guarding the western entrance to the Mediterranean. All the same, on this occasion I couldn't help feeling that if Spain were to enter the war, or if German forces were allowed to operate from there, this British fortress would receive short shrift. I had seen just how useless those elaborate fortresses in the Maginot Line had proved in the test of battle. I suppose I was very anti-fortress-minded, but it didn't seem to me that Gibraltar, with its teeming civilian population packed like sardines on the side of the rock, could hold out for long in face of a modern air attack.

When the aircraft came to rest, I found awaiting me a distinguished reception party, headed by Major-General Sir Colin Jardine, the military commander. They had no idea who was coming, merely that the aircraft contained a solitary V.I.P. Goodness knows whom they expected, but their hastily concealed disappointment as I emerged was very obvious. "I am very sorry," I said, "but I'm afraid it's only me."

Luckily I knew Colin Jardine, who had been senior to me at the Staff College, and there was no one whom I would rather have met at that moment. If I say that he was the best example of a genuine Christian who really led a Christian life I shall certainly be misunderstood. But that is exactly what I mean. When he heard that I was on my way to command a corps in the Middle East, he assumed the kindly, sympathetic manner adopted by a Harley Street specialist towards a patient who is seriously ill. At that time generals in the Middle East didn't as a rule last very long. Command in the desert was regarded as an almost certain prelude to a bowler hat. As Rommel is reported to have said once: "If only the British would leave their generals for a little longer they might learn more about desert warfare."

In the dusk I took off again for an all-night flight over North

Africa to Cairo. As we had to cross territory occupied by the Germans and Italians it was necessary to fly very high, which meant wearing an oxygen mask most of the time. It was a most uncomfortable and almost sleepless night, so when we landed near Mena I had a splitting headache and was hardly in the best of shape to take over the most exacting job of my life.

CHAPTER VIII

CORPS COMMANDER IN THE MIDDLE EAST

A STAFF officer was waiting for me on the airfield, and after breakfast we drove to General Alexander's H.Q. In the major reshuffle which had just occurred he had taken over the supreme command in the Middle East.

I had never had the privilege of serving under General Alexander, but I knew him well by reputation. Who didn't? By repute he was Winston Churchill's fire brigade chief *par excellence*, the man who was always being dispatched to retrieve the most desperate situations. He had commanded the final evacuation from Dunkirk and the withdrawal from Burma. I expected, therefore, to be confronted by some terrific fire-eater, but instead I was greeted by a quiet man with a very pleasant personality. He gave me the impression of being remote from the battle, and on the few occasions I met him subsequently I always felt the same, that he lived in a world of his own which few others were encouraged to enter. I never got to know him any better than I did at this first meeting in Cairo.

It was immediately obvious that, quite rightly, he had left the conduct of the campaign in the Western Desert very much to Montgomery. He told me that Monty was busy organising a strong mobile reserve with which to drive Rommel out of Egypt; that he had sent for me specially at Monty's request with the object of ultimately commanding this reserve. As I left to drive up to 8th Army H.Q. in the desert I thought that I had seldom met a more calm, unruffled and confident general, which was all the more remarkable because, according to the reports I had seen in the War Office, Rommel's victorious army was almost at the gates of Alexandria.

As I drove along the famous desert road, which I came to know so well, I kept passing vehicles bearing the red egg divisional sign of the 44th Home Counties Division. I had commanded this division at home and it was a cheering thought that here at least would be friendly faces; they had just arrived, and were in the process of moving up to the desert battle.

Monty was, as I expected, cheerful, alert and with that gleam of battle in his eye which always indicated that he was up against some tough military problem. From a professional point of view he was unquestionably enjoying himself. No time was wasted. I was taken straight to the map caravan which served as his mobile office and he outlined the situation. This was one of the most remarkable military appreciations I ever heard. Remember, he had arrived in Egypt only five days before; yet in this short space of time he had acquired a complete grip of the situation. Even to-day I can remember almost every word of it, and this is what he said:

" After several advances and withdrawals by both sides, the two armies, that is the German-Italian Army commanded by Field-Marshal Rommel and the 8th Army commanded by me, are now facing each other on a thirty-five-mile front about sixty miles west of Alexandria. Our defensive positions are on what is known as the El Alamein Line (this, incidentally, was the first time I had heard this historic name). The chief merit of our position is that both flanks are secure; on the right we have the sea, and on the left the Qattara Depression, where the going is so soft that it is impassable for a large number of vehicles. So no outflanking movements are possible and the enemy will have to break through our positions before advancing on Alexandria and the Delta.

" This position had been occupied by the 8th Army before I arrived, but I found the existing plan envisaged a further withdrawal of our left flank if necessary. I have stopped this, and ordered the 8th Army to fight and, if necessary, die, where it now stands. There will be no further withdrawal at all, and I have ordered dumps of supplies and ammunition to be built up in the forward areas. I believe that this has had a good effect on morale. The troops were getting bewildered; now they know where they are and what they have got to do. Rommel, my opponent, is undoubtedly suffering from a number of administrative headaches and is very short of petrol. I am certain, however, that he will launch one last all-out attack to smash the 8th Army and get through to the Delta. This may come any day.

" We have two corps in the line; 30 Corps on the right and 13 Corps on the left. The position of the former is strongly held in depth and protected by mine-fields. I do not anticipate any penetration in this part of the front. I haven't sufficient troops to hold the whole thirty-five miles in depth, so 13 Corps on the left is rather thin on the ground. This has been done purposely in order to tempt Rommel wide out into the desert where he will use more petrol. And it is against 13 Corps that he will undoubtedly launch his main attack.

" You, Jorrocks, are to take over command of this corps—13—and you will defeat Rommel and repel his attack *without getting unduly mauled in the process.* This is vital, because as soon as possible I want to build up a strong mobile reserve consisting largely of armoured divisions, on the lines of the German Afrika Korps. When this is equipped and trained I shall attack and hit Rommel for six right out of Africa. If you suffer heavy losses in this forthcoming battle it will delay the formation of this mobile striking force. I don't much like the existing plan on 13 Corps front. Go up and alter it as you think fit, but keep me informed of what you propose to do and I will come and see you at any time. In my opinion the key to the battle on your front is the Alam Halfa ridge which is now occupied by the 44th Division."

He then went on to describe to me his outline plan for " kicking Rommel right out of Africa," in order words, for the offensive which subsequently became known to the world as the battle of Alamein. Although this battle did not start until 23rd October, two months later, the plan he outlined to me that day, with one exception, was never altered to any major extent.

I thought I knew Monty pretty well by now, but this appreciation was an astonishing *tour de force* even for him. Well might the German general who was captured at Tunis say, " With the arrival of Montgomery war in the desert ceased to be a sport." What made him such a dangerous opponent was the way he planned his battles with an ice-cold brain. He was always working at least one jump ahead, not concerned so much with the current battle as with the next or the next but one. I can see him now, as I left the caravan, shaking his finger at me and saying: "Remember, Jorrocks, you are not to get mauled."

I left the caravan with the definite impression that prior to Monty's arrival the plan had been for the 8th Army if heavily attacked to withdraw still farther to the east. Monty has confirmed this in his book when he described his interview with the Commander-in-Chief, Middle East, General Auchinleck on the 12th August, 1942, after his arrival in Egypt. He states how he listened in amazement when Auchinleck put forward his plan that at all costs the 8th Army must not be destroyed in battle. If Rommel attacked in strength, as was expected soon, the 8th Army would fall back on the Delta; if Cairo and the Delta could not be held, the Army would retreat southwards up the Nile, etc., etc.

There is no doubt that Monty really believed this to be so, yet Field-Marshal Auchinleck has flatly denied that he ever said anything of the sort.

It is obviously highly impertinent, and even dangerous for a mere corps commander to intervene when two Field-Marshals fall out over a matter of fact, but, as I was involved in this controversy in that I took over command of the corps on the left flank which was presumably supposed to initiate this withdrawal, I have been at considerable pains to ferret out the truth. As I wish to remain unbiased, I have not approached personally either of the main contestants. Moreover even at the ripe old age of sixty-three I have no desire to have my head bitten off.

To understand the situation it is necessary to go back to 25th June, the day when Auchinleck decided to take over command of the 8th Army from General Ritchie. His personal intervention on the battlefield in this hour of need was the act of a great fighting commander, but while he was engaged in the day to day tactical battle, trying to halt Rommel's rapid advance eastward he was also responsible for the whole Middle East Command which involved not only the defence of the Delta, but also Persia/Iraq with its vital supplies of oil, the Basra base, Syria and Malta. All the time there was the distinct possibility of a German advance through the Caucasus into this area.

Few generals have ever had such a load to bear. At this time the situation in the Western Desert looked disastrous. Our troops and the German Afrika Korps were both moving eastward at full speed, sometimes in parallel columns. A defensive position had been prepared at Alamein but as only the 2nd South Africa Division and an Indian brigade group were available to man it, this was by no means impregnable. It wasn't even certain that we should get there first with the remainder of the 8th Army, let alone be able to retrieve from the existing chaos sufficient battleworthy formations to hold this position. I have always felt that the decision to stand and fight on the Alamein position was a bold one, as it involved bringing the only available reserve, the 9th Australian Division, forward from Alexandria with the risk that it also might become involved in the rout.

The decisive nature of the initial struggle which now took place at Alamein has never been appreciated by the general public, though General Alexander made the situation plain in his dispatch of 5th February, 1948 in which he wrote, "By this stand the survivors of the old Desert Army gained the vital time necessary for the arrival of the fresh divisions and improved tanks which were to turn the scale of battle." Had the battle-worn, exhausted and bewildered 8th Army not succeeded in halting Rommel's drive, we should most certainly have lost the Delta and Egypt, and the Mediterranean would then have become an Axis lake.

It can be argued with justification that this heroic stand was the turning point in the war. Complete disaster in the Mediterranean Middle East might well have resulted from any failure. Could we have retained our hold on the Persian Gulf? Because this tempting prize might have induced the Germans to switch their drive south of the Caucasus. India, cut off from Persian oil, would have been in the gravest danger. Axis pressure could have forced Turkey into the war against us. Faced with such a situation would Franco's Spain still have remained neutral? If not, Gibraltar must have fallen. Italy would then have been preserved for Fascism and the landings in North Africa would never have taken place.

It was the desperate fighting in the first fortnight of July, when the 8th Army rescued Egypt, which paved the way for our subsequent victories.

It was decided to stand at Alamein but obviously it was prudent to organise another position farther back on the outskirts of Alexandria and the Delta in case we were defeated at Alamein. This was developed into the G.H.Q. Line, as it was sometimes called. Even so, the rest of General Auchinleck's vast Middle East Command was now almost denuded of troops and the most vital area of all, far more vital than Cairo, Alexandria and the Delta, was that containing the Persian oil. In the words of Viscount Alanbrooke, who was C.I.G.S. at the time, "If we lost the Persian oil, we inevitably lost Egypt, command of the Indian Ocean and endangered the whole Indian-Burma situation." So surely it was only right for the C.-in-C. Middle East to prepare plans to keep the 8th Army in being at all costs, and if the worst came to the worst, to withdraw it southwards up the Nile.

I maintain that at this very difficult time General Auchinleck showed all the attributes of a very great commander. He stepped in personally to repair the breach in the Western Desert but at the same time ordered his staff, which was back in Cairo, to prepare plans in case his personal intervention in the battlefield failed. His opponent Rommel paid him an exceptional tribute when he wrote, "General Auchinleck had taken personal command of the operation in the Alamein position, conducting the battle with remarkable skill and tactically much better than Ritchie. His appreciation of the situation seemed admirably cool: he did not allow himself to be impressed by any of our measures and he did not have recourse to a 'second-class solution,' remaining unmoved by the demand of the fleeting moment. This became very clear in the time to come."

It is comparatively easy for a general to emerge as a great commander during a successful campaign when everything is going his way but nobody can don the mantle of a famous captain of war until he has survived a military disaster. Auchinleck had done just this. He stopped the rot by his personal intervention and by the middle of July the serious threat to Cairo and Alexandria had disappeared. In fact, from now on Auchinleck's mind was set on hitting back at Rommel and no further retreat was thought of.

At this time Major-General Dorman Smith was with him at Headquarters 8th Army as Chief of Staff while Lieut-General Corbett in Cairo acted as Deputy Commander-in-Chief. On the 27th July Dorman Smith prepared an appreciation for his commander in which " the intention " was that the 8th Army would defeat any attempt of the enemy to pass through or round it. There was no mention in this document of any further withdrawal, but even so Auchinleck at first refused his agreement because *it did not contain a sufficiently offensive spirit.* There was nothing defensive about Auchinleck at this period. He wanted to return to the offensive as soon as possible. But after further discussion Dorman Smith convinced him that reorganisation and training were required before the 8th Army could launch an offensive with any reasonable prospect of success. So the provisions of this appreciation, which envisaged an offensive defensive by the 8th Army, were followed.

As we now know the Prime Minister was moving heaven and earth to get the commander of the 8th Army to launch an immediate offensive. It says much for Auchinleck's moral courage that, at this time, when he was convinced that such an offensive would have little chance of success, and he was under a cloud, he refused to attack until he was satisfied that his troops were trained and reorganised. The 44th (H.C.) Division straight from the United Kingdom without any desert experience would inevitably have been in this attack. They might well erect a monument to Auchinleck who unquestionably saved them very heavy casualties.

It seems clear, therefore, that from the middle of July onwards Auchinleck never thought of any further withdrawal. Indeed on the 25th July he had issued a stirring order of the day in which he congratulated the 8th Army on having wrenched the initiative from Rommel, but in some curious way this does not seem to have penetrated down to the company commander/squadron leader level. Meanwhile his headquarters in Cairo was still laboriously churning out orders and instructions which were being worked upon by subordinate staff in case a further withdrawal should become necessary. In other words they were several weeks behindhand. There is no doubt that at this period defeatism was prevalent in the rear and particularly in Cairo.

But this does not explain how Montgomery came to believe that Auchinleck, even as late as 12th August, still envisaged the possibility of a further withdrawal. The answer lies, I believe, in a clash of personalities. The very qualities of self-confidence and cocksureness which made Montgomery the ideal man to inspire the 8th Army at this difficult period must have proved very irritating to Auchinleck who had been subjected to a terrific strain during the preceding months. I am not suggesting that he was exhausted. Far from it. It is to his eternal credit that his physique and morale remained unimpaired in spite of considerable buffeting, largely because he was always able to sleep peacefully, however difficult the situation might be.

Auchinleck, who a few days earlier had heard that he was to relinquish his present command—he had refused to accept the Iraq/Persia command carrying equivalent rank which the Prime Minister offered him—probably regarded his interview with Montgomery as an extremely painful experience to be got through as quickly as possible. Moreover, as Montgomery was under his orders until the 15th, when he handed over his command to Alexander, there was no need for him to go into the situation in the same detail as would have been the case if he had been handing over to his successor. This of course is pure supposition on my part as no one else was present at the interview, but I imagine that quite briefly he showed Montgomery on the map first of all the Alamein position and then the alternative lines behind, which were all part of the defence of Egypt—defence in depth in fact. But when Montgomery arrived at 8th Army headquarters he found a gloomy atmosphere, which is not surprising. The chief of staff, Freddie de Guingand, was having a difficult and confusing time with

Auchinleck back in Cairo and the 8th Army temporarily commanded by Ramsden, one of the corps commanders. Moreover, Montgomery found Graham, one of his chief administrative staff officers, working out flagged routes back to the G.H.Q. line. It is understandable that under these circumstances Montgomery should have come to the conclusion that a further withdrawal by the 8th Army was contemplated.

De Guingand afterwards assured me that there certainly had been a plan for a further withdrawal, but, when Montgomery took over, the 8th Army staff were in fact mainly concerned with plans for an offensive at Alamein. He felt that possibly quite unwittingly, he himself might have overstressed these withdrawal plans when making his report to his new commander. There can be no doubt, however, that almost at once Monty issued orders that any plans for a further retreat were to be destroyed and the 8th Army was to stand, fight, and if necessary die where it was. The effect of this order was magical.

CHAPTER IX

ALAM HALFA

THIS, HOWEVER, is all hind-sight. Let me now return to the lonely general leaving Monty's caravan for the greatest test of his life—with a sinking feeling in his stomach, for it was painfully obvious that the fate of the Middle East rested firmly in his hands.

On the way up to 13 Corps H.Q., which was right out in the desert, I had an opportunity of discussing the peculiarities of desert warfare with the young staff officer who had been sent to act as a guide. Pat Hobart belonged to the Royal Tank Corps and was a nephew of Major-General Hobart, the original commander of 11th Armoured Division, who achieved fame as the brain behind " the funnies," all those curious tanks, such as the flails, flame-throwers, bridge-layers, swimming tanks, and so on, which played such a notable part in the D-Day landing in Normandy.

Pat Hobart, though young in years, was a desert warrior of vast experience, so I couldn't have had a better mentor. Briefly, what he said was that the desert was a desperate place for infantry because there was practically no cover from view, and the tops of the small hills—the commanding features in the barren countryside—were so rocky that digging was difficult. The only way to construct a defensive position was in the first place to use explosives to blast the necessary excavations. Infantry could attack only under cover of thick smoke-screens fired by the artillery, or at night during the period of the full moon. (To this day veterans of the 8th Army talk about a " Montgomery moon " when it is full).

So the tank was the queen of the battlefield. The armoured formations operated against each other by day and then withdrew into laagers for the night to rest and carry out maintenance protected by the infantry who occupied all-round defensive positions known as " boxes "—at least, that is what they were called until the arrival of Montgomery, who disliked fancy expressions of this sort.

If either side suffered heavy casualties in its armoured formations, then it had lost the battle. It was as simple as that. Unfortunately at this period the Germans had more and better tanks than the 8th Army, so we had to be very careful. And it was precisely in this direction that the existing 13 Corps plan required amendment.

Both my chief of staff, Bobby Erskine, subsequently G.O.C. Southern Command, a tower of strength, and Major Freddy de Butts, in charge of intelligence, had no doubt at all about what Rommel would do.

They said: " Rommel will attack your position with the whole of the Afrika Korps somewhere between the left of the New Zealand Division and the Quaret el Himeimat, a sharp, outstanding hill which marked the left flank of the 7th Armoured Division position. Having penetrated your front—and the 7th Armoured are much too thin on the ground to prevent him penetrating—he will do one of two things; either carry out a wide, encircling movement right round the Alam Halfa ridge to cut the desert road beyond it, or make a minor wheel and attack north, crossing over the Alam Halfa ridge about point 102 which is at present unoccupied, and thus cut your corps in two. In our opinion he will adopt the second course, because he is too short of petrol to carry out the wide encircling movement; moreover, he would hardly dare risk leaving the strongly-held Alam Halfa ridge on his flank."

The existing plan was for the 22nd Armoured Brigade to counter-attack as soon as the Germans penetrated the position held by the 7th Armoured Division. In this brigade were concentrated all our Grants, numbering sixty. These were the only tanks which could compete with the German Mk. IIIs and Mk. IVs; they were known, in fact, as the E.L.H., Egypt's Last Hope, and I hated the idea of committing them head-on against a superior number of German tanks estimated at about 234. If we lost the E.L.H. then we had lost the day.

So I decided to fight a purely defensive battle, and ordered Brigadier " Pip " Roberts, their commander, to dig his tanks into a

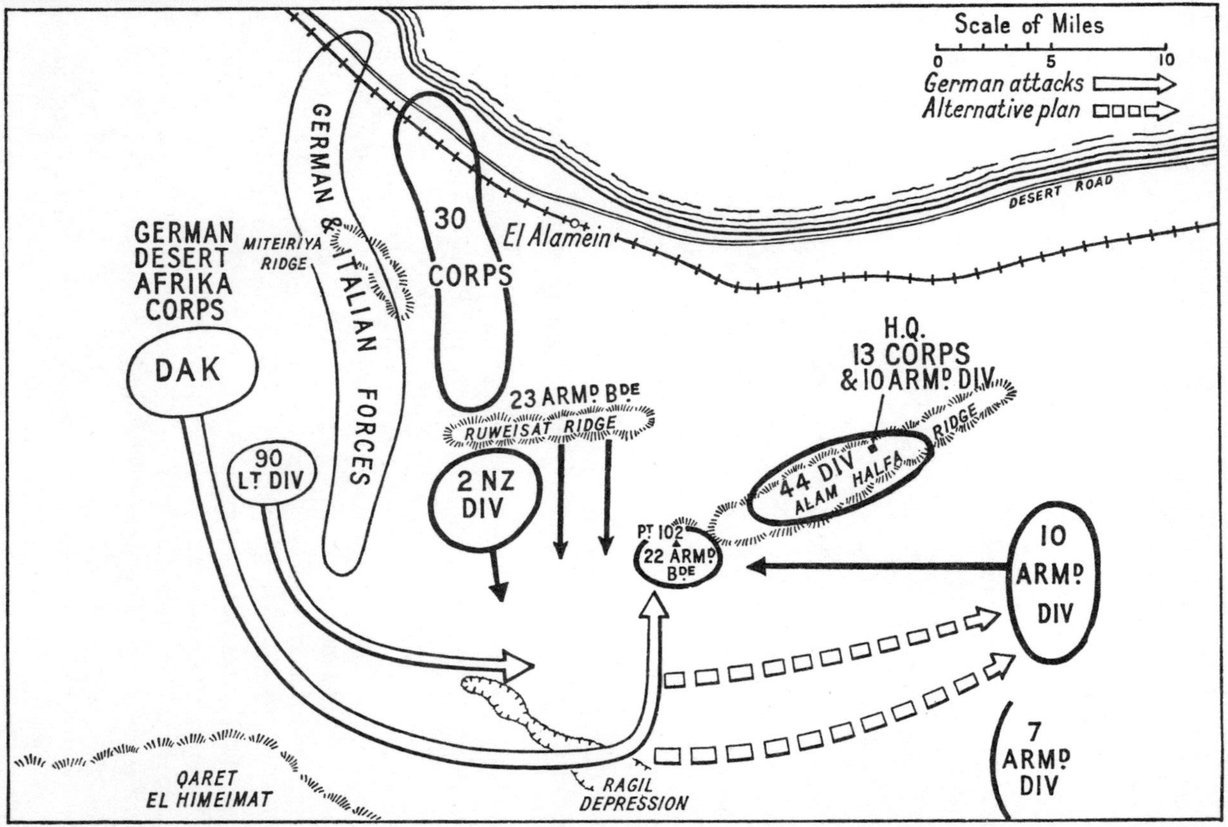

THE BATTLE OF ALAM HALFA

defensive position round point 102. Later on, when 10th Armoured Division, possessing sixty-six Grants, became available, I arranged for them to occupy a defensive position which would block the wide encircling movement, the other alternative Rommel might adopt. All my Grants were thus concentrated in one powerful, heavy, armoured division under the command of Major-General Alec Gatehouse, one of the most experienced tank commanders in the Middle East. He established his headquarters beside mine and we fought the battle from now on together. We felt, I think quite rightly, that we were well placed, for whichever way the enemy came he would run head-on into an armoured brigade, protected by anti-tank guns dug into a defensive position, while the other brigade would be available to operate against his flank and shoot up his soft-skinned vehicles. That was the plan.

Now began the most difficult period of my life. Very naturally the desert veterans, who had been fighting continuously in the Middle East, resented the arrival of Montgomery and myself. Since Dunkirk we had been sitting in England. What did we know about desert warfare? Anyway we looked all wrong. Our knees were white and, worst of all, we were wearing uniform, an almost unforgivable offence in the 8th Army, where the standard dress of the real desert type with sand between his toes was corduroy trousers, a khaki pullover and coloured scarf round his neck, the whole topped by the oldest and most battered cap he could find.

The situation was particularly difficult for me because the previous commander of 13 Corps, who had been shot down in an aircraft on his way back to Cairo to assume command of the 8th Army, had been "Straffer" Gott, a very popular man and a famous general. I was all too obviously a very inadequate substitute. Wherever I went I noted a speculative look in people's eyes, and there was a good deal of belly-aching at orders which I issued. In fact there were one or two distressing scenes before I could get things done.

To make matters worse, after I had been there about a week we had a visit from the Prime Minister, Mr. Winston Churchill. It was obvious from the start that the old warrior statesman did not think much of the new commander of 13 Corps. His unfavourable opinion was further enhanced when I explained my plan to fight a defensive battle which I tried to make clear by saying that it was really a case of " dog eat rabbit." While the Germans blunted their noses against our positions we would strike at their " rabbits," in the shape of their lorries, on which they depended for their supplies.

" That's no good," he said. " Trouble with you generals is that you are defensive minded. Why don't you attack? That's the way to win battles, not by sitting down in defence."

I couldn't help admiring the old man's pugnacity. It was precisely this spirit which had kept the country going during those dark days after Dunkirk. But his obvious disapproval of me and my plan did not improve my morale, which had already been subjected to some severe battering.

" Dog eat rabbit! " he muttered at intervals during the day. And before departing he turned to me and said: " You've got a very big responsibility on your shoulders, young man." I felt there was no need to tell me this.

I heard afterwards that on the way back to Cairo he turned to Monty and said: " He's no good, get rid of him." Monty replied, " Look here, sir, you stick to your sphere and I'll stick to mine."

This visit did an enormous amount of good to everyone except me. The troops loved the old man. I can see him now standing, with a sort of umbrella or sunshade over his head, saying to the only squadron of his old regiment, the 4th Hussars, which had survived the fighting: " Forty years ago I joined B squadron of the 4th Hussars—— " Unquestionably, with the exception of my own, everyone's morale was much higher after his visit. Monty must have realised that I had been through a gruelling experience, because he rang up that evening and was most encouraging.

Everyone was full of stories about the famous Afrika Korps composed of the 15th and 21st Panzer Divisions, who usually operated in conjunction with the almost equally well-known 90th Light Division, which, equipped with a high proportion of anti-tank guns, acted as handmaiden to the two armoured divisions. These three were Rommel's special pride; he had trained them himself and often led them into battle. There was a feeling of complete mutual trust throughout this hard-hitting group, and I would say that they were the best German formations I encountered in the war. What is more, they always fought cleanly.

There was an odd atmosphere about this desert war; never has there been less hate between the opposing sides: that is between the Germans and ourselves. Owing to the constant " to-ing and fro-ing " both armies lived alternately on each other's rations and used quite a quantity of each other's captured equipment.

Unfortunately, however, there had grown up a Rommel myth. He was regarded by our troops as a sort of ubiquitous and invincible figure. Nobody realised better than Monty that almost the first and most important thing which he had to do was to replace this feeling with a Montgomery fable. And this he set about doing in a characteristic fashion. Very soon the soldiers were discussing their strange, new commander, who wore curious hats and, while buzzing about all over the place, constantly stopped and spoke to them. What was even more surprising, he seemed to know what he was talking about. Apart from his immediate staff, the Monty impact started from the bottom upwards; the troops accepted him long before he became, as he ultimately did, popular with their officers, who naturally didn't immediately take to the hats.

Every night we expected Rommel to launch his attack, but nothing happened. The longer he delayed, the stronger we got, as more and more tanks which had been damaged were repaired and came from the base workshops. The 22nd Armoured Brigade now had ninety-two Grants, an increase of fifty per cent. I also had time to hold two exercises, so that everyone would be quite clear about their role in this new plan for a defensive battle. They were of great value and one of the brigadiers told me afterwards that when he wanted to know during the battle what was going to happen next *he looked up the exercise.*

Freddy de Guingand, Monty's chief of staff, arranged a small deception which had a major influence on the battle. In some parts of the desert the going was hard and firm, in others it was so soft that vehicles were often stuck, or at least had to churn along in bottom gear. So we all worked with " going maps " on which the hard and soft places were shown in different colours. The Germans had captured many of these maps in the course of their advance and they made great use of them. So de Guingand arranged for a fake to be printed for the area which we now occupied in which a particularly soft area just in rear of the 7th Armoured Division positions known as the Ragil depression was shown as good, firm going. This fake map, all dirty and covered in tea stains, was stuffed in an old haversack, then placed with soldiers' kits and the usual junk in a scout car which we arranged to have blown up in a minefield in the front line. Next morning the car had been ransacked and the map had disappeared. During the battle the main German line of communication ran through the Ragil depression, where the vehicles must have used up a lot of extra petrol. Later a captured German general Von Thoma said that before the battle of Alam Halfa they had captured a going map *which proved most useful to them*—the italics are mine.

During this preparatory period I got into hot water with Monty for describing to the assembled British war correspondents who were paying me a visit how we proposed to fight this battle on 13 Corps front. I did this deliberately, because if correspondents are briefed beforehand their dispatches are much more likely to be accurate, and this has an appreciable effect on morale. Nothing more infuriates soldiers belonging to some regiment which has taken a notable part in the battle than to read glowing accounts of the activities of some other unit which took practically no part at all, but, because it was in reserve, was more readily accessible to the Press. Good, accurate reporting is a great morale raiser, and never once during the whole war was my confidence abused.

Monty visited me several times and as always I was perfectly clear how he wanted the battle fought. On one occasion we were sitting in my map caravan when the A.D.C. popped his head inside and said, " Quick, sir, Stuka attack—— " So we both nipped outside and lay side by side in the sand. In these Stuka attacks, which came quite frequently, each aircraft, as it came screaming out of the sky, seemed to be directed at one personally. I couldn't help feeling this time that an unlucky strike which knocked out the commander of the 8th Army before he had really got into his stride might alter the whole war in the Middle East.

As usual the bombs fell at least half a mile away from where we were lying. Monty obviously irritated by our ostrich-like performance, said, " They won't be able to do this sort of thing much longer." He went on to give me a glowing account of the Desert Air Force commanded by Coningham. " We are just beginning to get command in the air," he said. " And as you know the Army and the R.A.F. must fight hand in hand. It is one battle, not two. Up to now the two headquarters have been separated, now they are side by side." Monty was the most air-minded general I ever met.

As the end of the month approached we entered the full-moon period—the attack must surely come now. On the evening of 30th August I visited the New Zealand Division and after eating tinned oysters with their famous commander, General Sir Bernard Freyberg, V.C., we went to visit the Maoris who were carrying out a large-scale raid on the Italians that night.

About 11 p.m. I set off in my jeep to return to 13 Corps H.Q. when suddenly the whole of the southern flank seemed to go up in flames; everything opened up. This was obviously it.

Sure enough, I returned to find the operations branch of my staff in full activity. Reports were pouring in that Rommel had attacked the 7th Armoured Division in force—just where we had expected him to come. For me this was a most exciting and dramatic moment, my first corps battle, and I would have given anything to have stayed there watching the battle develop on the operations map. But I had already learned one lesson, the value of sleep. The plans were all made. There was nothing I could possibly do that night, and it wouldn't be a very good example to my staff if the corps commander kept fussing round all night. It was far more important that my brain should be clear next day when important decisions would almost inevitably have to be made. So assuming a nonchalant air which I certainly didn't feel I said good night and walked over to the small hole in the sand where my valise awaited me. I didn't expect to sleep very much, but I had quite a good night's rest.

It was difficult, however, next morning to shave, dress calmly, and then *walk* over to the operations room. I would have liked to have leapt out of my valise and run over, but the appearance of an unshaven, out-of-breath corps commander would not have created a favourable impression.

Unfortunately that morning there was a haze overhead which prevented our air force from being used to full effect, but at ground level visibility was excellent. From my headquarters on the top of the Alam Halfa ridge it was possible through powerful glasses to study the enemy's movements and the mass of enemy tanks and vehicles moving slowly in an easterly direction was an impressive sight.

By approximately 11 a.m. we had definitely identified the whole of the Afrika Korps and the 90th Light Division in the south, so the other attacks which had been made, notably against 30 Corps front, were only diversionary. I rang up Monty and asked for the 23rd Armoured Brigade, with its 149 Valentine tanks, to come under my orders as promised. He agreed, so Brigadier Richards started moving his brigade to the positions which he had reconnoitred during the exercises. By 1400 hours he was there, all along the north side of the hill running between Alam Halfa and the position occupied by the New Zealand Division.

At 1300 hours the German columns halted, obviously to refill with petrol. Would they continue in an easterly direction, we wondered, in which case they would be embarked on the wide outflanking movement which Freddy de Butts had mentioned as the first possibility? But no, they turned north towards the Alam Halfa ridge. So Freddy had been right, and Rommel was doing exactly as predicted. We almost cheered as we watched, because if he carried on with this course his tanks would even pass through the aiming posts which we had put out in the desert to mark the different ranges for our tanks and anti-tank guns. We felt that from our point of view Rommel was behaving very decently.

At 1730 hours 15th and 21st Panzer Divisions launched an all-out attack on the 22nd Armoured Brigade whose tanks were well dug-in round the famous point 102. This was the key to the whole battle. Could the Germans with their superior numbers break through? Pip Roberts husbanded his resources and handled the battle with his usual skill. When the Germans made a slight penetration into his position he brought up his reserve armoured regiment, the Greys, which counter-attacked and drove them out again. As the light began to fail the German panzer divisions withdrew for the night into the Ragil depression. This fateful day, 31st August, had gone well for us and the crisis was over.

The remainder of the battle can be described in a few words. Next day a much weaker attack, which seemed to consist of only one armoured division, was launched against Pip Roberts's position; then, veering round to the west, it ran into the 23rd Armoured Brigade just over the crest and was driven back.

Visibility was now good, and a ceaseless stream of our aircraft pounded the Germans in the Ragil depression. Artillery fire was also concentrated against any German tanks and vehicles which were within range. The initiative had definitely passed to us, but I refused to allow any Grants to attack the German positions. Remember, I had been told at all costs not to get mauled. Time after time in the desert warfare the whole balance of the battle had been suddenly altered because of the severe losses caused when our tanks had run on to a German anti-tank screen. During the next two days the Germans tried over and over again to lure us out of our defensive positions, but to no avail. Why should we risk casualties, when the enemy was suffering severely as a result of our shelling and attacks from the air? An intercepted wireless message indicated that they had already lost over 100 tanks.

Monty came up to see me and decided that the New Zealand Division should attack due south on the night of 3rd September in order to start closing the door behind Rommel's forces. This was only partially successful for although the Maoris on the left got through to their objectives, many things went wrong with the attack of the right brigade, the 132nd Brigade, whose first desert battle this was. Nevertheless Rommel had seen the red light, and on the

4th the Germans started to withdraw, each vehicle pulling at least two others behind it. We harried them from the air and also with all the light tanks that could be mustered, but I still refused to allow one of my precious Grant tanks to take the offensive.

On 7th September, my birthday, the battle was called off leaving the Germans in possession of our forward mine-field and also of the Himeimat hill. Naturally both Monty and I have been criticised for not at once launching an armoured counter-attack. " Rommel's forces were streaming back in disorder. Now was the moment to destroy him "—that was the general feeling among many subordinate commanders. To some extent I shared their feelings, because from the corps point of view it was an infernal nuisance to have the enemy sitting on this hill from which he could observe everything that went on in the southern part of my sector. I should like to have driven him off Himeimat, which we could have done quite easily.

But Monty said no, and taking the larger picture he was, as usual, quite right. First of all, he was taking no chances. Several times before Rommel had snatched a last-minute victory when our tanks had run headlong into one of those famous anti-tank gun screens which the German 90th Light Division organised so quickly and skilfully to cover any withdrawal of the Afrika Korps. But more important still Monty's plan was to destroy the Axis forces. He realised that the 8th Army required a period for reorganisation and training before it could be launched in a major offensive, and this was the offensive which he was already planning. Part of the deception plan for this next battle, the battle of Alamein, consisted of constructing dummy pipe lines, dumps and so on, down in the south to make the Germans believe that the main thrust was coming in this sector when actually it was being launched from the north. " What is the good of constructing all these dummies if the Germans cannot see them ? " he said. " Leave them in possession of Himeimat. That is where I want them to be."

We derived considerable satisfaction from the thought of all the Italian women in Alexandria who had been having their hair specially done to greet the victorious Italian armies on their entry.

We also knew that Mussolini had arranged for a special white charger to be sent from Italy so that, mounted in suitable fashion, he could head the victory parade.

This was one of the few battles in which I fought that went exactly according to plan. When it was over I rang up Monty and asked him whether I could send a wire to the Prime Minister. "What do you want to say?" he asked. "Only four words," I replied. "DOG ATE RABBIT. HORROCKS." "Certainly not," he said. But I still believe that Winston Churchill would have been delighted to receive it!

On the day after the battle finished I was sitting in my headquarters purring with satisfaction. The battle had been won and I had not been mauled in the process. What could be better? Then in came a liaison officer from 8th Army headquarters bringing me a letter in Monty's own hand. This is what he said:

> "Dear Jorrocks,
> Well done—but you must remember that you are now a corps commander and not a divisional commander. . . ."

He went on to list four or five things which I had done wrong, mainly because I had interfered too much with the tasks of my subordinate commanders. The purring stopped abruptly. Perhaps I wasn't quite such a heaven-sent general after all. But the more I thought over the battle the more I realised that Monty was right. So I rang him up and said, "Thank you very much."

I mention this because Montgomery was one of the few commanders who tried to train the people who worked under him. Who else, on the day after his first major victory, which had altered the whole complexion of the war in the Middle East, would have taken the trouble to write a letter like this in his own hand to one of his subordinate commanders?

The psychological effect of this victory was terrific, for nothing succeeds like success, particularly in war. Troops will always follow a successful general. Monty had unquestionably won the first round in his contest with the Desert Fox; what is more, he had won it in exactly the manner in which he had said beforehand he would win it. Everyone felt that a new dynamic force had entered into the tired, rather stale, old body of the 8th Army. I, of course, also benefited from the change of heart, and from now on things became much easier.

One of the most fascinating studies of the last war was the contrast between these two great commanders, Montgomery and Rommel, each in his own way an outstanding general, yet utterly and absolutely different in almost every respect.

Rommel was probably the best armoured corps commander produced by either side. Utterly fearless, full of drive and initiative, he was always up in front where the battle was fiercest. If his opponent made a mistake, Rommel was on to it like a flash, and he never hesitated to take personal command of a regiment or battalion if he thought fit. On one occasion he was found lifting mines with his own hands. His popularity with the soldiers was immense, but a great many officers resented his interference with their commands. All this reads like the copy-book general but, in point of fact, this is not the best way to control a swift-moving, modern battle. Very often at a critical moment no one could find Rommel, because he was conducting personally some battalion attack. He tended to become so involved in some minor action that he failed to appreciate the general picture of the battlefield.

I would say, also, after reading a good deal about him, that Rommel worried too much. It is a curious fact that his health, which seemed to be all right in victory, began to deteriorate when the tide turned against him. This is borne out by a letter written to his wife on 29th October, 1942, during the battle of Alamein, in which he wrote: " At night I lie with my eyes open wide, unable to sleep for the load that is on my shoulders. In the day I am dead tired."

Generals who fail to sleep seldom last long. Auchinleck had proved of sterner stuff during his period of trial.

Monty was not such a dashing, romantic figure as his opponent; nor would you find him leading a forlorn hope in person, for the simple reason that if he was in command forlorn hopes did not occur. He had an extraordinary capacity for putting his finger straight on the essentials of any problem, and of being able to explain them simply and clearly. He planned all his battles most carefully—and then put them out of his mind every night. I believe he was awakened in the night only half a dozen times during the whole war.

Their handling of the battle of Alam Halfa makes the contrast clear. Having made the best possible plan to win the battle, yet at the same time to husband his resources, Monty dismissed Alam Halfa entirely from his mind and concentrated on the next one. His insistence on the fact that I was not to be mauled was typical of his forward thinking.

Rommel was suffering considerable administrative difficulties, particularly lack of petrol, and this was exploited by Montgomery to the fullest extent. Monty disposed his forces so as to force Rommel wide out into the desert, where he would use more petrol: the going map was planted for the same purpose. Furthermore, I am not convinced that the shortage of petrol was quite so acute as Rommel claimed in his book. My information, from the most reliable sources, is that two, or possibly three, petrol ships arrived in Tripoli on 28th August, giving him 400 k.m.s. worth of petrol per vehicle.

Rommel attributes his defeat to three main causes:

(1) Lack of petrol, which I have already discussed.

(2) Our superiority in the air. Yet on the first day, the 31st, when the battle was virtually decided, our air forces could not operate with maximum efficiency owing to bad visibility.

(3) He claims that surprise was essential, but owing to the unexpected strength of the defences which held up his initial attack, he was delayed, and the British, who usually reacted slowly, were given time to regroup.

There was never the slightest possibility of achieving surprise. Rommel did precisely what we expected and hoped he would do. No regrouping was necessary at all; in fact, he conformed exactly to the dispositions which we had practised in our exercises.

Finally, he says that Montgomery never really launched an attack against him during the whole battle and left him in possession of our original front line, which included Himeimat. I have already explained that he was left here because Monty wanted him to be able to see the dummy preparations for Alamein. While Rommel was leading his troops in person against our strongly-held defensive positions on the Alam Halfa ridge, Montgomery was planning the battle of Alamein. That was the difference between the two.

CHAPTER X

ALAMEIN AND AFTER

EVEN BEFORE the battle of Alam Halfa was over Montgomery began withdrawing troops from the line in order to build up 10 Corps, which was to form his mobile striking force. General Alexander had told me originally that I was to command this *corps d'élite*, but the more I thought about it the more I realised that I was not the best man for the job. 10 Corps was to consist of two armoured divisions and the completely motorised 2nd New Zealand Division. It would, therefore, be composed largely of the real old " desert sweats," and although I had, to a limited extent, won my spurs at Alam Halfa, I was still very much a " foreigner from the U.K."

It was most unlikely that an infantryman straight from home would be welcomed by the cavalry and tank corps formations which formed the hard core of this mobile force. It would take time to break down their prejudices, and time was all too short. So I went to see Monty before any final decisions were taken; I knew only too well that once he had made up his mind nothing on earth would alter it. I suggested somewhat tentatively that the obvious man for the command was Herbert Lumsden, who would be readily acceptable to everyone. A cavalry officer and a well-known amateur rider before the war, he had all the qualities required in a first-class steeplechase jockey, physical fitness, nerve, and the capacity to make up his mind in a split second. He had commanded the 12th Lancers brilliantly during the withdrawal to Dunkirk. Since then he had proved himself over and over again on the battlefields of the Western Desert.

But it was his long desert experience which was to prove the stumbling block. He could never bring himself to accept us new arrivals from England, and was in consequence inclined to play a lone hand. Anyhow, he was the obvious man and Monty at once agreed—though probably it had all been decided before I made my suggestion.

This meant that I should have only a subsidiary role in the large-scale attack now preparing. The front was still held by 30 Corps on the right and my corps, 13, on the left—in the south. The main attack was to be made on the right, and after 30 Corps had punched two broad corridors through the heavily-defended mine-fields, 10 Corps was to follow up and pass through. My corps was to attack also, and if we could break through, so much the better, but our main role was to mislead the enemy into believing that ours was the main effort and thus contain, in the south, as many enemy troops as possible; in particular 21st Panzer Division, which was in reserve opposite my sector of the front. It was impossible to prevent the enemy knowing that the attack was imminent. The best we could hope for was to deceive him about the time and place of the main effort.

Monty's very able staff, under the direction of Freddy de Guingand, worked out in detail the number and position of all vehicles and guns which would be required for the assault. These were concentrated in their proper places behind 30 Corps front very early on; but they were not the real operational vehicles. They were spares and, above all, dummies. Though the German aircraft photographed these concentrations constantly, they always remained the same, and there was no sudden increase just before the battle. As the assaulting divisions moved into position, their operational vehicles merely replaced the dummies, the change-over taking place, of course, at night.

In my sector dummy dumps and workshops began to spring up like mushrooms, all supplied by dummy pipelines and water installations. On the night of the attack it was arranged for the wireless sets of a complete armoured division to operate so as to suggest that large armoured forces were moving forward in this sector. In fact, I had the somewhat invidious task of trying to attract the enemy's attention to the place where I was due to attack.

During this preparatory period Monty was building up his

army on three basic principles which were drummed into all his subordinate commanders: leadership, equipment and training. The character and capability of all commanders were examined under the microscope, and a number of changes were made. Monty has often been accused of ruthlessness—of sacking people right and left. He certainly didn't suffer fools gladly, and he demanded from his subordinates the same high standard of military integrity which he set for himself, but I have never known him to be unreasonable. If an officer failed for some good reason, such as staleness or illness, he was always given a second chance. His detailed knowledge of quite junior officers was astonishing, even alarming on occasions.

The main change which occurred at the top was the arrival of Oliver Leese to command 30 Corps in place of Ramsden. I had hardly ever met Leese before but knew him to be a great character—reputed to have a wonderful flow of language on occasions—who had firmly impressed his personality on the Guards Armoured Division. He turned out to be a fine commander and an easy man to work with. He had the dubious reputation of being the only man who drove a motor car faster and more dangerously than I did. It was with great amusement, therefore, that a few months after he had retired I saw his name in the paper as opening the "road safety week of Wolverhampton."

The equipment situation improved rapidly and this is where General Alexander was such a help. I have seen him sitting in Monty's caravan making notes himself of all the many requirements of the 8th Army. Then, somehow or other and within an incredibly short space of time, they would start arriving. If one item more than any other helped to win the battle of Alamein it was the Sherman tank.

I feel that the time has come for the history of the Sherman tank to be made public, if only in tardy acknowledgment of the work of our tank designers, for whom nobody in the desert ever had a good word to say. "Why are our tanks always inferior to the Americans?" was the cry heard on every side. Yet the fighting part of the Sherman was built to British design. Although the American Grant was mechanically a great improvement on anything which had so far been produced, it had many drawbacks from a fighting point of view—chiefly the position of the gun which was housed in a sponson beside the driver and had only a limited arc of fire forward. If the gun had to fire to a flank, the whole tank had to turn. This meant that while the Grant was a useful tank in defence it was not really suitable for offensive operations. Moreover it had too high a silhouette and the wireless layout was inconvenient for the tank commander. At first the Americans would not accept our criticisms of their tank and make the necessary alterations. So 300 were constructed for us, and to our design, in the extension to the Lima Locomotive Works for which we paid in hard dollars—both for the works and for the tanks. This was, of course, in the days of cash and carry. Then came Pearl Harbour followed by lease lend and the Munitions Allocation Board in Washington allotted these 300 tanks to the U.S. ground forces.

At that time it was not considered diplomatic for us to claim that the improved fighting qualities of the Sherman were due to British brains, so our backroom boys—not for the first time—just had to grin and bear it. We did, however, claim credit for installing the 17-pounder gun in the tank during 1944. The Sherman was really a first-class example of Anglo-U.S. co-operation, the fighting part British and the mechanical side American.

This does not in any way detract from Roosevelt's generous action in handing them over to us after the fall of Tobruk, which no doubt had Marshall's backing as he was always a great friend of the British. By this time they had already been issued to the First U.S. Armoured Division in America. To remove these tanks from their own troops and hand them over to us was a fine gesture and their timely arrival in the Middle East tipped the scales at Alamein. At last we had a match for the German tanks.

Almost every day our artillery resources increased and there was plenty of ammunition, so there were no worries about inadequate equipment. Such riches had never before been accumulated in the Middle East.

Training, however, was not quite so good. Although the troops looked brown and fit, many of them were not really hard and tough. Moving always in lorries and long periods in defensive positions, were not conducive to extreme physical fitness. Nor was the standard of military training as high as it should have been. It was because of this that Monty was forced to modify his original plan for the forthcoming battle, to ensure that more was not demanded of the formations than they could do. Instead of first attempting to destroy the enemy's armoured formation, the original plan, he decided to make his initial attacks against the enemy's holding troops, the infantry divisions, and to use our tanks to hold off the enemy armour which was certain to counter-attack.

One evening as I emerged from the caravan lean-to which served as my mess I saw a cloud of dust in the distance which heralded the arrival of the 51st Highland Division. And next morning at reveille I awoke to the sound of the pipes. So started an association which was to last throughout the war; in fact, on almost my last night in Germany as a corps commander, several months after the war was over, I dined in their mess and they drank my health with Highland honours. I have always liked working with Scottish troops. To start with they are very suspicious and inclined to be obstinate, but once they make up their minds that, for a foreigner, you are a reasonable human being, then nobody in the world can be more helpful.

Major-General Douglas Wimberley soon became a familiar figure in the corps area. Sitting crouched in a jeep with his bony knees almost touching his chin, he was here, there and everywhere, watching over the interests of his beloved Jocks. He had two main objects. First, to repay with interest the debt incurred when most of the original 51st Division was captured at St. Valery, and secondly to keep the 51st a Scottish division in every way. If an appointment became vacant it was always filled by a Scotsman in preference to an Englishman, even though the latter might have the better credentials.

On 19th and 20th October Monty explained the plan to all officers down to lieutenant-colonel. I knew what to expect, because I had heard him speak on many occasions before, but the effect on this occasion was electrifying. Clear, and full of confidence, he

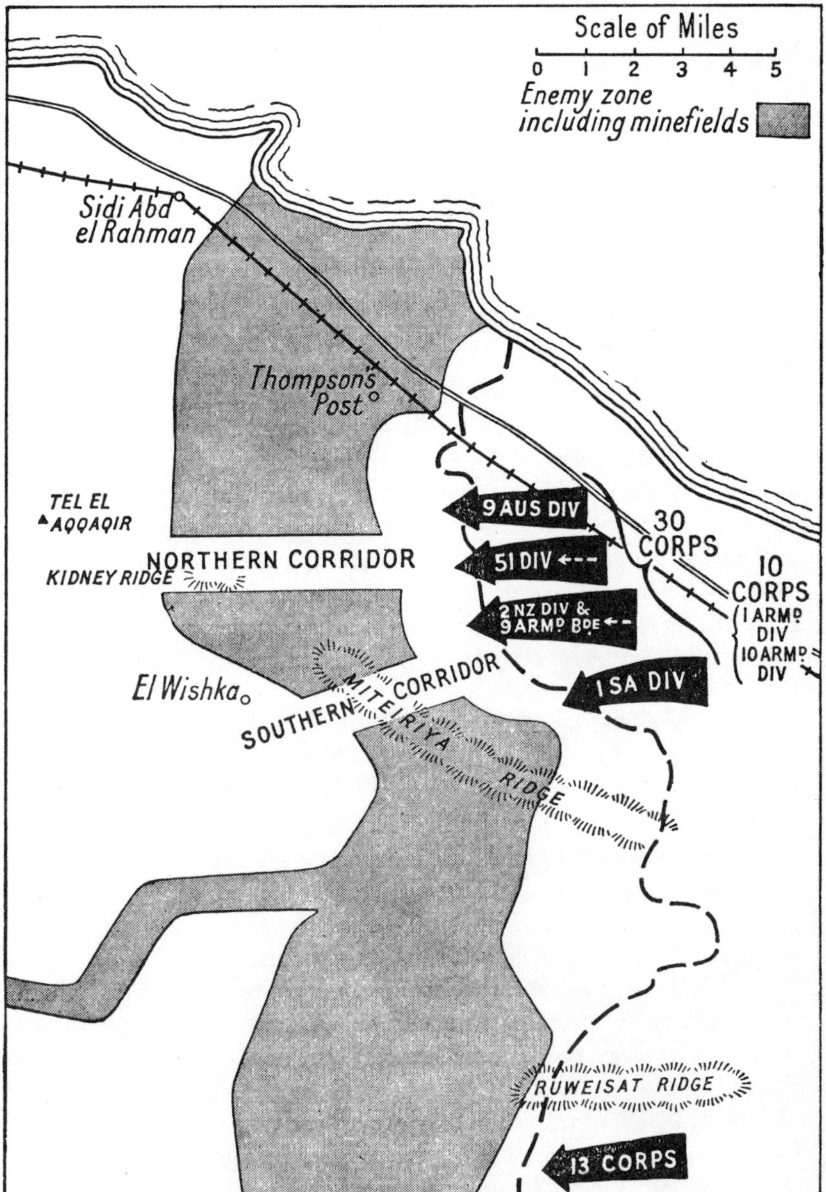

THE BATTLE OF ALAMEIN

explained that the initial attack would be made by the 9th Australian, 51st Highland, 2nd New Zealand and 1st South African Divisions from right to left. He then described the enemy situation, the deep mine-fields, anti-tank guns and so on. He stressed that there would be some very hard fighting, a dog-fight, in fact, which might last for up to ten days. After giving details about our great strength he drummed in the fact that everyone must kill Germans.

During the next few days all this was explained to every soldier taking part in the battle, and there is no doubt that the 8th Army entered the battle of Alamein in a state of great enthusiasm, almost exaltation. They had been told by their commander that this was the turning-point of the war, and they believed him.

October 23rd was D-Day. There was a lovely full moon, and the desert on a moonlight night was very beautiful. But our minds were on other things. We were waiting. And at 2140 hours exactly a thousand guns opened up in thunder and gun flashes flickered across the desert. There was practically no answering fire from the enemy, a clear indication that the deception plan had been successful. The Germans and Italians must have wondered what had hit them.

We launched our subsidiary attacks as ordered, but unfortunately the 44th Division and 7th Armoured ran on to some loose mines some distance on our side of the mine-field proper, and we did not obtain our bridgehead beyond the second mine-field until the second night. It has been suggested in some quarters, usually by people who themselves had no personal experience of desert fighting, that I was inclined to over-estimate the depth of the mine-field in the Alamein position. This may well be true, though the mine-fields on our operational map were plotted from our intelligence reports which were as a rule astonishingly accurate. Anyhow, as my role was strictly subsidiary to the main attack, I was not justified in taking risks.

My chief memory of the battle is an early morning visit to our bridgehead when the tanks of the 22nd Armoured Brigade were sitting in open formation being steadily shelled by the enemy. A small figure climbed out of the turret of a tank and walked over to my car. It was their commander, General John Harding. I hardly knew him at all, but I was immediately impressed with his calm competence. For thirty-six hours he had had practically no sleep but he seemed as fresh as when he had started. Here was a man, I felt, who would certainly go far; and he did.

Although the main thrust was being made by 30 Corps I had secretly hoped to break through in the south as well, but my hopes were dashed when Monty rang me up and said that under no circumstances was I to incur tank casualties. I was to make faces at the enemy, but offensive operations on my front were to be restricted to small-scale raids.

At intervals throughout the next few days he would ring me up an inquire how I was getting on. He always ended by asking whether there had been any tank casualties. While it is possible to fight a defensive battle without incurring casualties this cannot be done in an attack. So for the rest of the battle I confined myself to what in theatre parlance is called noises off. But from the wings I was a most interested spectator of the main performance being carried out by 30 and 10 Corps in the north. We had nevertheless played our part, because it was not until the night of the 26th/27th that the 21 Panzer Division was moved up to the north.

The battle lasted for eleven hard-fought days and it was Alamein that established Monty's reputation as a master of the set-piece battle. He kept himself balanced, i.e., always with sufficient troops in reserve, either by drawing formations from my front or by pulling divisions out of the line to regroup and rest. All the time he was changing the axis of his attacks. As soon as the Germans moved their reserves to blunt his thrust, he would halt it and initiate another elsewhere. This meant that the German reserves were forced into what he always called wet hen tactics—rushing hither and thither.

All battles have their crisis and this one came at 3.30 a.m. on 25th October. After three days' hard fighting we still hadn't completely cleared the two lanes forward and the situation had deteriorated badly, particularly in the south where a deep, hitherto unlocated, mine-field was discovered on the reverse slope of the

Miteiriya ridge. This lane through the mine-fields was congested and being heavily shelled by the enemy. A feeling was beginning to spread that we should never get through, and under the strain of forty-eight hours bitter fighting everyone was tired and on edge. The infantry complained bitterly that they had cleared the gaps in the mine-fields and suffered heavy casualties in the process, but now the tanks wouldn't go through.

"The only way to get them on is to put anti-tank guns behind them," was the sort of bitter remark that was heard. The armoured formations accused the infantry of never knowing where they were; in fact, of claiming to have reached certain objectives when they were still several thousand yards short. They felt very strongly that their precious tanks were being wasted.

"How can we debouch from bottlenecks formed by the lanes through the mine-fields when these are ringed round with enemy anti-tank guns? It is the job of the infantry to knock out these anti-tank guns and let us out." As an infantryman who had also commanded an armoured division, I could sympathise with both points of view.

During previous desert battles our tank commanders had been accused over and over again of charging recklessly on to the enemy anti-tank guns, and thus incurring heavy tank casualties. But, as long as the guns in the enemy tanks out-ranged ours, the German armoured divisions could sit back out of range of our guns and destroy our tanks one by one. Our tanks had to get in close before they could hope to do them any damage. With the arrival of the Shermans, however, the position had been levelled up as we now possessed a tank to equal the German models. Lumsden, the armoured corps commander, had therefore issued orders that there were to be no more Balaclava charges. A brewed-up tank is not a pleasant sight. Walking over the battlefield afterwards I counted in one stretch of a few hundred yards eighty-five tanks belonging to the 9th Armoured Brigade, all burned out.

I will not go into the details of this battle, which has already been described many times by those who played the leading roles, but it has always seemed to me that the moment when Montgomery emerged as a great battle commander came in the early hours of 25th October. It almost seemed as though an anxious hush had fallen over the battlefield—the first enthusiasm had waned. People were beginning to ask whether we should ever break through the deep crust of mine-fields which protected the German positions. They were beginning to look over their shoulders, a little anxiously, towards their commander. Any hesitation at this period would have been fatal, and Alamein might well have ended in a stalemate with our forces bogged down in a sea of mine-fields. But there was no hesitation. Montgomery faced the first real crisis of his career as a high-level commander with unflinching courage. This was the first concrete example of Monty's steely determination when things go badly, which is the hall-mark of a great commander. After a week's dour fighting the turning-point of the struggle came at 0100 hours on 2nd November, when the 151st and 152nd Brigades, under command of the 2nd New Zealand Division, attacked to punch the final hole in the enemy defences. The 9th Armoured Brigade was then to pass through, followed by the 1st and 7th Armoured Divisions. The operation was called Supercharge. This was a very critical moment, for these two brigades were almost the last infantry reserves available. Yet the enemy still showed no signs of cracking. That afternoon I visited 8th Army H.Q. and found Freddy de Guingand somewhat tense.

Sitting in a deck-chair with his cap over his eyes was Monty. A squadron of our medium bombers flew overhead, and Monty pointed to them and said: "They are winning this battle for me; the R.A.F. are doing a wonderful job." By this time "Mary" Coningham, that tough New Zealander who commanded the Desert Air Force, had achieved virtual air supremacy with his squadrons. All the German and Italian prisoners-of-war complained bitterly of the devastating effect of our continuous air attacks.

We waited anxiously for news of Supercharge. Just after dawn next day Freddie de Butts, my intelligence officer, came running to my caravan—"We're through!" he said. "Our armoured cars have broken out into the open country beyond. The Royals and the 4th South African Armoured Car Regiment have both reported by wireless that they are having a wonderful time shooting up streams of Axis transport heading for the west."

The battle was over, and Alamein had been won, but in eleven days, not ten, as Monty had prophesied. The success of Supercharge was largely due to the 9th Australian Division, who had carried out continuous attacks night after night in a northerly direction. In spite of heavy casualties they had almost destroyed the 164th German Infantry Division and had tied down in the northern area both 15th Panzer and 90th Light Divisions.

After the battle I went to see General Morshead, the Australian commander, to congratulate him on the magnificent fighting carried out by his division. His reply was the classic understatement of all time. He said: "Thank you, General. The boys were interested."

Rommel had not sufficient transport to evacuate the whole of his army, so many Italians were left behind to march into our prisoner-of-war camps. Badly equipped and extremely badly led, they had never had much heart in the war and were glad it was all over.

But we had more important things to worry about than rounding up Italians. The vital question was whether or not it would be possible to cut off the remnants of the German Army, which was certain to fight a series of stubborn rearguard actions to cover the withdrawal of their administrative units.

Monty has been criticised for allowing the Germans to escape and it is true that the pursuit started rather slowly. This, however, is a familiar phenomenon in war. Over and over again throughout history the full fruits of victory have been lost because of a failure to pursue the defeated opponent energetically after a hard-fought battle. The classic example was Napoleon's failure to follow up Blücher after the battle of Quatre Bras, as a result of which he lost touch with the Prussians and did not realise that, instead of going off at a tangent towards their own country as he had expected, they had withdrawn parallel to Wellington's army. This caused his defeat at Waterloo.

After a long drawn out, hard-fought battle there is always a natural tendency for the victors to relax the pressure: the battle has been won, so, " What the hell? " This is the time more than any other when commanders must go round " driving " and " driving " in order to get the pursuit into top gear. But in this particular case there were two additional factors which caused a slow start. It was a very dark night, making cross-country movement in the desert a slow and painful business, particularly for tired troops. Moreover, these highly-mechanised divisions were very dependent on supplies —petrol was their life-blood—and it was a tremendous task for the administrative echelons to get forward and join them through the maze of mine-fields and all the junk of the battlefield. I wonder how they ever joined up at all.

Eventually the pursuit got under way and then no time was lost. Two outflanking movements had been ordered, a short hook by the 1st and 8th Armoured Divisions directed on Galal with the object of cutting the desert road some fifteen miles west of Daba and a wider encircling movement by the 2nd New Zealand Division towards Sidi Hanesh. There were moments when it looked as though a big proportion of Rommel's Afrika Korps might be cut off, but the German rearguards were skilfully handled and our three divisions were constantly plagued by shortage of petrol. Meanwhile the 10th Armoured Division by-passed the trouble and moved straight up the desert road, occupying Mersa Matruh which had been vacated by the Germans.

Then, when things seemed to be going very well, the weather broke and violent rainstorms flooded the desert, which at once became quite impassable for wheeled and tracked vehicles. It was most unfortunate, for the 1st Armoured Division was practically within sight of the vital desert road. Not one of these three divisions could move a single yard; they might have been stuck in glue, and what is more, none of their supply lorries bringing up petrol, ammunition and food could get anywhere near them.

By the 9th, when movement again became possible, the enemy had slipped away. The same thing happened a few days later when the 7th Armoured Division was almost in a position to block the escape route on the escarpment at Sollum. Again rain intervened and Rommel's rearguards moving along the road got clear.

The pattern for the pursuit was now clear. Lumsden's 10 Corps and Leese's 30 Corps were in the van, while poor old 13 Corps became the 8th Army's Mrs. Mopp, left behind with the unpleasant task of clearing up the battlefield of Alamein.

The number of formations in a corps is always fluctuating, unlike the units in a division, which remain fairly constant. This was the period when I sank to my lowest ebb as a corps commander, for at one time the only formation in 13 Corps was one salvage unit. We got to know each other very well, for I visited them almost every day. It is a lonely feeling to be left behind. All we could do was to study on the map how the 8th Army was speeding along the coast road. Capuzzo, Sollum and Bardia, and by 11th November the Axis forces were out of Egypt. Tobruk was entered on 13th November. There was no delay once the pursuit really got going.

The main problem at this period was whether the 8th Army could overrun the important airfields in the Derna area in time for them to be used by our air forces and thus give air cover to a vital convoy which was sailing to Malta. It was a close-run thing. Malta was almost at its last gasp, but we won the race and the island was saved by about twenty-four hours. Benghazi was reached on the 20th, so the 8th Army had advanced 700 miles in fifteen days. But here there was obviously going to be a battle because the Axis forces were preparing to fight on the Agheila position. The desert veterans reminded us gloomily that twice before we had reached this position, but never got any farther.

Would we be more successful at the third attempt? We were. The attack started with active patrolling on the 11th December and by the 19th the German rearguards were streaming back.

By now Harold Young of the 12th Lancers had become my A.D.C. and we remained together, except for the period when I was in hospital, up to the end of the war. Few people realise what an important part an A.D.C. plays in the military hierarchy. He can be of the greatest assistance to his commander or he may be a complete menace. A general in battle leads a lonely life with immense responsibility resting on his shoulders. For much of the time he is putting on an act, disguising his innermost feelings.

He alone must make the decisions which affect the lives of thousands of his men, for battles cannot be run like board meetings.

A commander will spend a large part of every day driving round units accompanied by his A.D.C. and it makes all the difference if they get on well together so that the mask can be dropped when they are alone. An A.D.C. can act as a buffer between a commander and an all-too-importunate staff, but this has to be done with considerable tact or the A.D.C. will be accused of becoming swollen-headed. The sensible, sympathetic A.D.C. who is trusted and liked by both the commander and staff is worth his weight in gold, and he can do a great deal to make the wheels go round smoothly. I was very lucky with mine.

Later on in Europe Young was joined by Lord Rupert Nevill who in spite of a very youthful appearance turned out to be extremely shrewd. Both of them really became personal staff officers and I would say quite seriously that their contribution to the successful battles fought by my corps was out of all proportion to their rank and age.

I was now told that Herbert Lumsden was going back to the United Kingdom and I was to take over command of 10 Corps, then in reserve at Termimi some fifty miles west of Tobruk. Though my new command was admittedly in reserve it was at least several hundred miles closer to the battle and I was getting very bored with being out of it all.

My headquarters was eventually established outside the town of Benghazi on the embankment looking down on the airfield which had been so successfully raided by Major Stirling and two N.C.O.s of the S.A.S. I could also see the famous Benghazi-Barce narrow-gauge railway. This short strip of the line was most useful for moving stores, and was therefore highly prized by the administrative staff. So, when we had been forced to withdraw from Benghazi in face of Rommel's initial offensive, the officer in charge of the railway had removed a vital part of the one available diesel engine and thrown it into the sea. But the plan miscarried. As soon as the British had departed a wily Arab who had watched the whole proceedings dived into the water and retrieved the vital part, which he then sold to the Germans. The story, however, does not end here. When the time came for the Germans in their turn to beat a hasty retreat from Benghazi the same Arab was watching again. Sure enough a German officer this time threw the same vital part into the sea. It was once more retrieved and proudly sold to us at an increased price when we reoccupied the town later on. Had Benghazi continued to change hands in this mobile war a most deserving Arab would unquestionably have died a rich man.

We heard of great goings on in Tripoli. The arrival of the Prime Minister and the C.I.G.S. (General Sir Alan Brooke now Viscount Alanbrooke), victory parades and a magnificent address which Mr. Churchill gave to 30 Corps in which he said:

> "In days to come, when asked by those at home what part you played in the war, it will be with pride in your hearts that you can reply 'I marched with the 8th Army——'"

My first visit to Tripoli came on 15th February when Monty laid on a series of lectures, demonstrations and discussions so that the successful battle technique developed by the 8th Army, and particularly our system for joint Army/R.A.F. control, could be passed on to everyone. This was a great get-together for all of us, but my chief memory is of meeting for the first time that remarkable character, General George Patton of the U.S. Army. I found myself walking back to our hotel with Patton after Monty's initial address on "How to make war," so I asked him that he thought of it. He replied in a southern drawl, with a twinkle in his eye: "I may be old, I may be slow, I may be stoopid, but it just doan mean a thing to me!"

It was soon quite obvious that he was neither slow nor stupid. One of the remarkable things about him was the way in which, seemingly at will, he could put on two entirely different acts. Either the fine old southern gentleman and cavalry officer with his polo ponies, or the real tough guy with a steel helmet and two revolvers stuck in his belt. He was unquestionably a very strong personality and had terrific drive. His pet phrase, however sticky the battle might be, was "Keep 'em rollin' forward."

Montgomery and his three Corps Commanders before the battle of Alamein, October 1942. Left to right: Leese (30 Corps), Lumsden (10 Corps), Montgomery, Horrocks (13 Corps)

Explaining the plan for the battle of Alam Halfa to officers and men at 13 Corps H.Q., August 1942

The end of the left hook during the battle of Mareth; my command tank entering El Hamma, March 1943

After being wounded at Bizerta, North Africa

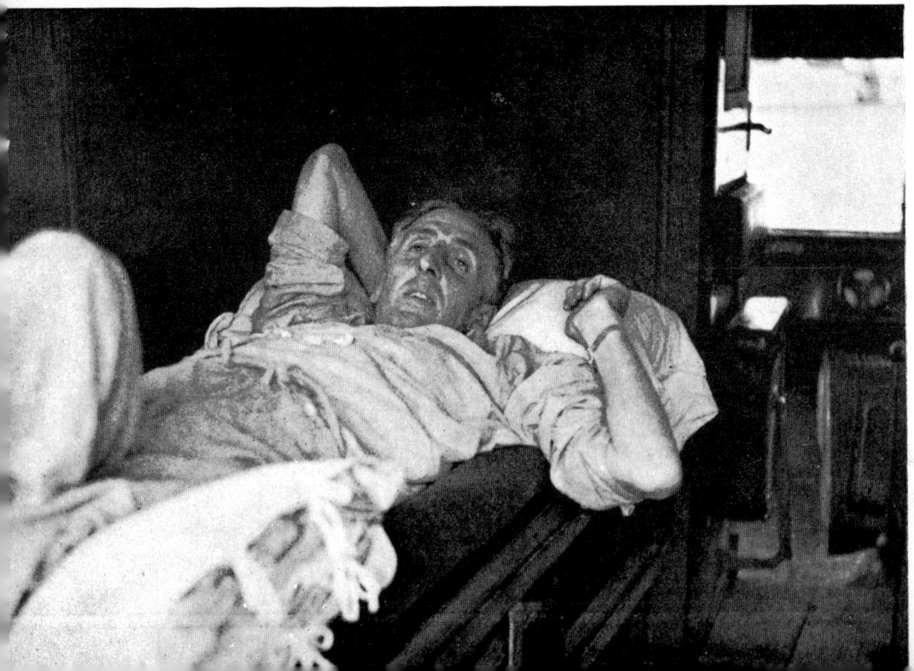

It was during this conference that we heard the news of the American reverse in the Kasserine Pass battle in North Africa. This we knew could have a big effect on us, because the closer we came together the more the operations of the 1st Army west of Tunis and the 8th Army west of Tripoli must merge into one campaign.

It was in Tripoli that I witnessed an example of the affection in which the 8th Army now held their commander. We were all seated in the Opera House for an entertainment given by a very high-level concert party headed, I believe, by Leslie Henson. Everyone had been looking forward to this immensely because visits from concert parties, let alone one of this calibre, had been rare events up to now. When Monty entered his box in the dress circle the audience of all ranks turned their backs on the stage and cheered for several minutes. When the performance was over the same thing happened again, only this time they chanted " We want Monty." The British soldier is not as a rule very demonstrative and his attitude to brass, unless it happens to be his own particular bit of brass whom he knows well, is normally far from complimentary. So this spontaneous outburst from a British audience was all the more remarkable.

The basis of all good generalship is the relationship built up between a commander and his troops. Napoleon's greatest and, as it turned out, almost his only asset on his return from Elba was the devotion of his army. His physical condition might have deteriorated, his military genius might have waned, but so long as his soldiers were prepared to die for him the French Army was still a formidable fighting machine.

And here in the 8th Army was the same outward and visible sign of the greatest battle-winning factor of all—a spirit of complete trust, confidence and affection within a formation. This sort of happy family atmosphere is common enough in divisions which have lived, trained and grown up together, but it is comparatively rare in higher formations. I know of only two in our army where it existed strongly during the last war—Montgomery's 8th Army and Slim's 14th Army. And it is significant that both men took over their commands at a time when things were going badly and morale was low.

Monty had the harder passage of the two to start with. As we know, the old desert sweats did not welcome him with open arms—far from it. Yet only a few months later, here in Tripoli was this remarkable demonstration of personal affection.

How had it been done? Cynics will say that Montgomery was successful, and that soldiers will always follow a general who wins battles. Wellington's troops never loved him, yet they would have followed him anywhere. I would say that there were four main qualities of leadership which bound the 8th Army to Monty.

First—When all was confusion he had the supreme gift of reducing the most complex situation to simplicity. More than any other man I have ever met he was able to sit back and *think* with the result that he was never deluded by " the trees."

Second—He took infinite pains to explain to every man in the Army exactly what was required of him.

Third—He was very tough mentally, both towards the enemy and, perhaps more important still, towards the political direction from the United Kingdom. No amount of urging would ever induce him to launch his army into battle before it was ready.

Finally—He was obviously a complete master of his craft, the craft of war.

CHAPTER XI

THE BATTLE OF MARETH

Rommel, working on interior lines, was now like a boxer fighting desperately to prevent the inevitable knock-out. Having landed a hefty punch with his right on the American jaw at Kasserine, he turned to deliver a sharp left hook against the 8th Army at Medenine—but he was too late. Monty was balanced and waiting for him. After ineffectual efforts to pierce our positions the Germans withdrew with the loss of fifty-one tanks which they could ill afford. This was a model defensive battle second only to Alam Halfa. The defensive position had been so well chosen that the Germans defeated themselves. I took very little part in the battle as 10 Corps was still behind, but I came forward with a small headquarters to organise the defence of the main administrative area at Ben Gardane, just in case the Germans tried a wide encircling movement against our rear. Nothing of the sort developed and we had to be content with listening to the battle on the wireless and hearing the rumble of guns in the distance.

On reading through what I have written since Alamein it sounds as though I was a very bellicose person, but this is not so. Nobody, if he is honest, likes fighting, and the closer to the front you are, the less you like it. All the same, if there is fighting to be done it is unpleasant to be left out. This doesn't apply just to generals, who are comparatively safe compared with the front-line troops, but to all ranks as well. On many occasions N.C.O.s and men who had recovered from their wounds and had been sent to some reinforcement unit in the Delta escaped and thumbed lifts for over a thousand miles in order to rejoin their units at the front.

Medenine was Rommel's last battle against the 8th Army—a few days later he flew back to Germany.

In spite of the failure to disrupt our forward movement the Axis Powers decided to make a determined stand on the Mareth line, which had originally been constructed by the French to protect Tunisia against attack by the Italians from Libya. The main defences stretched for twenty-two miles from the sea to the Matmata Hills. At the eastern end by the sea, the Wadi Zigzaou had been widened and deepened to form a tank obstacle, and was covered along its whole length by a complicated system of concrete and steel pill-boxes protected by wire obstacles and deep mine-fields.

The soft sand and the broken ground of the Matmata Hills made it impossible to get round the flank of this formidable position, except by a very wide detour of some 150 miles round the left flank towards the Wadi Merteba, a valley with steep hills on either side leading towards El Hamma. The designers of the position decided that such an outflanking movement was virtually impossible because the going was so bad, but all the same they had constructed a switch-line defensive position to block the valley leading to El Hamma. The coastal strip was held mainly by the Italians with 90th Light Division and 164th in the vicinity and 15th Panzer Division in reserve.

Monty's plan was for 30 Corps to attack the Wadi Zigzaou with 50th Division and 23rd Armoured Brigade, while the New Zealand Division plus the 8th Armoured Brigade, General Leclerc's Free French and several additional gunner regiments, which made it virtually a corps, was dispatched round the left flank to burst through the switch line, called " Plum," and outflank the Mareth position via El Hamma. 10 Corps, with 1st and 7th Armoured Division under command, was in reserve ready to exploit success towards Gabes.

On the evening of 20th March Monty invited us to dinner at his tactical H.Q. to show us the film *Desert Victory* which he had just received. As we sat in a wadi watching the performance, all around us were the guns firing the opening salvoes for the battle of Mareth. It was an odd sensation watching two battles at the same time.

At 2230 hours, supported by a terrific artillery bombardment, the attack went in, and after some hard fighting the 50th Division

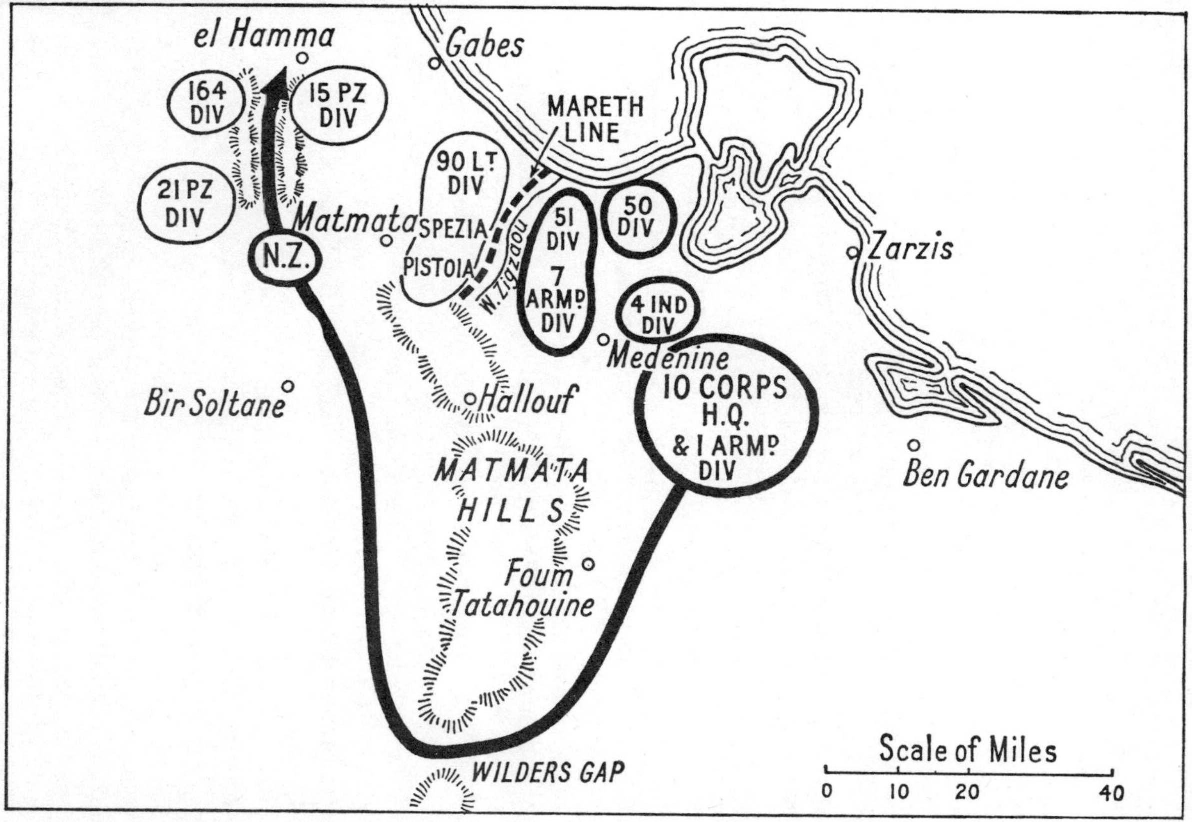

THE BATTLE OF MARETH

secured all its objectives. But during the next two days little progress was made. The main source of trouble was the infernal wadi, which made it very difficult to get tanks or anti-tank guns forward to the infantry bridgehead on the far side. It became a death-trap, still remembered with horror in many households in the north of England, whence the bulk of 50th Division came.

On 22nd March heavy rain added to their difficulties, and when 15th Panzer Division counter-attacked, the Geordies and Yorkshiremen were forced to withdraw by sheer weight of tanks. In spite of the utmost bravery, the main thrust in the coastal plain had failed and the crisis in the battle had now arrived.

At 0800 hours next morning I was summoned to a conference at 8th Army H.Q. where Monty explained a complete change of plan. The 15th Panzer Division and 90th Light Division were now firmly committed to the coastal plain. 30 Corps was to break off its attack, but do its best to keep these two German divisions tied down on their front.

The main effort was now to be made round the left flank. I was to go round with my corps H.Q. and the 1st Armoured Division and take command of the New Zealand Division which was then preparing to carry out a final assault on the "Plum" position. We were then to smash through to El Hamma. It looked as though the Italians who were holding this switch-line had been reinforced by the 164th German Division plus 21st Panzer Division, but we were promised the full weight of the Desert Air Force behind us in our assault.

Monty made it quite clear that this was the turning-point in the North African campaign and whatever happened we simply had to break through to El Hamma.

I was delighted. This was an operation after my own heart. As we left the conference Oliver Leese turned to me with a smile and said, "Off you go, Jorrocks, and win the battle"—a very generous gesture from a commander whose attack had failed. Freddy de Guingand took me on one side and said, "It's all right you going off like a dog with six tails, but I am a little worried about your reception. The New Zealand corps has done all the hard fighting, now you are going to arrive at the last moment, take over the whole show and carry out a spectacular victory. I cannot see you receiving a very warm welcome, and we don't want the attack messed up by friction."

He was right; General Freyberg, the New Zealand commander, would have every right to feel aggrieved. After all, he was a world-famous figure and a most courageous general who had forgotten more about soldiering than I was ever likely to know. So I suggested to Freddy, that contrary to the principles of war, it might be better to address all messages and orders to us both, and I felt certain we could work out the battle together on those lines. From then on Freddy, with his usual tact, called us Hindenburg and Ludendorf.

I set off with my small tactical headquarters on the long 150-miles drive past Foum Tatahouine—a desolate spot reputed to be the worst French peace-time garrison, where troops were only sent as a punishment—then through the mountains via Wilder's Gap. My desert-worthy car got through all right, but it was obvious that some of the vehicles belonging to the 1st Armoured Division were going to have a difficult journey, and time was all-important. As a matter of fact, their last vehicles arrived only thirty minutes before the attack was launched. Speed was so essential that we arranged for the ammunition lorries in many cases to drive right up to the gun positions instead of dumping their shells at the wagon lines which were farther back. It was a risky proceeding because the gun positions were overlooked by the enemy in the hills on both sides of the valley and the lorries were liable to be shelled in the forward areas. I was much amused at the R.A.S.C. drivers who, quite undeterred at finding themselves in this exposed position, leant out of their lorries as they drove past the wagon lines and called out to the gunners, " Come on, you base wallahs." These R.A.S.C. drivers were a remarkable body of men and their contribution to the final victory was considerable. Many of them had been long-distance lorry drivers before the war and seemingly they could go on for ever without sleep. As one of them said to me, " As long as I have a wheel in my hand I am all right."

On arrival I met the frigid atmosphere which Freddy had

anticipated, but I explained that there was no question of my being sent round to run the New Zealand attack; the main reason was that the number of troops now involved in this left hook was more than one divisional headquarters could handle. It was my corps H.Q. rather than me that was required there.

Freyberg was much too good a soldier to allow personal feelings to interfere with his handling of the battle, and whatever he may have felt inwardly at the arrival of a comparatively unknown, skinny corps commander, he co-operated most nobly. After consulting Monty, we decided on a blitz attack straight up the valley. The New Zealand division and 8th Armoured Brigade supported by every gun we had were to attack at 1600 hours with the sun behind them, a most important factor in desert fighting: up to the present the Germans had always had this advantage, but now it was our turn. The air support was on a scale never attempted before by either side during the war. The continuous low-flying attacks organised by Harry Broadhurst, the new commander of the Desert Air Force, were to form the pattern of army/air co-operation for future battles in Europe.

The 1st Armoured Division was to follow behind and pass through the New Zealanders when the crust had been broken. It would continue to advance until dusk, then halt and wait for the moon to rise before continuing the advance right through the night. The whole point of this night advance was that the valley was ambushed by the hills on either side which would prove a death-trap in daylight. I remember Freyberg turning to me and saying, "If we punch the hole will the tanks really go through?" (shades of Alamein!) I said: "Yes, they will, and I am going with them myself."

The battle went like clockwork. My chief memories are of our fighters and bombers screaming in at zero feet, the first time that this had been attempted in the desert.

Then the tanks of the 8th Armoured Brigade, Staffordshire and Sherwood Rangers Yeomanry, commanded by Roscoe Harvey, advanced up the valley in open order. They thought they were being launched on a second Balaclava, but there was no hesitation.

The New Zealanders emerged from their trenches where they had been lying up all day and swarmed forward. What magnificent troops they were.

Finally the really awesome sight of a whole armoured division moving steadily forward. It impressed me, so what must it have looked like to the German defenders? Tanks and still more tanks moving continuously towards them. This was the sort of attack which the Germans themselves always tried to carry out, the real "*schwer-punkt*," everything concentrated in great depth on a comparatively narrow front. There was some very hard fighting, particularly by the Maoris on Hill 209, which was too steep for the tanks, but nothing could withstand this punch—air, artillery, tanks, infantry—in fact everything we had got.

It was the most exciting and worrying night of my life. As my small tactical H.Q., consisting of three tanks, took up its position in the armoured mass, I realised very well that if this attack went wrong, there was no doubt as to whose head would be on the block. I could hear the arm-chair strategists in their clubs in London saying "Heavens! The man must be mad. Fancy trying to pass one armoured division through an enemy armoured division. And in the dark too." Because that was what we were trying to do.

And, of course, in the cold light of day, viewed from England, they would be quite right; but in reality it wasn't quite so mad as it seemed. The Germans as a rule do not react very quickly to something new, and in this attack two new techniques were being tried out. Never before had they been subjected to such devastating low-level air attacks and they were shaken, or so it seemed. Because the 8th Armoured Brigade, leading the New Zealand assault with their Balaclava charge, had not suffered such heavy casualties as might have been expected. Then on top of this was the unusual employment of armour by night.

All round was the rumbling of tanks, vague shapes looming out of the dusk. I started very bravely with the upper part of my body sticking out of the turret of my tank, but as the advance went on I got lower and lower until only the top of my head was visible. There was too much stuff flying about for comfort, though most of the enemy fire was going over our heads into the area which we had just vacated.

Then suddenly it was dark, and we halted. This was the most trying time of all: we couldn't even risk that 8th Army panacea for all ills, a brew up. We just had to sit, deep in the enemy positions, and wait. I got down into the tank to see how my crew, the gunner-operator and driver were feeling. They were cheerful and completely unimpressed by the fact that they were taking part in a unique military operation: they might in fact have been driving up the long valley at Aldershot. In moments of crisis the phlegm of the British soldier is very reassuring.

This long halt seemed to go on for ever: then a pale dusty moon began to make its appearance. And at last, thank goodness, we were off again. It was just possible to make out the dim shape of the tanks in front and on either side and there was a great deal of ill-aimed firing all round. At times the tanks were crunching over occupied enemy trenches, and we could see terrified parties of Germans and Italians running about with their hands up. But we hadn't time to bother about prisoners.

Our progress was desperately slow. That was my chief worry. If we didn't succeed in getting through in the dark, the situation in the morning didn't bear thinking about. We should be surrounded by the enemy and dominated by the hills on either side of the valley.

The reason for the continuous halts soon became clear: the valley was intersected by wadis, many of which were tank obstacles and it was not easy for the leading regiment to find crossing places. Sometimes this necessitated getting on to a one-tank front. But we steadily rumbled on and this difficult night advance was brilliantly carried out by the 1st Armoured Division. As the night wore on the noise of the firing came more and more from the rear, and suddenly I realised that we were through—the impossible manœuvre had come off. It was an unforgettable moment.

The Germans, consisting of the remnants of the 21st Panzer and 164th Division, were now in our rear, sandwiched between us and the New Zealand division, and we were faced with a hastily-manned, last-ditch position round El Hamma itself.

It was an incredible situation. The New Zealanders were still fighting hard clearing up pockets of resistance; while the 21st Panzer Division was attacking our tail. This had been foreseen and the rear of the 1st Armoured Division was protected by a strong anti-tank screen, including some of our new 17-pounder anti-tank guns. I went back to watch them come into action for the first time, and very effective they were—the answer to the German 88.

The Germans opposite the Wadi Zigzaou, the sector occupied by 30 Corps were now in danger of being cut off, but once more the weather intervened to save them. Our attacks on El Hamma were delayed by dust storms and the enemy managed to escape up the coastal road.

Monty said afterwards that this was the toughest fight since Alamein. 15th and 21st Panzer Divisions suffered a tremendous hammering from which they never really recovered. 164th Division lost most of its heavy weapons and vehicles. At least three Italian divisions lost so heavily that they ceased to be of any fighting value. The total bag of prisoners amounted to 7,000, of whom 2,500 were Germans, almost all captured at El Hamma.

On 29th March, 1943, when the battle was practically over, a car drove up to my headquarters in the desert near El Hamma and out stepped a square, squat figure in unfamiliar uniform. There was, however, a sort of familiar Slav look about him which took me back over twenty years to my days in Siberia and Russia after the First World War. Russians are as a rule unmistakable, for they all seem to have come off the same assembly line with their low chassis, tough, square bodies, short legs and expressionless faces.

He was, as I expected, a Russian general who was paying a courtesy visit to our 8th Army. Even so there was something curiously menacing about him with his stubby revolver strapped to his belt. But I was glad to see him as I wanted to get a first-hand account of their colossal victory at Stalingrad where the 6th German Army, some 300,000 strong, had been written off. I was also feeling very pleased with myself, and eager to describe my recent victory to this visitor from another theatre of war. I thought even a Russian would have been impressed by the remarkable feat carried out by our tanks in passing right through a German armoured division at night.

Not a bit of it. He showed not the slightest interest and in fact gave me the impression that, as far as he was concerned, our operations were chicken feed. He seemed far more impressed by the fact that I spoke Russian for he immediately broke into a long, detailed account of warfare on the eastern front. Unfortunately my knowledge of the language was so rusty that I was able to take in only the gist of what he was saying, but he nevertheless whetted my interest to such an extent that since then I have taken every opportunity of studying that fearsome Russo-German theatre of war.

The main thing which has always struck me is that there were in fact two wars, ours and the Russians, which might have been taking place on different planets for all the resemblance there was between them.

We reckoned in the 8th Army that for quite long periods in the desert we led a fairly spartan existence, particularly during the blistering heat of midsummer. We were operating at the end of long lines of communication, and battle requirements such as ammunition, petrol, medical and R.E. stores had to be given first priority, so luxuries were, quite rightly, restricted to the minimum. One pint of water for all purposes was far from lavish. As a result I did not have a bath for three months, and one of my staff officers had not had one for six—a fact which became painfully obvious towards the end of that period.

As something had gone wrong with the refrigerating plant at the base there was no fresh meat and I have depressing memories of continuous, hot, bully-beef, which is never at its best when melted; biscuits, stews, and those horrible "V" cigarettes of dreadful memory. Luckily for us the desert was a clean place in which to fight, so these privations had no effect at all on our health, which with the exception of periodical epidemics of jaundice was excellent. They were, in fact, minor irritations, that was all, and, compared with the conditions which prevailed in the east, particularly during the German withdrawal from Moscow in December and January,

1941, and above all in Stalingrad, we were living in the lap of luxury.

Nowhere in the west, not even when the 1st British Airborne Division was almost surrounded at Arnhem, was there such appalling suffering as during those ten weeks of bitter, winter weather between 20th November, 1942, and 2nd February, 1943, when the 6th German Army was cut off by the Russians at Stalingrad. Rations were reduced to one slice of black bread per day and one tin of vegetables between sixteen men. The only meat that was available came from the dead horses which lay frozen stiff in the snow. Soon even these were so scarce that starving German soldiers were blown up in mine-fields trying to crawl through and get to one of the remaining carcases. Medical supplies ran out and, as everyone was lousy, typhus spread rapidly.

CHAPTER XII

END IN AFRICA

THE NEXT obvious place where the enemy might try to hold us up in the advance from El Alamein was in the twelve-miles wide Gabes Gap, a natural defensive position consisting of the Wadi Akarit dominated by some steep-sided hills. If this was held in strength we would be faced with another full-scale battle.

On 30th March I was driving round the front in my armoured car, while 10 Corps probed the enemy position, when a wireless message came through instructing me to report immediately to 8th Army headquarters. On arrival I was shown into the map lorry where were seated Montgomery and Eisenhower. As this was the first time I had seen our new C.-in-C. I was very interested.

Monty introduced me, then said: "Jorrocks, I want you to explain the situation on your corps front to General Eisenhower." Monty knew the situation as well as if not better than I did, so I presumed that this was part of an act designed to show the new, inexperienced commander from the U.S.A. how the veteran 8th Army worked—" Corps commander reports latest situation," etc., etc. So, harking back to the old days, I delivered what I hoped was a short, snappy, military appreciation in the approved Staff College manner, ending with the conclusion: " The Wadi Akarit position is too strongly held to be bounced and we shall have to stage a proper set-piece attack before we can break through."

While delivering this military peroration I was surreptitiously studying General Eisenhower, the completely unknown American general who had recently been appointed to command us all. Why had he been selected, I wondered? Was he a military genius? Obviously not—but he certainly had something.

The contrast between these two men could hardly have been

greater. Monty, the commander, the complete master of the art of war: the man who made it his business to win battles; small, alert, tense, rather like an intelligent terrier who might bite at any moment. Eisenhower, a large, friendly, shrewd person with a broad grin, who was a co-ordinator rather than commander.

By the time I left the lorry I had already partially succumbed to the Eisenhower charm. His most endearing quality was his complete selflessness. It was obvious even then that he was concerned with only one thing—to win the war—and that the last person to count with him was General Eisenhower.

He was not a military genius—he never pretended to be. Nor had he, at that time, had any practical experience in command, but he was prepared to let the experts like Monty get on with the battle while he welded the different nationalities into a workable team.

To my mind they were perfectly placed. At the top the co-ordinator; in the field the commander. Neither would have been a complete success in the other's job. In fact I doubt whether anyone but Ike could have succeeded in driving his difficult team of Monty, Patton and Bradley to final victory. Men don't rise to command great armies in war unless they are strong men who do not lightly brook interference with their plans, and these three were no exception.

There was a delightful story going round the 8th Army. Monty, having changed the original plan for the invasion of Sicily, was summoned to Algiers for a conference. On arrival at the airfield he said to Bedell Smith, Eisenhower's chief of staff, who had come to meet him, "I expect I am a bit unpopular up here!" Bedell Smith replied: "General, to serve under you would be a great privilege for anyone: to serve alongside you wouldn't be too bad. But say, General, to serve over you is hell!"

Whether there was any truth in this I cannot say. But I have yet to meet the really successful commander who wasn't hell to serve over.

On 6th and 7th April, 30 Corps launched a full-scale attack on the Wadi Akarit position, and after some hard fighting, particularly by the 51st Highland and 4th Indian Divisions, they smashed their way through. It was now the turn of my mobile 10 Corps to burst out of the bottleneck and sweep forward over the fertile coastal plain of Tunisia towards Tunis.

The hills across the Gabes Gap were like a gateway opening on to an enchanted garden. In front of us was an open plain with small, white villages, olive groves and cultivation. It seemed all wrong that war should descend on this pleasant land. Up to now, with the exception of Tripoli, most of the fighting had taken place in the arid desert, populated by a few scraggy Bedouin, who appeared from nowhere to stand beside some desert track offering for barter the smallest hen's eggs I have ever seen in my life. Otherwise there was no one, and we soldiers could wage our beastly war without interfering with anyone.

From now on it would be different; we were entering a country inhabited by French colonists. Sfax and Sousse were pleasant little seaside towns, and as each was liberated the authorities staged a suitable and very French welcome. At Sousse I found myself standing immediately behind Monty while the French mayor read a long speech of welcome. Around us were crowds of inhabitants, flags, guards of honour, in fact, all the trappings of a liberation ceremony.

After the speeches, as was usual on these occasions, a very charming young French girl moved on to the stage and presented Monty with a beribboned bouquet. So far all had gone according to plan. But suddenly, as Monty shook her by the hand and said, "Thank you, mademoiselle," we all heard a shrill girlish voice saying, "Plees kees me."

This certainly was far from normal procedure. I glanced out of the corner of my eye at my commander, wondering how he would react. I need not have worried. After a brief pause Monty bent down most gallantly and kissed her on the cheek. We heard afterwards that the young lady refused to allow her fiancé to kiss her for twenty-four hours, and wouldn't even wash her face as she did not wish to remove the touch of "*Le Liberateur.*"

I had my suspicions that this charming ceremony was not entirely unpremeditated, and, sure enough, we discovered that Monty's A.D.C., John Poston, who was killed almost at the end of

The futility of war: Caen in August 1944

The King meeting regimental commanders of the 82nd U.S. Airborne Div. at 30 Corps H.Q., September 1944. Left to right: the author, H.M. the King, the divisional commander General Jim Gavin, the regimental commanders

Normandy 1944. With Brigadier George Webb and Harold Young, my A.D.C.

Commanding 30 Corps during the Rhine crossing, March 1945

the war, had organised the whole incident, and had spent the previous afternoon happily rehearsing the young lady.

It was during our advance towards Sousse that we made our first physical contact with the U.S. forces, who were operating alongside 1st British Army in North Africa. An excited British voice came up on the air from one of the 12th Lancers armoured car patrols:

" We have made contact with friends on our left! "

The voice of a suspicious senior officer was then heard to say: " What do you mean, friends. What friends? "

" Friends to whom Smokey went," came the answer.

Smokey referred to a 12th Lancer officer called Smokey Douglas who had been flown over to act as liaison officer with American forces under General Patton with whom we were likely to make first contact, as the two armies were converging rapidly. Then came a fresh voice, and there was no doubt to what nationality it belonged:

" Sure, we're Smokey's friends."

So the big link-up had taken place, and the remainder of the Axis forces were now encircled in the north-west corner of Africa. A few days later I drove over in my armoured car—keeping my fingers crossed in case we should hit a mine, as this particular road had not been cleared—to contact our 1st Army, which had occupied the old, historic town of Kairouan, and here I met Charles Keightley, the commander of the 6th British Armoured Division (afterwards General Sir Charles Keightley who commanded the forces at Suez).

Here was the perfect example of the value of British Staff College training. Charles Keightley and I had been instructors there together; we were great friends and understood exactly how each other's mind worked. There was no likelihood, therefore, of any misunderstanding between our two formations, and from then on I had no anxiety about my flank.

It must have looked to the world outside that all we had to do now was to move in for the kill. But it wasn't as simple as that.

The German and Italian forces were holding very strong defensive positions and if they intended to stay put and fight it out, then this, the last hurdle, might prove the most difficult of the whole African campaign—certainly as far as 8th Army was concerned.

On 16th April orders were issued by 18th Army Group for the final offensive to take place. All the Allied forces in turn, British, French, and Americans in the 1st Army and our own 8th Army were to attack in a wide arc all round the imprisoned Axis troops. Practically every available formation was to be committed. It was rather like the closing stages of the battle of Waterloo, when Wellington gave the order " The whole line will advance."

The 8th Army was to go in first, so on the night of the 19/20th 10 Corps launched a full-scale attack on the Enfidaville-Takrouna position. After some hard fighting we captured both these places and made a little progress beyond, but were then held up by one of the strongest defensive positions I have ever seen. The coastal plain narrowed into a funnel, overlooked by a series of almost vertical hills: these were wired, mined and held by the enemy. It was a horrible place to attack.

It was the New Zealanders who captured Takrouna. This 2nd New Zealand Division commanded by General Freyberg was unquestionably the most experienced and formidable fighting machine in the 8th Army. No man was even considered for a commission unless he had been in at least six actions, and a high proportion of the men had been wounded two or three times. They were equally at home in left hooks, day or night attacks: in fact in every type of battle which a division might be called upon to undertake. Yet even for them Takrouna was a truly formidable objective.

It consisted of steep slopes, half-covered by boulders surmounted by a high rock pinnacle with a flat top on which were stone buildings and an Arab tomb, occupied in strength by the enemy. The sides of the pinnacle were almost sheer.

A platoon of Maoris was given the final task of capturing Takrouna, but by the time it reached the foot of the pinnacle only two sergeants and seven other ranks were left. Somehow or other these few men scrambled up one at a time led by a most gallant sergeant called Manahi, and captured the whole feature. The enemy casualties were 150 prisoners and forty to fifty killed, all by this handful of men.

A few days later I visited Takrouna myself and it was all I could do physically to get to the top. How the Maoris did it wearing full equipment and in face of tough enemy opposition, I simply do not know. Incidentally, while I was on the top there was a sudden roar over my head and the New Zealand divisional artillery brought down a beautifully tight concentration within 200 yards of where we were sitting. Their head gunner, Steve Weir, told me afterwards with a grin that there certainly had been a call for defensive fire, but he had turned the whole lot on just to show the corps commander what the N.Z. gunners could do.

I have mentioned this fight in some detail because in my opinion it was the most gallant feat of arms I witnessed in the course of the war, and I was bitterly disappointed when Sergeant Manahi, whom we had recommended for a V.C., only received a D.C.M.

We were now ordered to sit tight while the main effort was made on the 1st Army front. Monty showed me the plan for these operations and asked me what I thought. I was not very hopeful. Too many units were attacking on too wide a front and there didn't seem to be sufficient strength to break through anywhere.

" I quite agree," said Monty. " I want you now to work out a plan to break through to Tunis by a strong attack up the coastal plain." Next day he flew back to Cairo to discuss plans for the invasion of Sicily.

The next few days were among the most unpleasant of my life. Under me were two very able and experienced divisional commanders, Freyberg and Tuker, who commanded the New Zealand and 4th Indian Divisions respectively, and they both hated the idea of the forthcoming attack up the coastal funnel. A division in war soon becomes very much like a family, and this was particularly so with the New Zealanders and the Indians. The father of the family is the divisional commander. He is, of course, devoted to his men, and they develop confidence in his judgment. They trust him and if he orders a particular operation, come what may they will try to carry it out.

Both Freyberg and Tuker knew that this attack would result in very high casualties. I was, therefore, a far from popular figure when I arrived to discuss the plan and give orders. Unfortunately for me, in my heart of hearts I sympathised with them. That has always been one of my great weaknesses as a commander. I have too much imagination and can see too much of the other man's point of view.

There was no doubt that we could break through, if we had to, but at a heavy cost. I also hated the idea of blunting the cutting edge of what we honestly believed to be Britain's best army. We had come 1,800 miles and fought many hard battles, and by now the whole show worked like a piece of well-oiled machinery. As I went round in my armoured car studying the country in front of me I could see no other way out than a direct attack, and our losses were bound to be heavy. But on no account must I show anyone what I felt, and this proved a tremendous strain.

I think by now everyone was feeling edgy. Divisional commanders were irritable, rows would break out between staff officers who normally worked together in the greatest harmony. There was an end-of-battle feeling—so near and yet so far. It was simply maddening.

Monty returned from Cairo on the evening of the 26th in a very irritable frame of mind. He didn't like the existing plan for the invasion of Sicily and here was 10 Corps apparently stuck at the last ditch. As a matter of fact he was far from well and retired to bed next day with a high temperature. I was accused of belly-aching, a favourite Monty expression when a subordinate disagreed with him, and was told to get on with the battle as ordered. As a parting shot, before leaving his caravan, I said, "Of course we can break through, but there won't be much left of your fine 8th Army when we have done it. Why can't we make an attack on 1st Army front where the country is more suitable for a break through than it is here?" Monty merely grunted and out I went.

So for the next three days I continued to drive, encourage and cajole my most unwilling team into this thoroughly unpleasant operation. Then miraculously everything changed.

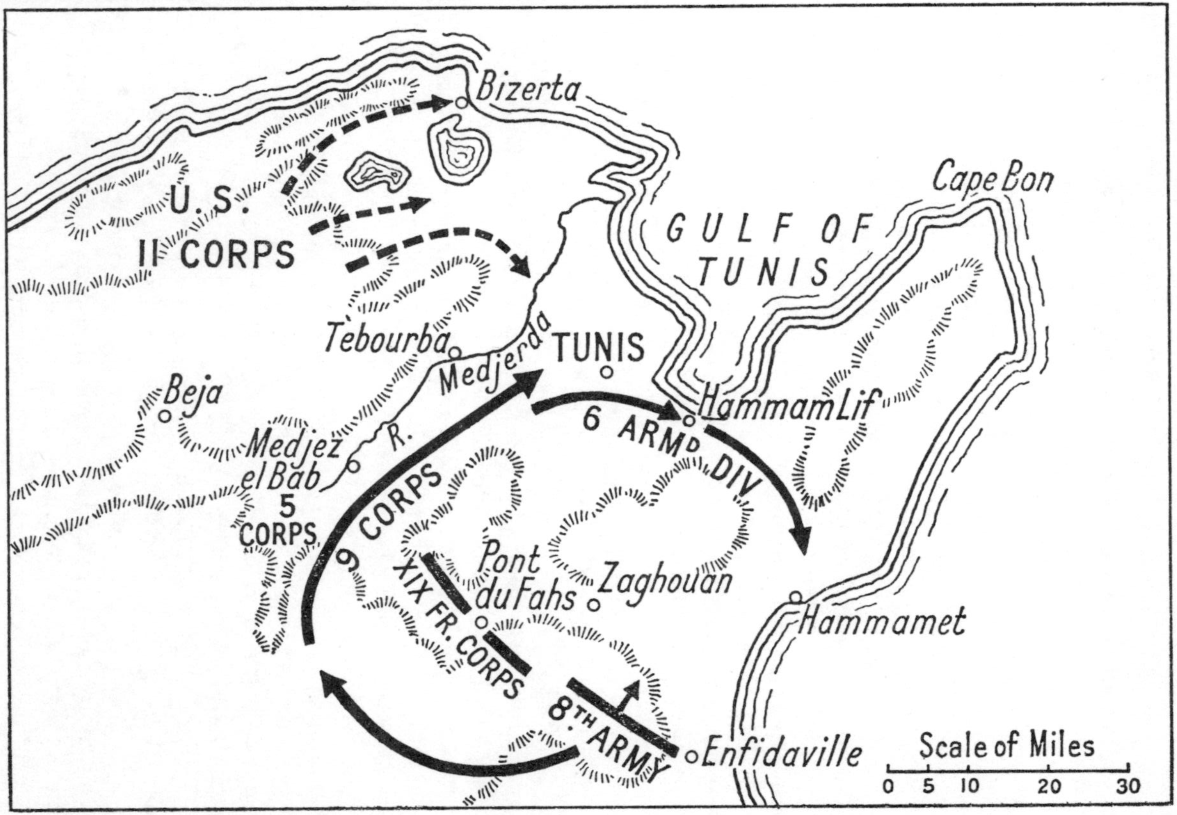

THE END IN AFRICA

On 30th April I was once again ordered by wireless to report forthwith to 8th Army headquarters. Sitting on the grass outside Monty's caravan was Admiral Ramsay, an old friend from the days when he had been flag officer Dover. He winked at me and said, "You are in for a bit of fun, my boy!" Inside the caravan were Generals Alexander and Montgomery standing in front of a map. Monty turned to me and said: "The whole weight of the final attack is being shifted from here round to the 1st Army front, from where the final *coup de grâce* will be administered. You will go off to-day, taking with you the 4th Indian Division, 7th Armoured Division, and 201st Guards Brigade, and you will assume command of the 9 Corps in General Anderson's army. You will then smash through to Tunis and finish the war in North Africa."

When I inquired what had happened to Crocker, the commander of 9 Corps, I was told that he had been wounded during a demonstration and would be out of action for a few weeks.

My heart leapt. This was the real art of generalship—a quick switch, then a knock-out blow. How much better than battering our heads against the strong Enfidaville position. And what luck for me that I should be selected for the job. Then my better nature asserted itself and I began to feel very sorry for poor John Crocker who, after bearing the brunt of all the fighting in North Africa, was to be deprived of the final fruits of victory.

At 3.15 I was off, taking with me a small staff, and by that evening I had entered a new world, because the 1st and 8th Armies were as different as chalk from cheese. It is astonishing how each army in battle develops its own personality. These two most certainly had. They looked different and felt different.

There was no doubt that the 8th Army was by this time a very efficient force, but it was the scruffiest-looking army you could imagine. The vehicles were battered and old, and round them hung a collection of old tin cans each of which had an important role to play in the by now famous desert brew.

Few people, certainly among the officers, wore uniform, and when they did it was patched and holed. The Americans when we first joined up, poured over, complete in full uniform and equipment and wearing their steel helmets, to have a look at the famous, victorious 8th Army. And what did they find? A curious sort of gypsy encampment! Montgomery like his distinguished predecessor Wellington paid little attention to dress. As Gratton who served in the 88th during the Peninsular War wrote:

> "Provided we brought our men into the field well appointed with their sixty rounds of ammunition each he (Wellington) never looked to see whether trousers were black, blue or grey; and as to ourselves we might be rigged out in any colour of the rainbow if we fancied it."

These words might well have been written about the 8th Army in the desert. It is a curious fact that two of Britain's most successful armies, Wellington's and Montgomery's were also two of the scruffiest which ever went to war.

The 1st Army looked much more like an army. Their vehicles were fairly new and painted green, not yellow like ours. Headquarters were camouflaged, everyone wore uniform. In fact this was the army with which I had trained in the U.K. up to nine months before.

Coming from the 8th Army I didn't expect to be exactly welcomed with open arms because, as I knew only too well, there was no love lost between the two. But I was getting used to this sort of situation by now.

I have no doubt that many people will be surprised to read so often of dislikes, jealousies and personal animosities, but just because people go to war they don't change their natures. In fact the unpleasant traits in people's characters tend to be emphasised. Everyone is living under considerable strain for most of the time. On the battlefield the niceties of peace-time civilised behaviour disappear, and the naked emotions, fear, hatred and jealousy are apt to emerge. Bitter animosities flare up suddenly; in the 1914 war the gunners and infantry were constantly at loggerheads, in the desert it was the infantry and tanks who did not get on.

A regiment may imagine that the one next to it, by failing to capture some objective, has uncovered a flank, and as a result a bitter hostility grows up between them which may last for years. These are the sort of things which happen in war and it is no good pretending they don't.

In this case I could quite understand why the 1st Army so disliked us. They had experienced some hard fighting in that difficult North African mountainous country and had come through a gruelling test with great credit. If you have any doubt about that, read the account of the battle of Tebourba, when the 2nd Battalion the Hampshire Regiment held out for four days though attacked by German forces which outnumbered them by four to one, supported by modern tanks and with complete air superiority.

Yet the 1st Army had no spectacular gains to show for all their hard fighting, and the papers were full of the victorious drive of the 8th. We had captured the headlines, and by this time were insufferably conceited. When I met a senior 1st Army general a few weeks before, he greeted me by saying sarcastically, " You must be having a wonderful time rounding up the Italians in the desert."

So bitter was this feeling that later on, when 78th Division, the famous 1st Army " Battle Axe " division, came under Montgomery's orders during the invasion of Sicily, they bore proudly on their vehicles the words, " We have no connection with the 8th Army."

These things have to be faced, and on arrival at 9 Corps headquarters I assembled as many people as I could and explained that I had not come there as a superior being from a superior army to teach them anything at all. I knew very well the difficulties they had been through. I couldn't help the fact that I came from the 8th Army, and I probably wasn't as bad as they thought. Anyhow, here I was and they had better make the best of me. This cleared the atmosphere considerably, because everyone laughed.

I had been warned that General Anderson, the 1st Army commander, was a dour Scot and a difficult man to serve, but as far as I was concerned no one could have been nicer. He was quite clear about what I was to do: " Capture Tunis "—it was as simple as that. Then he went on to enumerate the forces he proposed to place under my command, namely: two infantry divisions, the 4th British and 4th Indian with 160 Churchill tanks and two armoured divisions, the 6th and 7th, supported by the whole tactical air force commanded by "Mary" Coningham, and an immense weight of artillery. My spirits soared. If I failed to break through with this immensely powerful force under command, then I deserved to be shot.

From the map it seemed that the obvious place to launch the assault was from Medjez el Bab, up the valley via Massicault, and St. Cyprian, straight through to Tunis twenty-five miles away. As this was the sector of the front occupied by 5 British Corps I made their headquarters my first call. Fortunately for me their commander was Charles Allfrey, another ex-instructor from the Staff College, whom I knew well. He was one of the most popular officers in the British Army and nobody could have been more helpful. The capture of Tunis was the result of the closest co-operation between our two corps, 5 and 9.

Allfrey at once took me on a personal reconnaissance of the whole front. Everywhere we went I could see curious glances at my desert-camouflaged car, which somehow looked rakish and indecent surrounded by the dark-green 1st Army vehicles.

This country was entirely different from the desert where I had spent the last nine months. It looked far more like England, with its growing crops and small hills broken by the mountains on either side. But to see the country meant visiting the forward units who held positions overlooking the Medjerda valley. This is not as a rule a popular procedure with the forward troops, to whom there is nothing more irritating than too brave generals who refuse to take the normal precautions and stand upright, wearing a red cap, in the front line, thus inevitably inviting retaliation from the enemy artillery—the shells descending on the heads of the unfortunate troops usually after the general has gone. During the First World War we used to have a notice-board in our trenches bearing the words, "Please remember we *live* here."

On this occasion I removed my red cap and explained to the troops that I would take every precaution, but that I simply must see the country. If after my departure they were shelled—well, I was sorry, but it was the fortune of war.

The more I saw of this country the more convinced I was that here was a wonderful opportunity to employ the type of attack which, given the right sort of terrain, can be irresistible. This was to advance on a narrow front in great depth, so that there are always more men and more tanks to maintain the momentum. This endless procession, when seen from some enemy trench which is being steadily shelled (we had one gun to every seven yards of front) and attacked from the air, must surely strike despair into the hearts of even the stoutest of defenders. So I decided to attack on a 3,000-yard front with the two infantry divisions followed by the two armoured.

Zero hour was 3 a.m. on 6th May. On the previous afternoon I moved into a small command post which had been dug into a hill reasonably close to the start line. Some hours later I was sitting with my feet on the table, sipping a short drink and reading a novel, when the canvas screen which served as a door was pushed aside and in came General Alexander, who must have had a long, exhausting drive to get up to me.

Obviously dusty and tired, he said rather testily, "You don't seem to have much to do." I looked at him in surprise and replied: "If I had anything to do now, sir, we should have lost to-morrow's battle before it ever started."

Nevertheless I much appreciated his visit and he impressed on me the importance of speed and of not allowing the enemy to draw us off from the direct route to Tunis.

I never felt so confident about any battle before or after. Everything went like clockwork. The two infantry divisions punched the initial breach, and at 7.30 a.m. I was able to order the two armoured divisions forward. By midday we were through the crust and the tanks were grinding their way forward down the valley towards Tunis. It was a most inspiring sight to see these two well-trained and experienced armoured divisions being used in a role for which armoured divisions were specifically designed—to exploit a breakthrough deep into the enemy's heart. They worked like efficient machines, aircraft, guns, tanks, infantry and vehicles each fitting into the jig-saw of battle in its proper place.

I do not claim this as a great feat of generalship; it was nothing of the sort. I was merely fortunate to be in command of a battle in which victory was a foregone conclusion. On 7th May the advance continued, and as I was standing beside the road a soldier wearing the famous brown beret of the 11th Hussars leant out of his vehicle and shouted, " First in again, sir! " The 11th made a habit of being first into captured towns.

But whether or not they succeeded on this occasion is open to doubt. Their claim is hotly disputed by the Derbyshire Yeomanry, another armoured car regiment. It is almost certain that the leading troops of these two regiments entered Tunis by different routes at exactly the same moment. Later we became quite blasé about liberating cities.

The confusion in Tunis must have been unique. The town was full of German soldiers, who were completely surprised by the speed of our advance: some were even walking the streets arm-in-arm with their girls. A few of the most stout-hearted opened up with tommy-guns, or tried to organise the defence of some house; others just surrendered. Irretrievably mixed up with these local battles were thousands of inhabitants who gave full vent to their joy at being liberated.

I heard all this at second-hand because I never entered Tunis myself. When at 4 p.m. a report came through that the town had fallen, I went off to Charles Keightley's headquarters to turn his 6th Armoured Division away south-east through Hammam Lif to Hammamet, in order to cut off the Germans who had escaped into the tip of the Cap Bon Peninsula and separate them from those who were facing the 8th Army. I arrived at Hammam Lif just in time to watch the Welsh Guards clearing the top of the hill which dominated the one road through to the south-east.

In my eagerness to get on I didn't pay sufficient attention to where our front line was, but went off with my A.D.C. on a personal reconnaissance. Suddenly eight figures with hands above their heads jumped up almost at our feet. To my disgust I realised that they were very frightened Italians. Had they been stalwart members of the Afrika Corps it would have been different; we could have escorted them back proudly into our new lines. But for the corps commander to return with eight weedy, miserable Italian prisoners in tow would have made me the laughing stock of the entire corps. So, feeling rather ashamed of myself, I handed them over to my A.D.C. and went back alone by another route.

This was almost our last battle. Driving throughout the night the 6th Armoured got through to the coast at Hammamet next morning. As we had complete air superiority I ordered Charles Keightley to forget all about open spacing and to drive along this one road nose to tail, two abreast if necessary as long as he got there quickly. That was all that mattered.

General Anderson arrived next morning, and as we sat together on a hill watching the armoured division pouring along the road below us, he turned to me and said: "I have waited a long, long time for this."

Next day the surrender started. First of all a trickle, then a flood of Germans and Italians poured into our lines. Many of them were driving their own vehicles; they were well fed, quite well clothed and perfectly cheerful. This is a side of the German character which I find it difficult to understand. The previous day they had been fighting well, there was no shortage of food, ammunition or equipment. So why should an entire army, apparently without any orders, just lay down its arms and surrender?

By 13th May some 217,600 Germans and Italians had done so. Under similar circumstances I feel certain that quite a number of our formations would have gone on fighting in the mountains for ages. And if the Germans had elected to do so it would have taken us a long time to winkle them out, and they might well have interfered with the time-table for the landings in Sicily. The same sort of thing occurred when we entered Germany in 1944; white sheets were hanging out of every house. Yet no one would deny that the Germans are first-class troops who fight with great courage. I can only imagine that they are too well disciplined; as long as everything is proceeding in the orderly manner to which the German mentality is accustomed they will go on for ever. But once the command structure breaks down and orders do not come through, then they are not prepared to think for themselves in the same way as the more independent-minded British.

The final curtain in North Africa came down on two particularly fitting scenes. First, the original Desert Rats, the 7th Armoured Division, were in at the final kill; and secondly, those stalwart opponents the German 90th Light Division, insisted on surrendering to the New Zealanders.

A few days later I returned to the 8th Army and moved back with my corps to Tripoli. The next month was a pleasant interlude in the turmoil of war, rather like a period of convalescence after a serious operation. The whole corps relaxed, refitted, reorganised, and bathed, while the remainder of the 8th Army was busily preparing for the invasion of Sicily. My caravan was on the coast and twice a day I used to drive out into the Mediterranean in my amphibious jeep and swim.

By now Tripoli had become a main medical area and some twelve base hospitals had been erected in the vicinity. Hospitals meant nurses, British girls whom many of the corps had not seen for a very long period. Every evening, outside their camps, were parked rows and rows of jeeps waiting to drive the sisters to parties in the different officers' messes. This was all very well but it didn't seem to me that the troops were getting their fair share, so I invited all the matrons to lunch. This I regard as my bravest act of the whole war. I have always found one matron frightening, but here I was alone with twelve!

However, as a result of that lunch party they all responded nobly, and we were able to organise a twice-weekly dance for other ranks only. These proved an enormous success, because it meant a great deal to men who had not spoken to a British woman in some cases for years to be able to dance with one again.

This was too good to last and sure enough I was ordered to establish a planning headquarters in the Ecole Normale just outside Algiers in order to prepare for a landing in Italy.

But the trouble was to find out where. Every evening we attended a conference which was known as "the children's hour," when a representative from General Eisenhower's Supreme Headquarters arrived to tell us what new plot had been hatched for our benefit during the day. There seemed to be a certain number of suitors for the hand of 10 Corps. At one moment I was placed under command of General Mark Clark's 5th U.S. Army: then next day a wire would arrive from Monty's headquarters in Sicily informing me that I was still under 8th Army and was to report at once for orders. Eventually General Eisenhower stepped in and we were firmly wedded to General Mark Clark for the landing at Salerno.

To celebrate the occasion I flew down to 5th Army's headquarters where I received an almost royal reception. My first experience of serving in an American formation was a particularly happy one, because Mark Clark's chief of staff was the famous Al Gruenther (afterwards Supreme Commander at S.H.A.P.E.), reputed to be one of the best bridge players in the U.S.A. Whether or not he was a maestro at bridge, he certainly had all the qualities that go to make a superb staff officer—a first-class brain, great charm and a phenomenal memory. His only weakness was that he tended to do everything himself and not to decentralise sufficiently. The amount of work he got through in twenty-four hours would have killed most people, but he seemed to thrive on it.

Although we were very sorry to leave the 8th Army I was glad that at last someone had decided under whose orders we were to come and where our next operation was to take place, because time was running out. Any form of combined operation involving an opposed landing needs the most meticulous planning beforehand. Ships have to be loaded well in advance and what goes into the hold first, comes out last. So careful loading tables are required to ensure that the right sort of ammunition, stores, and, shall we say, bridging equipment, are available when required. An operation of this sort is really the military equivalent of taking up a small-sized town, putting all the people with their different requirements into ships and then landing them on an open beach complete with all the necessary services, food, water and so on. And then in addition providing them with the means to make war.

It was these loading tables which proved my undoing. As the

beaches at Salerno were certain to be heavily attacked by the German Air Force we were trying to decide whether or not to include as part of the air defence plan a new form of smoke-screen which was claimed by the Americans to be extremely effective. If we took it, we should have to leave something else behind, because, as usual, shipping space was strictly limited. At the beginning of June I went to Bizerta to watch the 46th Infantry Division carry out a full-scale rehearsal of its assault on the Salerno beaches. While talking to the divisional commander in his headquarters I heard the air-raid warning sound. Here was obviously a golden opportunity to see whether this U.S. smoke-screen was really effective or not, so we all went out into the street and watched it rolling steadily over the town. Suddenly out of the smoke emerged a low-flying German fighter with all guns blazing away into the blue—with no particular target at all. A sledgehammer hit me in the stomach. I lost control of my legs and collapsed on to the ground, but even then I don't think I realised that I had been hit. I discovered afterwards that the bullet entered the top of my chest—I must have been leaning forward at the time—and then, starting with my lungs it pierced almost every organ in my stomach and intestines, emerging at the bottom of my spine. It was pure bad luck; no one else in the party was even scratched. Here was further proof of that old military adage " If your name is on a shell or bullet, there's nothing in the world that you can do about it—it will get you in the end."

I retain only two memories of the next twenty-four hours. The first was when I was lying on the floor of divisional headquarters with a group of people standing round. Recognising the face of the divisional A.D.M.S.—the chief doctor—I asked him if I would be well enough to take the corps to Salerno. He shook his head. Luckily for my peace of mind it never entered my head that at this time he thought I was going to die.

Some hours later I became aware of a strange face bending over me and an American voice saying delightedly: " General, you are *not* going to die. I didn't think it was possible until I operated—but you are not "—and he kept on repeating " not "—" going to die." This turned out to be Colonel Carter, the head surgeon of an

American field hospital on the outskirts of Bizerta to which I had been taken. I came to know Carter very well during the ensuing weeks and no man could have done more to save my life. He was one of the leading surgeons in Dallas, Texas, from where the whole hospital came. I developed a great affection for these cheerful Texans who were so friendly to the "Limey" general who had suddenly appeared in their midst. There was no doubt in their minds, nor in mine after a few weeks of their company, about which was the best State in the U.S.A. and who was really fighting this war—Texas and the Texans.

Apparently the outside world also believed that my number was up, as the troops say, but luckily this never entered the heads of the two people most concerned, Colonel Carter and myself.

Dick McCreery arrived one day to say that he had been appointed to command my corps during the Salerno fighting, but the only other visitor whom I remember distinctly was my A.D.C., Harold Young, who had established himself somewhere in the vicinity of the hospital and came in to see me regularly. If only I hadn't been feeling so ill, the next few weeks should have been amongst the most interesting of my life. I occupied the corner of a general ward with a constantly changing population of troops from every country taking part in the war, friend and foe. The toughest of all, unquestionably, were the French goumier from the North African mountains, on whom pain and discomfort seemed to have no effect whatever. One day, unknown to me, Colonel Carter got hold of Harold Young and said that my wound was not healing satisfactorily. He could do no more for me in the field and reckoned I should be got back into a base hospital in the U.K. as soon as possible. This must have presented quite a problem for Harold because we were both by now very much out on a limb: everyone is so busy in war that anyone who disappears from the military scene is soon completely forgotten. He realised that the only chance was to see someone at the top so, undaunted, he set off on his own for Supreme Headquarters in Algiers. It says a great deal for his initiative—or cheek if you like—that this young British captain succeeded somehow in bluffing his way into the office of

Eisenhower's famous chief of staff, General Bedell Smith. Although I didn't know Bedell Smith very well at the time, this made no difference to him at all. He responded at once and in a few days I was flying home to England in the forward half of a U.S. aircraft accompanied by Harold, Colonel Carter and a U.S. nurse. The rear was occupied by General Bradley going back to U.K. to start work on the invasion of Normandy in which he commanded the U.S. assault forces.

We stopped for one night at Marrakesh close to the Atlas Mountains, where I was privileged to occupy Churchill's room in Mrs. Taylor's villa. When we resumed the flight the weather deteriorated rapidly and although I was well doped with morphia Harold and the nurse had to take it in turns to hold me down so as to keep me in my bunk. However we survived, and after changing planes at Prestwick we ultimately made a perfect landing on the airfield at Farnborough near Aldershot. I was then whisked away in an ambulance to the Royal Cambridge Hospital, Aldershot.

I have always been a fatalist and feel convinced that some good fairy must have taken a hand in directing me to this particular hospital where I came under the care of that magnificent surgeon, Edward Muir, of King's College Hospital, now surgeon to the Royal Household. I owe my life to his skill and devotion. He carried out five major operations on my midriff and as a rule visited me at least five or six times each day. The relationship between a patient and his surgeon is of vital importance. I relied on Muir to such an extent that I became miserable if he even went outside the hospital precincts. He was backed up by some splendid nursing, notably by Miss Wilkinson and Miss Piercey amongst others.

The real crisis of my life came when I was recovering from my third operation in a convalescent home at Somerley, near Ringwood in Hampshire. After subjecting me to a lengthy examination the Southern Command surgical specialist announced that at least one more operation would be necessary, but I should have to wait a minimum of six months before this could be done.

" It would be bad surgery," he said, " to do it in your present condition." I was appalled. This meant that my days of active command in the field were over. I had no intention, however, of giving up without a struggle, so I returned smartly to the attack. "Bad surgery," I said, "only applies to peace-time. Surely your job is to get me fit enough to return to the battle." The argument went on and on endlessly. Eventually driven almost mad by this intractable general bouncing about in his bed the specialist went to the window and stood with his back to me saying nothing at all. I realised only too well that this was the turning-point in my whole military life. I simply couldn't bear the thought of lying about doing nothing month after month while the war was reaching its climax. Suddenly he spun round on his heels and said: "All right, have it your own way. You know the risks. I'll ask Muir to operate but if he does not want to do so you will have to abide by his decision."

I sighed with relief. Muir agreed to carry out this difficult operation, contrary, I suspect, to his own wishes.

For fourteen months I alternated between the Cambridge hospital and Somerley. Towards the end of this long period I became a sort of tame parrot in the hospital. Everyone knew me and all sorts of people used to drop in for a chat. This had its amusing side. All the nurses had been invited to a New Year's Eve dance in a nearby officers' mess, but had run into difficulties because matron had decreed that everyone must be back in their quarters by 11 p.m.

Eventually a deputation of nurses came to see me. Their plan was simplicity itself. As all the doors would be closed to them after 11 p.m. those wishing to return to the hospital in the early hours of the morning would get in through my window which was conveniently placed on the ground-floor. No one in authority, they thought, would have any suspicion that a general's room was being used for this illicit purpose. I, of course, agreed, and all went well. Nurse after nurse returned successfully.

Then came disaster. The head night-sister spotted one of them emerging from the door of my room and immediately gave chase. The nurse being younger gained a short lead, slipped into her room and jumped into bed. Sure enough the door opened and in came sister. The nurse apparently put up a magnificent performance of a girl awakening from deep sleep. But to no avail. The sister merely said tartly, "Do you usually go to bed with your hat on?" The poor nurse was on the mat next morning.

During all this time I had heard nothing from my late commander, who must have been desperately busy preparing the Normandy landings, but when I was allowed to leave hospital and become an out-patient I was at once invited to spend a night at Monty's billet near St. Paul's School. I did my best to impress him with my complete recovery but without much success. "You haven't recovered yet," he said. "Go away and get fit. Then we shall see."

CHAPTER XIII

RETURN TO THE WAR

By THE end of July, 1944, I was almost well again. In fact on 31st July, I attended the Cambridge hospital for my final injection, and though the medical board had refused to classify me A1, I was to all intents and purposes fit for active service.

Ever since D-Day, 6th June, I had watched the battle of Normandy unfold very much on the lines which Bedell Smith, Eisenhower's chief of staff, had predicted when I had visited his headquarters at Bushey two days after the landings had taken place. I knew enough about war to realise that some very bitter fighting must be taking place as the Normandy beach-head was surely but very slowly expanded. The battle of the build up in fact.

Could the Germans concentrate troops in Normandy more rapidly than we could land them on the beaches? The whole operation might almost be reduced to this simple fact. The success of this, the largest combined operation in history, depended more on the R.A.F. and the Royal Navy than it did on the Army. The initial landings on D-Day had been a triumph of naval planning and seamanship, while the air effort provided by the British and U.S. Air Forces was on an unprecedented scale.

All this I had watched with growing impatience. Then, on 1st August, I received a telephone call from the War Office to say that Monty was sending his aircraft back for me the next day and I was to fly out to France to take over 30 Corps in the British Liberation Army.

This was splendid news, particularly as it meant I was to get command of 30 Corps, that veteran formation of the desert.

Monty hadn't wasted any time. Before the arrival of this message we had arranged to leave the Farnborough Park Hotel, where we had been staying so that I could be near the Cambridge hospital, and move to a small, very attractive cottage which belonged to my wife at Compton in the southern outskirts of Winchester. Now, instead of all three going together, I saw my wife and daughter drive off before going up to Northolt to await the arrival of Monty's aircraft. When the pilot showed me the course he proposed to take to Normandy I realised that we passed over Winchester, and he agreed to circle over our cottage at tree-top height so that I could wave good-bye. Almost my last sight of England was my wife and daughter in the garden of Yew Tree Cottage. My daughter was jumping up and down beside a white table-cloth which they had stretched out on the lawn. We then straightened out and were soon over the Channel on our way to the Normandy beach-head.

I don't know what I had expected to find across the Channel, but my first sight of the Normandy beaches was very stirring. Offshore there was intense maritime activity, ships at anchor, ships unloading at the monstrous Mulberry harbour—monstrous that man should have had the impertinence to throw down such a challenge to the sea and construct, in a few days, his own artificial harbour where none had existed before. It had been a truly Churchillian conception and here it was working away below me, playing a vital role in the battle of the build up.

Small boats were darting about and hundreds of D.U.K.W.s were driving backwards and forwards between the sea and the beach-head. The area inland from the beaches looked just like a dusty ant-heap with stores, troops and vehicles moving about in every direction. And all the time aircraft were taking off and landing on strips which had been hewn out of the Normandy countryside. If it hadn't been for them none of this could have existed at all. Without almost complete air superiority we could never have dared to risk the concentrations of men and material which I saw below me.

I was looking down on the last major combined operation of this sort that can ever take place. In my lifetime there had been many, starting at Gallipoli, and here was the end of the chapter in

Normandy. For in these days of thermo-nuclear warfare, no commander will ever dare to present his opponent with such a tempting target for an atomic missile.

By the time we landed on one of the dusty airstrips my first mood of exhilaration had passed and doubts had begun to assail me. This always happened when I was on my way to take over a new command. I felt lonely. The intense military activity all round me was in such striking contrast to the peaceful hospital existence of the past year that I had entered a strange world. Fourteen months was a long time to be out of it all. Would I find myself completely out of date? The thick hedgerows of the Normandy bocage were very different from the desert, even from the Medjez-El-Bab valley and Cap Bon.

Would I know anyone, I wondered? The B.L.A. was composed mainly of formations which had trained in England, with only a very small proportion of my old friends from the Middle East. All the people whom I had come to know so well were in the 8th Army, and must be somewhere in Italy. A great nostalgia for the old sweats with sand between their toes, and their coloured scarves, swept over me. Then, as we drove along in a jeep with ceaseless rows of traffic on all sides we were halted by a passing column of tanks. A dusty, grinning face looked down at me from a turret and I heard a voice saying, " Glad to see you back, sir! "

I suddenly felt much better. That young officer could not know how much his friendly greeting did to improve the morale of his corps commander.

As I continued on my way to 21st Army Group Tactical Headquarters I saw more and more familiar faces. The people I had last seen in Africa were now seemingly in Normandy. Later, when I remarked on this phenomenon to Graham—that old war-horse who had fought through the desert campaign as a battalion commander and brigadier in the 51st Highland Division, and was now commanding the 50th Division—he said in his dry Scots voice, " General, you ought to know by now that you always meet the same people battle-fighting."

Of course he was right. Nobody enjoys fighting. Yet the forward area in any theatre of war, the sharp end of the battle, as we used to call it, is inhabited entirely by young men with a gleam in their eye who actually do the fighting. They are comparatively few in number, and they are nearly always the same people. They had been in the desert, they had been in North Africa and Sicily. Now they were in Normandy, and they wouldn't have had it otherwise.

At last we arrived at Monty's tactical headquarters. It was in a small orchard, a place of complete peace and calm, in marked contrast to the turmoil outside. Some green humps under the trees indicated the presence of a few lorries and caravans covered by camouflage nets, but that was all. There was no scurrying: in fact, there were no signs of military activity at all. It was incredible that this little orchard was the hub from which the hundred miles' battle-front peopled by 1,580,000 troops was controlled.

Then the door of a caravan opened and out came two figures, Eisenhower, the Supreme Commander, and Montgomery, commander of all the ground forces. They were talking earnestly as they walked slowly towards me. I wondered whether General Eisenhower would remember me after all these months, as I had met him only half a dozen times previously. But when he saw me the familiar Ike grin spread across his face and, shaking me by both hands, he said: "Jorrocks, there's nobody I am more glad to see out here than you."

This was a gross exaggeration: I could think of many people who would have been of much greater value to him at that particular moment but it was a typical Eisenhower gesture, warm and friendly, and it gave me the feeling that I was back in the team at last.

After he had gone Monty took me into his map lorry, where I underwent a minute scrutiny, which, I felt, concerned my physical fitness. Had I really recovered sufficiently to be entrusted with the command of a corps in battle? This was what he was considering. And knowing how shrewd he was I felt uneasy because every now and then I had bouts of high temperature combined with sickness. I was afraid that if Monty discovered this I should be on the next plane back to England.

I must have passed the test, for he turned to the map to give one of those military appreciations which I had come to know so well.

I had also been studying him, and wondering how he was standing up to the strain of this difficult time. From what I had heard in England criticisms about his handling of the battle were growing, people were getting impatient and the Press were turning hostile. Monty had many enemies, and it looked as though the pack was moving in for a kill. This was all very different from the adulation of the 8th Army days.

Yet it seemed to leave him completely unmoved. He explained to me that the battle was developing almost exactly in accordance with the plan which he had given out at his final conference in St. Paul's School, London, a couple of weeks before D-Day. This plan was basically simple—for the British and Canadians to go on attacking in the eastern sector so as to draw to their front the bulk of the German reserves, particularly their panzer divisions, and thus enable the Americans in the western sector to capture the Cherbourg peninsula and break out in a southerly and south-easterly direction.

At that time, on the British sector, fourteen British and Canadian divisions were opposed by fourteen German divisions and 600 tanks, while nineteen U.S. divisions were faced by only nine German divisions and 110 tanks. So the constant attacks on the eastern sector had fulfilled their purpose, and the U.S. forces were at that time breaking out of the beach-head. The whole front would then swing round, hingeing on the eastern flank, and advance to the River Seine. The days of the bitter, close-quarter fighting were nearly over.

Of the Germans Monty said that, as usual, they had fought very well, but thanks to the continuous operations of the British and U.S. air forces it was almost impossible for them to move up reserve divisions by day or to stage a large-scale counter-offensive. Most of their reinforcements were forced to move by night and were then thrown into the battle piecemeal.

I asked him about the German commanders and he said there were rumours that Rommel had been wounded and Von Rundstedt sacked. He added that Von Rundstedt was a very experienced and able commander, but that he was probably now getting too old and set in his ways for a life-and-death struggle like this.

I got to know Von Rundstedt quite well after the war, when he was in the German generals' prisoner-of-war camp in Western Command. I was G.O.C. at the time and I went down on several occasions to fight some of the battles over again with him. To start with, he was suspicious, as he had never heard my name at all, which was hardly surprising because as one of the supreme enemy commanders he dealt in rather higher coinage than British corps commanders. He was particularly bitter about Hitler, and complained that when we landed in Normandy the Fuehrer had refused him permission to use his reserve panzer divisions to counter-attack the beach-head.

" I was not allowed to use them without getting permission from the Fuehrer in his headquarters on the eastern front. What did he know of the battle in Normandy? We rang up every few hours, but he refused until it was too late, until, in fact, you had your anti-tank guns and many tanks ashore. I practically had to ask him whether I was to put a sentry at the front or back of my headquarters," he added bitterly.

Von Rundstedt was chronically short of cigarettes but was much too proud to mention the fact. So we used to leave packets on the table by the door when we went out. I felt no particular hatred for the old field-marshal. We were both professional soldiers, and as far as I knew he had always fought cleanly. He was, however, a typical Prussian general of the old school. I once said to him: " Have you any complaints? Is there anything I can do to improve the living conditions in your camp? " He replied: " Yes. Some of the German generals in this camp are not the sort of people with whom we are used to mixing. I would be grateful if you could have them removed to another camp."

" Who are these undesirable generals? " I asked.

" General doctors and general engineers," he said. " It is most unpleasant for us real generals to be forced to live with people like that." Needless to say, no steps were taken to effect this particular improvement, and I left them all to get on together as best they could.

After taking my leave of Monty I reported to my army commander, General Dempsey, at 2nd Army headquarters. Our two careers had been closely linked. I had twice taken over from him in staff appointments before the war, and he had taken over 13 Corps from me in the Middle East. From now on, with the exception of one short period during the battle of the Reichswald, I was to serve under his command up to the end of the war.

Dempsey hated publicity of any sort, and had such a quiet, self-retiring personality that at first it was difficult to get to know him, but the longer I served under his command the more I liked him and admired his quick brain and complete grasp of the current military situation.

He was also much tougher than he looked. I remember his arriving at my headquarters during a hectic battle. He gave me my orders with his normal lucidity, and then, as usual, confirmed the main points in writing (he wrote left-handed). In fact, he seemed his usual self. It wasn't until some hours after his departure that I heard that the small Auster aircraft in which he travelled round the front had turned over on landing and had been written off. Though he must have been badly shaken, he never even mentioned this mishap during his visit.

At this time 8 and 30 Corps were attacking alongside the Americans, and opposite my corps loomed the famous, or infamous, Mont Pinçon. This hill feature, 1,200 feet high, dominated all the surrounding country. It was, in fact, the hinge of the whole battle on our sector of the front. From its top the Germans had the most wonderful observation of everything we did, but, once it was in our hands the tables would be turned. We were still some distance away, but it was obvious that sooner or later 30 Corps would have to assault this formidable bastion.

My first task was to get the feel of the corps. After visiting a number of units it soon became clear that the gloss had been taken off that magnificently-trained army which had sailed across the channel in June. Seven weeks hard fighting in the difficult bocage country with its small fields and thick hedges, so much better suited to defence than to offence, had taken their toll. This was particularly so in the infantry, which seemed to have lost the sharp edge of its offensive spirit. This is bound to happen after a long period of close-quarter fighting, because the offensive power of any infantry unit depends entirely on the leaders.

It would be safe to say that out of a section of, say, ten men, two lead, seven are perfectly prepared to follow where they are led, and one would much prefer not to be there at all. This, of course, is only a rough average and varies in different units. One of the reasons why so many generals objected to men being asked to volunteer for special cloak-and-dagger private armies was that it was always the leaders who volunteered. In these special formations, composed of the picked men of the whole army, each leader represented only himself, because they were all of the same type; but in his regiment he was worth almost a whole section, for he was the man the others would follow.

As the leaders take the most risks they tend, unfortunately, to become the first casualties, and as more and more of them are killed or disappear into hospital so the offensive power of their unit wanes. This was the position in Normandy at the beginning of August. Another disturbing feature was the comparative lack of success of the veteran 7th Armoured and 51st Highland Divisions. Both of them came again later on and finished the war in magnificent shape, but during the Normany fighting they were not at their best.

The problem of what might be called divisional psychology requires constant attention in war. A division may go into its first battle well trained and full of enthusiasm, but lacking in front-line experience. If it can have a quick success when it is still at the peak it will probably develop into a magnificent fighting formation. But some divisions never recover from a first unfortunate battle, or from being left in the line too long. To decide on the right moment at which a division should be pulled out of the line for a rest requires nice judgment on the part of the superior commander. The danger signal comes when the troops begin to say: "Is nobody else fighting this war?"

The 7th Armoured and 51st Highland Divisions, after being lionised in the U.K., came out to Normandy and found themselves faced with an entirely different type of battle, fought under different conditions of terrain. And they began to see the difficulties all too clearly. A racing enthusiast once described this condition to me as " like an old plater who won't go in mud." All the more credit to them that they eventually staged a come-back and regained their Middle East form.

There seemed to me to be two ways of helping to put the punch back into the corps. First, to use to the fullest possible extent the magnificent artillery support which was now available, and secondly to explain to as many troops as possible how well the battle was really going. I therefore spent my first few days with 30 Corps rather like a U.S. politician on a whistle-stop tour, going round and talking to the officers and N.C.O.s of all formations, and showing them the latest situation on a large map which was usually hung on the back of a lorry. It was hard work, but I am certain that it paid a good dividend.

30 Corps had unquestionably the most experienced and battle-worthy corps headquarters in the British Army. My B.G.S. (Chief of Staff) Pete Pyman (now Lt.-General Pyman, subsequently Deputy Chief of the General Staff at the War Office), was that rare bird, a first-class staff officer and also a commander. These two qualities are not often combined in one person. Like my Brigadier Q (Chief Administrative Staff Officer) George Webb, he came from the Royal Tank Corps. George Webb, who was killed later in the campaign, had a genius for administration. The popular conception of an administrative staff officer is of someone built more for comfort than for speed, but George Webb, who before the war had represented England at athletics, was one of the most energetic men I have ever met. Hardly a day passed that he did not visit some unit in the front line—" Just to keep in the picture," as he used to say.

He could always be calculated to do the unexpected. I discovered one day, to my surprise, that I was the owner of a 30 Corps farm, run by Webb to supply our medical establishments with fresh milk and eggs. After each battle all the stray cattle were rounded up into this farm and looked after by men with farming experience until their rightful owners could be found.

One day a senior officer standing by the roadside was astonished to see lorry after lorry passing by, each full of cattle. "What on earth is this?" he asked an officer by his side. "30 Corps farm, sir, moving up," was the reply. It was probably the only completely mobile farm which has ever existed.

Every day we were closing up on Mont Pinçon. On 4th, 5th and 6th August the 43rd (Wessex) Division slowly fought its way forward in very hot, sultry weather against the most stubborn German resistance. Unfortunately their casualties, particularly in officers, were distressingly high. The 5th Wilts., for instance, was reduced to 500 men commanded by a comparatively junior officer. By the evening of the 6th, the 43rd had reached the foot of Mont Pinçon and it looked as though we were in for a tough fight before we got to the top, as the whole feature was strongly held. But as I returned to my headquarters that evening Pyman came running towards me. Now senior staff officers are not in the habit of running round their headquarters, so I wondered what had happened.

"We've got it, sir!" he called out while still some distance away. "Got what?" I said. "Mont Pinçon," he replied. I couldn't believe it. He told me a message had come through that two troops of tanks belonging to the 13th/18th Hussars were now on the top of the hill. They reported, however, that they were feeling very lonely as there was a thick mist all round them and they could hear the Germans moving about everywhere. Pyman also added that he had been in touch with the 43rd Division, and the 4th Battalion of the Wiltshire Regiment were now on their way up to join the tanks on the top.

This was wonderful news. It seemed almost impossible that this key position should have fallen into our hands like a ripe plum. Here is how it happened.

Captain Denny, who commanded the leading troops of tanks working with the 43rd Division, discovered a narrow track winding up the hill, and reported by wireless to his C.O., Lieut.-Colonel

Dunkerley, that this was apparently undefended. He was immediately ordered to have a go. The track was so narrow that one tank toppled over into a disused gravel pit, but the others ground their way steadily upwards, until they broke out on to the top. So, thanks to the initiative of one young officer, the most important tactical feature in Normandy had been captured by six or seven tanks. Meanwhile the 4th Wilts., who were almost at the end of their tether after some forty-eight hours' continuous fighting, were being galvanised into activity by their C.O., Lieut.-Colonel Luce, who led the transport column himself. In single file in the dark this battalion somehow struggled to the top of the hill.

It was a great achievement which had a profound effect on morale. Even from the early days in the U.K. this feature had stood out as the main bogey in the Normandy campaign. On all the models of the countryside which had been used for training purposes in England Mont Pinçon had always loomed large. During battles men's minds tend to become fixed on some particular feature in front of them which gradually assumes an almost impregnable and sinister character. Mont Pinçon had looked like this. Its capture made all the difference to me. From now on we were able to overlook the Germans. I used to sit on the top with my chief gunner, Stewart Rawlins, beside me, with 300 guns at the end of our wireless mast. If any units were held up, we were able to concentrate in a few minutes the fire of these guns on the enemy. And we blasted the tanks and infantry forward with artillery fire. It was a very hard time for the gunners, who were never out of action day or night. The only way they could carry on was to form two teams for each gun by rounding up every available man; cooks, drivers, orderlies were all roped in to serve the guns.

I have often said in lectures since the war that, although I am an infantryman, I would say that the Royal Regiment of Artillery did more to win the last war than any other arm. Time after time their young forward observation officers would step into the breach and take command of some forward infantry unit whose commanders had all become casualties, while the technical skill with which huge concentrations of fire were switched rapidly from one part of the front to another was never equalled in any other army. The Germans never succeeded in achieving anything like it.

We started with limited objectives, but gradually the fighting loosened and soon daily objectives were several miles ahead instead of just a few hundred yards. During the next fortnight the Germans suffered one of their greatest defeats of the whole war, second only to Stalingrad (where General Paulus's 6th German Army was totally destroyed). In the Falaise pocket of approximately ten by twenty miles were concentrated the best part of 100,000 German troops, and all around them the Allied forces were pressing in, Canadian, Polish, British and U.S. from the south. Although the eastern neck was never quite closed the destruction of enemy equipment was prodigious. During the ten weeks' fighting in Normandy the Germans suffered half a million casualties of whom 211,000 were taken prisoner. Forty-three divisions were destroyed and their losses in equipment amounted to over 2,000 tanks and assault guns. Meanwhile the outer prong of the American encircling movement had reached the Seine: their 20 Corps crossed the river near Fontainebleau and 15 Corps turned north-west along the river bank.

As we also approached the river from the west, it became a tricky problem to disentangle the British and U.S. lines of communication which crossed each other. I had decided to breach the River Seine on my front with the 43rd Division at Vernon, and was in the process of issuing the necessary orders to General Thomas, the divisional commander, when I began to feel very unwell. The skeleton was emerging from my cupboard. I was in for one of my bouts of pain accompanied by sickness and a high temperature which usually lasted for anything up to a week. I managed to complete the orders without Thomas suspecting anything, and then retired to my caravan, where I was soon bouncing about with a rigor.

A few minutes later the door opened and in came my A.D.C. to say that Field-Marshal Montgomery was coming up to my headquarters first thing next morning. This was the worst possible news. If Monty saw me in my present state I was almost certain to be sent home, unfit for active service. So I told him to send a message to ask the Field-Marshal to postpone his visit as I would be very busy away from my headquarters during the next few days.

A couple of hours later the caravan door opened again and to my horror in came Monty. " Ah, Jorrocks," he said, " I thought that something odd was happening so I came up to see for myself." He then went on, " I know why you sent that message. But you needn't worry. If we can get you fit out here there is no question of you being invalided back to the U.K. But I am not taking any chances. Your caravan will now be moved to my tactical headquarters and you are not to move from it back to your corps until I give you permission. There is nothing you can possibly do for the next few days anyhow. Thomas has got his orders and will get on with the battle much better without the corps commander fussing round him."

So my caravan was established next to Monty's, and during the next few days every medical specialist in the army came to see me. Each day Monty paid me a visit, and these talks proved more than usually interesting because this was the time when the big argument about the future conduct of the war was going on between Monty and Eisenhower.

Monty argued like this: " The Germans are now completely disorganised as a result of their defeat in Normandy. If we can prevent their recovering, there is a good chance of the war being won in the autumn of 1944. We should, therefore, stage a powerful thrust, preferably up the coastal plain, which must keep on and on without a pause, so that the Germans never get time to draw breath. We shall then be able to bounce a crossing of the Rhine before they can get their defences organised. We can encircle the Ruhr from the north, cut it off from Germany, and the war will then be over."

Eisenhower considered this narrow thrust to be too risky, and eventually decided to advance on a broad front up to the Rhine. This was a safer course, but it had two main drawbacks. First, the war could not possibly be won before 1945, which meant prolonging it by at least six months. Secondly, as a result of this broad front policy, almost all the available formations would be in the line all the time, and there would be very few reserves available to meet any unforeseen eventuality, such as the Germans' counter-offensive in the Ardennes, for instance.

Which plan was right?

I have thought about this a great deal and in my opinion each commander was right—in his own sphere. Monty, as the ground forces commander, was right from the point of view of the actual fighting. His plan might well have succeeded. But it could have done so only if unceasing pressure was brought to bear on the Germans the whole time. This meant that every lorry and supply aircraft in the theatre would have to be made available to bring up petrol, food, ammunition and all the many requirements of modern war, so that the mobile thrust would never have to halt for lack of supplies.

The only way to get all this transport would be to halt a large proportion of the U.S. divisions in France, and remove their vehicles in order to maintain this thrust, which would be, after all, a predominantly British affair. Had anything gone wrong with Monty's plan—and there was, of course, a distinct element of risk—the political repercussions would have been great. So Eisenhower, as the Supreme Commander, was correct to turn it down at his level.

Many people may disagree with me, but that is my opinion.

Anyhow, Monty was ordered to stage as powerful a thrust as possible up the coastal plain using his own resources, and the spearhead of this was to be 30 Corps. I was released from my pleasant bondage at Monty's tactical headquarters on 26th August, and returned to prepare for as exciting a role as any commander could wish.

CHAPTER XIV

ADVANCE TO BRUSSELS

When I arrived back at 30 Corps headquarters on 26th August, 1944, the 43rd Division had crossed the Seine at Vernon. My orders were to break out and seize the crossings over the River Somme, some seventy miles distant, before the Germans had time to organise the defence of the river.

The Germans had never quite given up the idea that our main cross-channel assault would come in the Pas de Calais area, so the coastal belt was still thick with their troops, perhaps 150,000 of them. 30 Corps was to drive north across their lines of communication, by-passing any serious opposition which might be encountered. All that mattered was speed.

But on my left the nearer you came to the coast the thicker the German troops would be. So whereas the 19 U.S. Corps and 30 Corps were likely to have a fairly easy passage, 12 Corps would find the going much tougher, while the Canadians who were advancing up the actual coastal belt itself were bound to have hard fighting before they could clear the Channel ports—which was their primary task.

As I had never fought alongside an American formation before, I visited the 19 Corps commander to discuss our mutual boundary. He was most co-operative, over coffee. I once asked an American commander how it was that the U.S. troops had so much better coffee than we could produce. He looked at me with a twinkle in his eye and replied: " Well, General, ours has the advantage of starting by being coffee." He was quite right.

I told the U.S. corps commander that if, in order to get on quickly, his troops had to come into my sector there would be no hard feelings, and he reciprocated. This friendly arrangement, however, nearly led to difficulties, because a few days later he had crossed the boundary to such an extent that if his troops had come any farther my right formation would have been unable to move at all. I was wondering what to do, because after all I had given him an open invitation, when fortunately I remembered that 1944 was the U.S. presidential election year.

So I sent him a wire, "Delighted to have you in my sector, but if you come any farther I will vote for Dewey." He never moved another yard.

On 29th August we burst out of the bridgehead on the Seine and set off on our chase northwards. This was the type of warfare I thoroughly enjoyed. Who wouldn't? I had upwards of 600 tanks under my command, and we were advancing on a frontage of fifty miles: Guards Armoured, 11th Armoured Divisions and 8th Armoured Brigade were scything passages through the enemy rear areas, like a combine-harvester going through a field of corn, with my old friends 50th Division clearing up the mess behind them. Small battles to overcome hastily-organised enemy defences at villages and cross-roads were going on right across this wide front. But there was no main enemy defensive position.

Our artillery would drop into action while the tanks carried out an encircling movement across country. If this was not sufficient, which it usually was, then the lorried infantry might have to debus and attack. In all the villages and towns we were given the most rapturous welcome—"*Les anglais, les liberateurs*" had arrived, and nothing was too good for them. It proved a wonderful tonic for the troops after the bitter fighting in the Normandy bocage.

Everywhere the Resistance movement leapt into action and they proved of the greatest assistance, taking over care of German prisoners, providing guides, guarding bridges and vulnerable points. Had the Germans tried to carry out a similar advance through the British Isles, what a frightful thorn in their flesh our Home Guard would have been. We were lucky enough to have the French and Belgian equivalent working on our side, but progress would have been much slower if they had been against us. The only trouble was that their estimates of the number of German troops in the vicinity were so exaggerated that eventually we came to divide the total by five.

There were many bizarre incidents. One of our self-propelled guns (a gun on a tank chassis) broke down and had to be left behind in a small French village. By the time it had been repaired some forty-eight hours later the whole corps had gone on its way, and the gun-crew were the only British troops in the neighbourhood. But before setting off to join up with his regiment again the sergeant succumbed to an urgent appeal from the local Maquis to assist them in rounding up several hundred Germans who were reported to be still holding out in a large wood nearby. After a combined reconnaissance it was agreed that the gun should fire a concentration at one corner of the wood while the Maquis attacked from another.

But when the plan was put into operation the Maquis understandably came to the conclusion that the artillery support was inadequate. The British sergeant then decided to do the whole operation with his own crew. So having fired for four minutes at the corner of the wood, the gun-crew, less the driver, jumped out and, running as fast as they could to get close to their own concentration, disappeared into the wood. Half an hour later they emerged with seventy German prisoners. On hearing this story the infantry said cynically that it was the only time in history that the gunners had ever followed up one of their own barrages.

It was impossible to command a mobile operation of this sort from my headquarters, so, during the advance, my command post was a tank. The gun was taken out and replaced by a small table where we could sit and study the maps. My staff consisted of one young staff officer (G.S.O. 2), a signals officer and my A.D.C., and I never saw the rest of the corps headquarters for over a week. This sort of command structure has only been made possible by the improvement in wireless communication.

It was the task of the staff officer with me to keep my chief of staff, who was back at the main headquarters, informed by means of coded messages how the battle was going, and pass on the gist of any orders I had given verbally to the divisions. In addition I had an escort of three tanks. This may sound unduly cautious, but each of our armoured columns was advancing up one road and disregarding entirely what lay on the flanks.

There is a popular conception, encouraged, I suspect, by certain war historians who have never had experience of armoured warfare in the field, that an armoured division moves across country rather like a fleet at sea. This is a completely false picture. Whenever possible armoured divisions move along roads because progress is much faster, and they deploy across country only when opposition is encountered. In order to visit the different divisions and brigades I had to move from one road to another, and as none of the Germans had been cleared from the intervening country, I could not have done so without an escort of some sort.

We advanced only about twenty-one miles on the 29th, which wasn't good enough if we were going to bounce the crossings over the Somme. So at 4.15 p.m. the next day I arrived at the headquarters of the 11th Armoured Division and ordered "Pip" Roberts, the divisional commander, to continue the advance throughout the night in order to capture the bridge at Amiens, some thirty miles away, by first light next day. This may seem a curious way to employ an armoured division, but I was a great believer in using tanks at night. I tried it on three occasions and was successful each time. It has a shattering effect on the morale of the enemy for them to wake up in the morning and find that some hundreds of tanks have penetrated deep into their positions under cover of darkness.

Roberts had been in command of the armoured brigade in North Africa when I had ordered Charles Keightley's 6th Armoured Division to carry out a similar night march in order to cut off the Germans in the Cap Bon peninsula, an operation which had been completely successful. But there was one big difference. Then the drive had been carried out in bright moonlight, now it was pouring with rain, which meant practically no night visibility at all.

This was asking a lot of the 11th Armoured Division. Driving a tank is a very tiring business, and the drivers had already been on the go for some thirty-six hours. But Roberts never hesitated. The division halted so that all tanks and vehicles could refill with petrol, and then started off on what proved to be one of the most fantastic night drives of the war. Drivers could barely see the vehicle in front of them. Utterly exhausted they fell asleep at each halt and very often, during this night of confusion, German vehicles and Germans were intermingled in our columns. But somehow or other the division went steadily on. Nothing mattered except that our tanks were penetrating ever deeper into the German positions.

Early next morning I arrived at divisional headquarters expecting to find chaos. Not a bit of it. The leading elements of the division, with the help of the local Maquis, had captured the bridges over the Somme intact, the tanks had crossed and were in the centre of Amiens, while the lorried infantry brigade was at that moment moving into the town to take over from them. This was a remarkable performance which could have been achieved only by a very highly-trained division—but Pip Roberts was probably the most experienced British armoured commander and certainly one of the best.

Having given me his report he said, "I have a surprise for you, General." And from behind one of the lorries was led a scowling, unshaven and very ugly German officer dressed in black uniform. I would have disliked him at sight, even if he had not looked like a senior S.S. commander (which he wasn't). Roberts was exactly like a proud farmer leading forward his champion bull. He told me with great pride that his prize exhibit was General Eberbach, commander of the 7th German Army, whom the 11th Armoured had captured in his pyjamas during the night advance.

With the Somme behind us we were now approaching the Belgian frontier. My big moment came on 2nd September, when I arrived at the headquarters of the Guards Armoured Division at Douai. The Guards make a fetish of understatement, and with long practice have developed a remarkable capacity for never showing any emotion under any circumstances. But on this occasion even they were slightly shaken when I gave their next day's objective as Brussels, for Brussels was seventy miles away. We had certainly come the full cycle from the hedge-to-hedge fighting in Normandy.

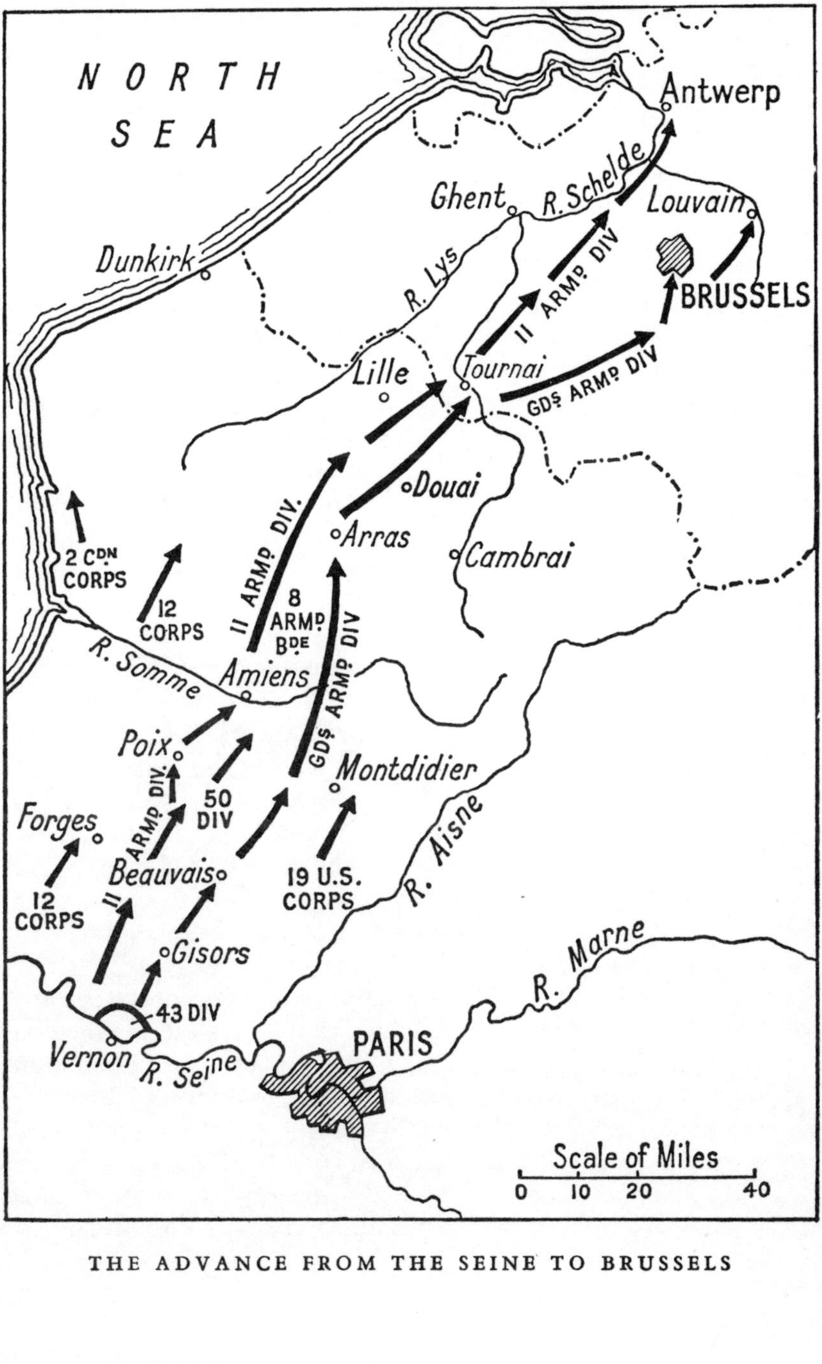

THE ADVANCE FROM THE SEINE TO BRUSSELS

There was a feeling of excitement, for it is not every day that a commander or a division is given the opportunity of liberating one of the great capitals of Europe. Brussels—what a prize! Next day the race was on, a pursely domestic affair between the Welsh Guards group (infantry and tanks) advancing on the right and the Grenadier group on the left.

This—the return to Belgium after our ignominious departure in 1940—was a moment to which I had been eagerly looking forward. I was not disappointed. As I crossed the frontier just behind the advance guard I saw a young Belgian standing by the road with tears streaming down his cheeks. Seeing the red band round my cap he ran towards me, seized me by both hands and said, " I knew you would come back! I knew the British would return! "

I was particularly touched by this, because almost the last words I had said to the sad-looking groups of Belgians whom we had left behind on our way back to Dunkirk were, " We will come back."

We had kept our promise.

As the day wore on it became obvious that it was to be a neck-and-neck race between the two groups. Then, just before dusk, the Welsh Guards and some armoured cars of the Household Cavalry entered Brussels. On the left road the Grenadiers had run into a lot of trouble at the small town of Pont à Marcq, which was defended by a hard core of Germans who had no intention of surrendering without a hard fight. In the ensuing battle the King's Company and No. 2 Squadron of tanks lost twenty-two killed and thirty-one wounded (including four officers) which marred for them the glory of the entry into Brussels.

The Belgians, after four years of German occupation, had become used to the movements of troops through their capital, so when on the evening of 3rd September, they heard the rumbling of tanks in the streets they hardly bothered to look out. As far as they knew the Allies had not even entered Belgium yet, and the war was still many miles away. As one Belgian described it to me, " I glanced out of the window quite incuriously, and then my attention became riveted. These tanks looked different. It couldn't possibly be the

Americans or the British? Yet could it? Suddenly I realised that we had been liberated, and like everyone else in Brussels that night I went mad."

From every house people poured into the empty streets, until it was almost impossible for the tanks to get through. There were flowers, fruit, champagne, girls on the vehicles and such kissing as has probably never been seen before or since! By now we had all become connoisseurs of liberation ceremonies, which had been going on in every town and village since we had crossed the Seine; but everyone agreed that the welcome by the citizens of Brussels had never been equalled.

What is more, it was no flash in the pan. Those kindly Belgian people took our troops to their hearts and into their homes. They were short of food and coal, yet before long nearly every officer and man had a Belgian home where he could go for meals, for the night or, indeed, to spend his leave. Months after we had left Belgium applications continued to come in from all ranks to spend leave not just in Brussels, the leave centre, but often in some small village on the outskirts. What the British soldier really likes is to " get his feet under the table," and there were many tables available in Belgium in 1944-45.

In 30 Corps at that time was a brigade composed of Belgians who had escaped to Britain, where they had been equipped and trained by us. Their commander was the famous Brigadier Piron, who was mainly responsible for the renaissance of the Belgian Army after the war. I was very anxious that they should share in this liberation ceremony, so when I entered the city early next morning I was escorted by some armoured cars from Piron's brigade. It must have been a wonderful moment for those men as they returned to their capital in triumph. When the crowds cheered and waved, I kept pointing to them and calling out " *Belge, Belge*," and the citizens of Brussels were delighted to see their own countrymen among their liberators.

My first problem was to find somewhere to establish my headquarters in comparative peace, so that we could get on with the war. The Guards had achieved their objective and captured Brussels, but

I had still to co-ordinate the activities of the 11th Armoured and 50th Divisions and 8th Armoured Brigade.

This became increasingly difficult as we penetrated into Brussels itself. Girls and still more girls seemed to be perched on the top of our wireless vehicles. Then I ran into Brigadier Gwatkin, who told me that his 5th Guards Brigade was all round the Palace of Laeken, which was still inhabited by the Queen Mother. He suggested that the park round the palace would be a most suitable place for our headquarters vehicles, as it was surrounded by railings which would offer some protection from the madding crowds.

The Queen Mother could not have been more helpful, and very soon 30 Corps headquarters was once more operational in the grounds of the palace. That night we invited her and her lady-in-waiting, la Baronne Carton de Wiart, a relation of our famous General de Wiart, V.C., to dinner. It was a rough-and-ready meal eaten off the usual six-feet tables in our small mess tent, but Queen Elizabeth told me afterwards that she never enjoyed any dinner as much.

During the next few days she wandered round talking to all and sundry, and became almost our fairy godmother. As our corps sign was a wild boar, she presented us with a baby boar from the Ardennes, whose name was Chewing Gum. His nose, when pressed against one's hand, felt just like this essential ingredient to the American way of life.

On the next day, 4th September, I was ordered to fly back to a conference at 2nd Army headquarters. The small two-seater Auster aircraft which I used on these occasions was parked at the extreme end of a large airfield near Brussels. I was told, however, that the Germans were still in occupation at the far end, from which a rather unpleasant 88 mm. A.A. gun fired at uncertain intervals. My pilot, a gunner major, was anxious about my safety, so, as soon as we were in the air, he took violent avoiding action, much to my discomfort.

I then settled down to study my notes for the conference. After about half an hour I happened to glance up and saw that my pilot was looking a very worried man. I asked him what was wrong and he replied that his compass was not working and he had no idea where we were. This was a shock, because at that time there was only a comparatively narrow corridor occupied by the Allies stretching back to the rear. After flying round for a few minutes trying without any success to spot a familiar landmark, I suggested that the only thing to do was to come down and ask. So choosing the largest available field we made a very bumpy but safe landing. Within a minute or two we were surrounded by civilians, who to my horror showed me on the map that we were fifty kilometres *behind* the enemy lines.

I asked them whether there were any Germans in the vicinity and they said, "No—the nearest are a couple of kilometres away." Even that was a bit too close for my liking, so we hurriedly took off, bumping across the field and just missing the trees on the far side. Our troubles weren't over. A little later the pilot explained apologetically that he was getting short of petrol, so we had to make another emergency landing—this time, I am glad to say, behind our own lines. I arrived at the conference three hours late, having been last seen heading straight for the German lines.

By this time I had rather lost confidence in my pilot, and debated whether to risk the return journey with him or not. He obviously was wondering the same, and he looked very relieved when I climbed into his plane. Afterwards I was glad that I had done so, because he was killed a few weeks later.

By 30th September, 30 Corps had covered 250 miles in six days. The Guards Armoured Division was in Brussels, the 11th Armoured Division was in Alost, directed on Antwerp, and the 50th Division was strung out to the rear, protecting our left flank and collecting thousands of German prisoners who were now trying to break out from the coastal area in order to get back to Germany.

Pip Roberts asked me to define his objective in Antwerp, and pointed out that an armoured division is not the best formation with which to occupy a large port. He was correct, but I had no other troops available. So, with vivid memories of the important part ports had played in the desert campaign, I said: "The docks. Go straight through to the Antwerp docks and try and capture them before the Germans can carry out any large-scale demolitions," which is exactly what he succeeded in doing.

At the time this seemed the obvious objective, but I realise now that it was a serious mistake. My excuse is that my eyes were fixed entirely on the Rhine, and everything else seemed of subsidiary importance. It never entered my head that the Scheldt would be mined, and that we should not be able to use Antwerp port until the channel had been swept and the Germans cleared from the coastline on either side. Nor did I realise that the Germans would be able to evacuate a large number of the troops trapped in the coastal areas across the mouth of the Scheldt estuary from Breskens to Flushing.

Napoleon would no doubt have realised these things, but Horrocks didn't. His mind was fixed on the Rhine. I am not suggesting that with one armoured division I could have cleared both banks of the Scheldt estuary, but I believe that I could have seriously impeded, if not stopped altogether, the evacuation of the German 5th Army. As it was, the German General Schwabe succeeded in evacuating some 65,000 men belonging to eight shattered German divisions, using this route.

If I had ordered Roberts, not to liberate Antwerp, but to by-pass the town on the east, cross the Albert Canal and advance only fifteen miles north-west towards Woensdrecht, we should have blocked the Beveland isthmus and cut the main German escape route. Roberts was ordered to, and did in fact, secure a bridgehead over the Albert Canal, but was subsequently forced to withdraw in face of increasing German resistance. He had not sufficient troops to seize the docks, clear the town and occupy the bridgehead.

With the capture of Brussels and Antwerp 30 Corps was ordered to halt. The reason given was that we had out-run our administrative resources. No port had yet been opened anywhere. The first, Dieppe, did not come into operation until 7th September, and then only for a trickle of supplies. It did not build up to the figure of 6,000 tons a day until the end of September. We were still receiving all our supplies from the beach-head some 300 miles away, and we were told that supplies, particularly of petrol, were running short.

This was a tragedy because, as we now know, on the next day, 4th September, the only troops available to bar our passage northwards consisted of one German division, the 719th, composed mainly of elderly gentlemen who hitherto had been guarding the north coast of Holland and had never heard a shot fired in anger, plus one battalion of Dutch S.S. and a few Luftwaffe detachments. This meagre force was strung out on a fifty-mile front along the canal.

To my mind 4th September was the key date in the battle for the Rhine. Had we been able to advance that day we could have smashed through this screen and advanced northwards with little or nothing to stop us. We might even have succeeded in bouncing a crossing over the Rhine. But we halted, and even by that same evening the situation was worsening. A General Chill, with his 85th German Division, had reached Turnhout in Holland on his way back to Germany to refit. On hearing that Brussels had fallen, and without any orders, he turned round and moved his division down to the line of the Albert Canal. He also placed teams of officers and N.C.O.s on all the roads to round up the German stragglers and reorganise them into efficient fighting units.

By 7th September he had succeeded in collecting quite a formidable force. He must have been a man of great initiative. But worse still, General Student's Parachute Army, headed by the 6th Parachute Regiment, commanded by the redoubtable Van der Heydte, was being rushed down from Germany to bar our progress. So from 5th September onwards the German forces on the Albert Canal increased rapidly.

It is easy to be wise after the event, and I was only a corps commander with no overall responsibility; but I believe that if we had taken the chance and carried straight on with our advance instead of halting in Brussels the whole course of the war in Europe might have been changed. On 3rd September we still had 100 miles of petrol per vehicle, and one further day's supply within reach, so we were not destitute. But there would have been a considerable risk in advancing farther north with only these supplies and a lengthening line of communication behind us.

When we were allowed to advance on 7th September, the situation had worsened drastically. We were no longer sweeping up through the coastal plain; we were fighting hard again. Every day fresh German formations appeared against us, and within three days, instead of being on a fifty-mile front, which is excellent when in pursuit, the Corps was concentrated on a five-mile front engaged in a tough battle.

The Guards Armoured Division took four days to advance over the next ten miles up to the Meuse-Escaut Canal where the Irish Guards by a most successful *coup de main* captured a small bridgehead, which was at once named "Joe's Bridge" after Lieut.-Colonel Joe Vandeleur, O.C. their 3rd Battalion. This was very different from their previous record of 250 miles in six days. The Germans had been given time to recover and we had missed our chance.

CHAPTER XV

ARNHEM I

ON 11th September I received orders for the advance to Arnhem and realised that once again 30 Corps was to play a leading role. The outline plan was for the 2nd British Army to advance approximately seventy miles to seize the Grave-Nijmegen-Arnhem area and then penetrate still farther northwards to the Zuider Zee in order to cut off all the enemy forces in the Low Countries from those in Germany. It was an exciting prospect because, if successful, it would go far to end the war as we should then be in an excellent position from which to outflank the Ruhr. The whole operation was given the code name of Market Garden—" Market " was to be carried out by the 1st Airborne Corps commanded by " Boy " Browning—Lt.-General Sir Frederick Browning—operating as part of the 2nd Army, and " Garden " by the ground forces, consisting of 30, 8, and 12 Corps.

The three Airborne Divisions were allotted the following tasks:—

1st British Airborne Division (which included the Polish Parachute Brigade) to seize Arnhem Bridge and establish a bridgehead to the north of the river.

82nd U.S. Airborne Division to capture Grave bridge, the railway and road bridges at Nijmegen and to hold the high ground south-east of the town.

101st U.S. Airborne Division to capture and dominate the road leading up to the Grave from Eindhoven to the north.

30 *Corps* consisting of the Guards Armoured Division, 50th and 43rd Infantry Divisions, 8th Armoured Brigade and a Dutch brigade, was ordered to break out of the existing bridge-

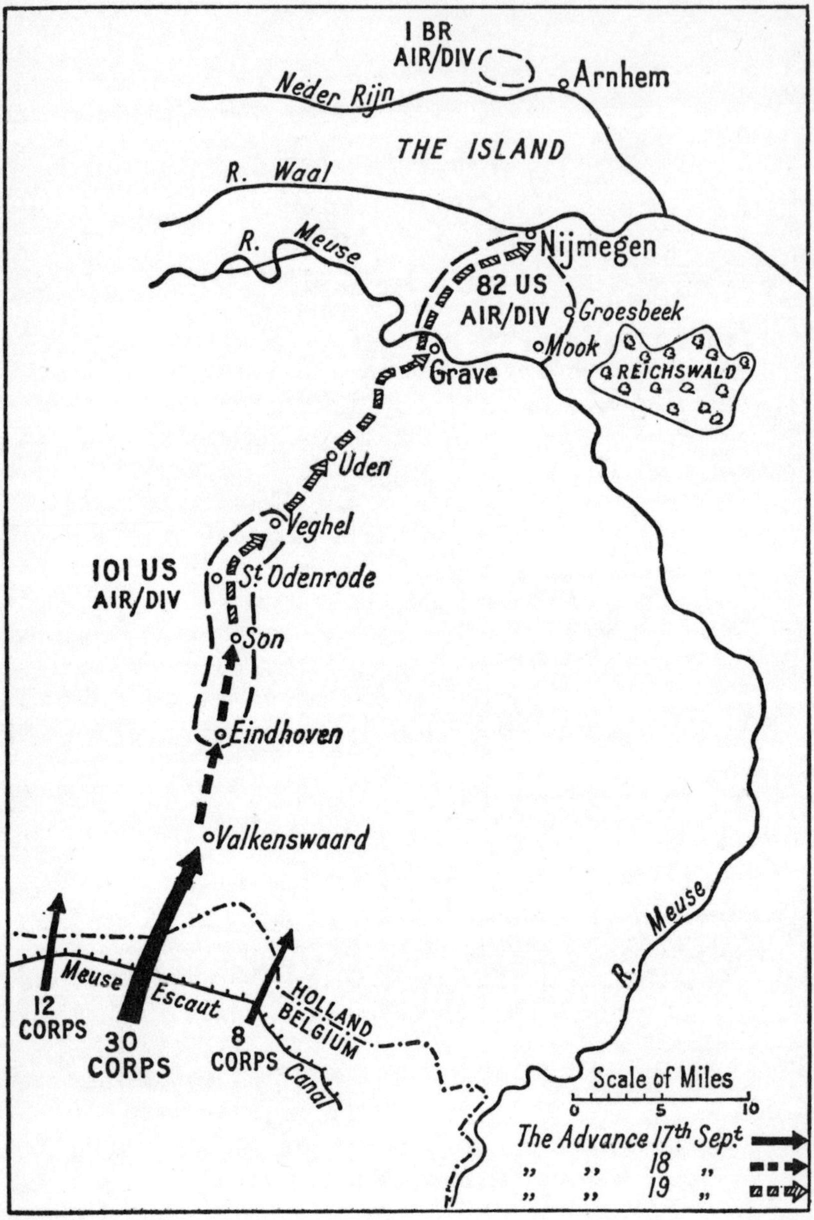

THE BATTLE OF ARNHEM I

head, pass through this airborne carpet which had been laid down in front of us and seize the area Nunspeet-Arnhem.

8 and 12 Corps would be on our right and left flanks respectively, but as most of the available resources had been allotted to us it was realised that they would not be able to advance so quickly, and we should be operating on our own for a considerable period.

During the next few days my staff were working almost round the clock as there was very little time available in which to tie up a complicated operation of this sort. But, as usual, somehow or other they accomplished this seemingly impossible task and all was ready by D-Day.

At 11 a.m. on Sunday morning, 17th September, 1944, I climbed up an iron ladder leading to the flat roof of a large factory on the south bank of the Meuse-Escaut Canal which was to be my command post for the opening stages of the battle. It was a peaceful, sunny, Sunday morning and apart from the occasional swish of an 88-shell passing over our heads, or the chatter of a distant machine-gun, there was no indication that any enemy was in front of us at all. Looking back I could see, carefully camouflaged and hidden in the woods and farms, some of the 350 guns which were waiting for my word to open fire. It had not been possible in this case to give a definite zero hour beforehand because airborne operations are dependent on the weather and may have to be postponed at the last minute.

So, sitting on the roof and waiting, I had plenty of time to think. I knew that we were opposed by some tough German paratroops under the command of the redoubtable General Student, and I remembered that the essence of Montgomery's plan had been to keep up a continuous pressure and never give the Germans time to recover from their defeat in Normandy. Yet we had been forced to halt in Brussels for three days, and now another week had been taken up with preparations for this battle. Market Garden could not possibly have been laid on any sooner, but these halts had given the Germans time in which to recover, and their resistance had been stiffening ever since we had advanced from Brussels. I felt quite confident, but I was under no illusion that this was going to be an easy battle. I disliked having to launch this attack on a Sunday, not, I am afraid, because of any religious scruples but because no assault or attack in which I had taken part during the war which started on a Sunday had ever been completely successful.

I had three main worries.

First—To break through the German defences in front of me. This was not so simple as it looked. Reinforcements, mainly of paratroops, were arriving from Germany daily. The country was wooded and rather marshy which made any outflanking operation impossible. The only thing I could do was to blast my way down the main road on a comparatively narrow front with as much air and artillery support as I could get.

Secondly—Even when we had broken through, the country did not favour a rapid advance because it was intersected with waterways. Between us and Arnhem there were three canals all capable of taking the largest barges, and in addition three immense rivers, the Maas (or Meuse), the Waal and the Lower Rhine. All the bridges were, we knew, prepared for demolition. Could we get there before the enemy blew them up? If not we should have to bridge them ourselves, and this would mean a large number of sappers involved in immense engineering projects, all of which would take time and might seriously delay our advance; yet the essence of the plan was speed to get to the airborne troops as soon as possible.

We had done our best to provide for every eventuality by concentrating a vast amount of bridging material in the Bourg Leopold area—no fewer than 9,000 sappers and 2,300 vehicles. Air photographs of each bridge had been carefully studied and preparations made to rush forward both men and materials as required.

Thirdly—It looked as though we should have to advance on one road only, and in the corps were 20,000 vehicles. This meant the most careful traffic control. Elaborate arrangements had been made to treat this one road almost as a railway. Traffic control posts with breakdown gangs and first-aid detachments, complete with wireless and line communications, were to be established behind the leading troops. No unit was permitted to put a column of more than five vehicles on this vital road without getting a timing from a movement office in my headquarters. As we were likely to be out in the blue on our own, I decided to take with us as much food, petrol and ammunition as we could carry. It turned out that this was a wise precaution.

In spite of these difficulties, however, I was confident that we should win through. The troops were in great heart. I had an experienced and very able staff, and the end of the war seemed to be approaching rapidly.

Then I heard on the wireless that the airborne divisions were on their way. Suddenly the armada appeared overhead. Hundreds of transport planes in perfect formation, many towing gliders, droned steadily northwards, protected on all sides by fighters, like little, angry gnats which filled the sky. It was a comforting thought that some 30,000 airborne troops were being dropped or landed from gliders in front of us.

As soon as the air armada came into view I ordered " Zero hour 1435 hours." At 2 p.m. precisely there was a sudden, deafening roar and a noise as though an express train were passing overhead. Our guns had opened their counter-artillery programme, and the battle of Arnhem was on. Under cover of the preliminary artillery bombardment the Irish Guards started moving into position just short of the start line.

I could imagine the drawn look on the men's faces, a look which is only seen before an attack. Being British they were of course making jokes. I once saw four men in an armoured carrier cross the start line for an attack wearing those black top-hats which Germans keep for funerals. This showed a macabre sense of humour, but it was typical. However much the troops may joke, they are under no illusion about what lies in front of them.

I always hated the last few minutes before zero hour and kept on going over in my mind again all the detailed plans, wondering whether everything possible had been done to give the leading troops a fair fighting chance.

At 2.35 p.m. exactly Lieutenant Keith Heathcote of No. 3

Squadron 2nd Battalion Irish Guards—a tank regiment—ordered " Driver advance " and one of the greatest break-outs in history had started. A hundred yards in front of Heathcote's tank rolled a curtain of fire from some 350 guns. In front of this again was an endless stream of R.A.F. Typhoon fighters pouring their rockets into the German defences. From my command post the whole battlefield was visible and for the first ten minutes all seemed to be going well. But just when we were congratulating ourselves that our blasting tactics had proved successful, the whole situation changed.

Within two minutes the Irish Guards had lost nine tanks, and the whole advance was held up by accurate fire from enemy anti-tank guns. I could not help a fleeting feeling of admiration for the fighting qualities of the Germans, for in spite of a terrific battering both from the ground and the air, they were still fighting stubbornly. Such feelings however, had no place in battle, and in the meantime a Homeric struggle was developing in the woods to my front.

The Typhoons came roaring in from all angles at zero feet, the barrage whistled overhead. In fact the din was appalling, tanks, trucks, planes, shells, rockets, machine-guns all raging and blazing. In the middle of it all, apparently enjoying themselves, were the famous Vandeleur cousins, Colonels Joe and Giles, who commanded the 3rd and 2nd Battalions of the Irish Guards respectively. Though continually shot at, they stood by their scout cars and issued their orders with far less tension than they might have displayed during a Trooping the Colour parade on the Horse Guards back in London.

The tanks were held up, but the Irish Guards (3rd Battalion Infantry) who had been riding on the outside of the tanks driven by their fellow " Micks " of the 2nd Battalion, were getting tired of being shot at, and as so often happens with these great fighters, they suddenly lost their tempers. An eyewitness reported afterwards that he ". . . had never seen Guardsmen or officers so angry. The Krauts got rough treatment that day."

The young R.A.F. pilots were superb and the Typhoons literally shot the infantry on to their objectives, the rockets landing within 200 yards of our leading troops. Nothing could stand up to this and after some bitter infantry fighting the enemy crust was pierced. By that evening the head of the Guards' Armoured Division had entered the first Dutch town, Valkenswaard.

I regard this battle as a classic example of perfect co-operation between the R.A.F. and the Army. No corps has ever had better air support than was provided for me that day by No. 83 Group of the Tactical Air Force, commanded by Harry Broadhurst, who though young in years was a veteran in army/air co-operation; he had taken an active part in the long advance from Alamein to Tunis, and understood the ways of the army better than most.

That evening the Germans started counter-attacking the hinges of our break-through, but this had been foreseen and the 50th Division could be relied upon to deal effectively with these attacks. So the 17th ended happily. Our casualties had been fewer than might have been expected and we had punched a hole in the German defences.

But to get a proper understanding of this battle we should now take a look over the hill and see what was happening behind the German lines; though I had no idea of this at the time.

First of all, let me kill the myth which was so prevalent after the war that the Arnhem operation was given away to the Germans beforehand by a Dutch traitor. This is nonsense; it came as a complete surprise to them. Here is the story as I have been able to piece it together from several different sources which I have every reason to believe are accurate.

About this time, some seventy miles to the north, General Model, the German C.-in-C., and his senior staff, were sitting down to lunch in the Hotel Tafelberg in the small Dutch town of Oosterbeek, six miles west of Arnhem. Suddenly an officer jumped to his feet crying: "Look out! Bombers!" They ran to the window and saw, not bombers as they had expected, but a sky full of coloured parachutes, for the dropping zone of the 1st British Airborne Division was only a couple of miles away. It was an awkward moment, and if the commander and his headquarters were not to be overrun by British paratroopers, there was no time to lose.

Model's car was sent for. As he ran out of the door his bag, which had been hurriedly packed, burst open, and all his belongings were strewn over the ground. Staff officers rushed to their commander's assistance, and within a matter of minutes he was driving away at a furious speed to the headquarters of the 2nd S.S. Panzer Corps, commanded by General Willi Bittrich which, unfortunately for us, was quite close at Zutphen only twenty-eight miles north-east of Arnhem. I say unfortunately because it was this corps which turned the scales against us in the subsequent fighting. Quite unknown to me, and, as far as I can make out, also to our Intelligence service, a few days before, the 9th and 10th S.S. Panzer Divisions had arrived in the Zutphen area to refit, after suffering heavy losses during the fighting in Normandy. They might have been sent almost anywhere else, but no! Fate—or whatever you like to call it—decreed that they should arrive just at this moment in an area from which they could intervene rapidly in the Arnhem battle.

Though both these divisions had suffered heavy losses in France, they still retained sufficient tanks and self-propelled guns to be more than a match for our extremely gallant but lightly-equipped airborne troops. Moreover, when in Normandy they had been specially trained in an anti-parachute role; so the dice were loaded against us from the start. It was also particularly unfortunate that Model should have had a grandstand view of the 1st Airborne drop, because he was thus able to take immediate steps to deal with this unexpected situation. He was used to plugging gaps as he had come from the eastern front, so, where a less experienced commander might have panicked, Model did nothing of the sort. He made a first-class appreciation of the situation and started active counter-measures at once. He realised from the outset that the real threat lay in the rapid advance of 2nd British Army headed by 30 Corps. If this could be held off, he then had sufficient troops to deal with the lightly-equipped 1st British Airborne Division.

Our main weakness lay in the long, slender and very exposed lines of communication which ran south from Nijmegen, so he concentrated his main strength against these. The 59th German Division was ordered to attack them from the west, while the 15th and 41st Panzer Divisions were to move in from the east. He also dispatched the 10th S.S. Division due south to stiffen up the defences in the low-lying piece of country between Nijmegen and Arnhem, which, because it was almost entirely encircled by the rivers, Lower Rhine and Waal, came to be known in the British Army as "The Island." This division was to operate against our head while the others moved in from both sides against our tail.

One further piece of good luck came the German way. General Student, who was commanding the parachute army against which we were fighting, wrote in his book as follows:—

> "Two hours after the air armada first appeared in the skies over Holland, the Allied operation order for Market Garden (the code name for the battle of Arnhem) was on my desk. It had been captured from a glider forced down near Vught—which was my command post. It was the same as in 1940 during the 1st German Airborne operation in Holland, when a German officer, despite the strictest injunctions, carried the operational order on his person. It fell into Allied hands, and enabled the Allies to conduct a thorough study of German parachute tactics, which was the main reason for the heavy German parachute troop losses in Crete."

The capture of this vital document was a great boon to the Germans, who knew exactly what we intended to do. Before leaving the German side of the battle, one last picture—Hitler's headquarters. How had the Fuehrer taken the news of this thrust into the under-belly of his Reich? This is how an eyewitness described the scene.

> "On the previous day, 16th September, a very important conference had taken place at Wolfschanze, Hitler's headquarters in East Prussia, when the Fuehrer had outlined his plan for the Ardennes offensive. All was calm. But the next day things were very different. As reports of the airborne landings came in, excitement mounted. The major part of the daily situation conference was taken up with discussions of the air

landing, constantly interrupted by telephone calls as fresh reports came in. Hitler himself was chiefly impressed with Model's narrow escape, and he became increasingly worried about the safety of his own headquarters. In his own words—' At any rate this business is so dangerous that you must understand clearly: if such a mess happened here—here I sit with my whole Supreme Command: here sit the Reichsmarshal (Goering), the O.K.H., the Reichsfuehrer S.S. (Himmler); the Reich Foreign Minister (von Ribbentrop); well then, this is the most worth-while catch, that's obvious. I would not hesitate to risk two parachute divisions here if with one blow I could get my hands on the whole German Command.' He then screamed ' Holland overshadows everything else.'

" As reports of more air landings arrived the Fuehrer became violent and raged about the failure of the Luftwaffe. As a result of all the excitement Holland was given top priority and every available reserve formation in Germany, and even as far afield as Denmark, was alerted and ordered to move down to defeat the British/U.S. penetration."

It was the arrival of these formations which finally turned the tide against us as more and more pressure was exerted along 30 Corps' line of communication which subsequently stretched from Nijmegen some sixty miles back to Belgium.

The story of the magnificent fight of the 1st Airborne Division against overwhelming odds is now well known, so I do not propose to go into any details here. The armoured reconnaissance regiment of the 9th S.S. Panzer Division seized Arnhem Bridge just thirty minutes before the arrival of Colonel Frost's 2nd British Paratroop Battalion. Frost could not force his way over the river, but by holding the houses north of the bridge for three precious days he prevented the Germans using the bridge themselves. Their 10th S.S. Panzer Division was thus forced to cross the river by the ferry farther to the east, and this delayed their arrival at Nijmegen until after we had captured the town. The remainder of the 1st Airborne Division was gradually driven back by sheer weight of numbers until it was sealed off into a tight perimeter on the north bank of the lower Rhine in the neighbourhood of Oosterbeek.

To return to my immediate battle. After some hard fighting on the 17th, the Guards broke through and reached Valkenswaard just inside Holland. On the next day, 18th September, after another sharp battle they made contact with the southern end of the aerial carpet in the shape of the 101st U.S. Airborne Division, which had been given the task of seizing and keeping open our main road northwards between Eindhoven and Veghel, a distance of some twenty-five kilometres. Their landings behind the enemy lines on the 17th had been extremely successful.

In the words of the divisional historian:—

> "The entire regiment came down in full view of one commander. Men landed close to their friends and close to their equipment. Battalions were assembled and operating in less than an hour. Considered from any standpoint it was the most successful landing that the division had ever made in either training or combat. An entire parachute regiment, in bright sunlight, landing on a single field is a pretty sight and if the field happens to be behind enemy lines it is also a reassuring sight. Between 1300 and 1330 hours 6,769 men were jumped with casualties of less than two per cent for personnel and five per cent for equipment.
>
> "The glider landings an hour afterwards were not so fortunate. Of the seventy gliders that were towed off from England, only fifty-three came in without accident."

As the guardsmen rolled rapidly northwards towards Nijmegen they were greeted at the canal bridges and cross-roads by cheerful groups of tough-looking paratroopers from the 101st U.S. Division, the men whose job it now was to protect our life-line to the rear.

By 10 a.m. on 19th September the Grenadier Guards Group (1st Motor Battalion and 2nd Tank Battalion), now in the lead, made contact with the second strip of our aerial carpet—the 82nd U.S. Airborne Division, who, to our great joy, had captured intact the road bridge over the Meuse at Grave. Had the Germans succeeded in destroying this bridge our advance might easily have been delayed for several days, for the broad river would have proved a formidable obstacle.

In addition to this success the 82nd, having captured another important bridge over the Maas-Waal Canal at Heuman, were holding the high ground about Berg en Dal to the east of the main road, and had penetrated to within 400 yards of the road bridge over the Waal in Nijmegen itself. At this point they had encountered stubborn resistance from the 10th S.S. German Division.

The town of Nijmegen is completely dominated by these two immense bridges over the river Waal, by the road bridge on the east and by the railway bridge on the west. To capture one of these, or if possible, both, was vital to our plan, and the fighting which now developed in Nijmegen was bitter in the extreme. Indeed there was a desperate urgency about this battle which I rarely experienced before or after.

To the north of us, on the far side of yet another water obstacle, the lower Rhine, were 10,000 British airborne troops. From them we had had no word, and airborne troops are lightly equipped. So, unless we could relieve them quickly, they must surely perish. This feeling was communicated to everyone from general right down to private soldier, to guardsman or U.S. paratrooper, and most gallantly they responded to the urgent need.

The Grenadier Guards Group and a battalion of the 505th U.S. Parachute Regiment combined in an immediate attack on the road bridge, which to our astonishment, was still intact; but in spite of the utmost bravery little progress was made. The Germans had fortified the open squares and had constructed a tight perimeter of defences around the southern end of both the vital bridges. Huner Park, which dominated the southern edge of the road bridge was particularly strongly held.

They also set fire to every fifth building until some 500 houses were blazing fiercely. Into this hell plunged tanks, Guards and U.S. paratroopers, but all to no avail. By midnight it was obvious that the bridges could not be captured by direct assault.

During the afternoon I met General Browning, who had landed

with the airborne corps which he was commanding. From then on we co-operated closely and took all the major decisions together. We now decided to outflank the bridges from the west by carrying out an assault crossing over the broad River Waal near the power station, some 800 yards down-stream from the railway bridge. This was a most hazardous operation but here lay the only chance of capturing the bridges intact. It is to the credit of General Jim Gavin, the commander of the 82nd U.S. Airborne Division, that this appallingly difficult task was accepted without the slightest hesitation.

At first light on 20th September, the 504th U.S. Parachute Regiment and the 2nd Battalion Irish Guards (Tanks) started clearing the western suburbs of the town and by midday they arrived on the river bank. Now took place what many of us consider to have been one of the finest attacks ever carried out during the last war.

It was a sunny afternoon with clear visibility, and the Germans were holding the far bank of the swiftly-running river which at this point was quite 400 yards wide. Yet at 3 p.m. the leading U.S. paratroopers entered the river in British assault boats which they had never seen till that moment. Supported though they were by fire from the tanks of the Irish Guards, and approximately 100 guns, they nevertheless suffered heavily and only half the leading wave, some in boats, some swimming, succeeded in reaching the far bank. Yet this mere handful of men charged up the steep embankment and secured a small bridgehead a couple of hundred yards deep. Gradually more and more troops were ferried across until by evening they had penetrated a mile inland to the village of Lent, where the railway crosses the main road. They had thus cut off both bridges from the rear, a truly amazing achievement.

Meanwhile the Grenadier Guards and the 505th U.S. Parachute Regiment had been busy. In accordance with fresh orders issued the night before by Brigadier Gwatkin, commander of the 5th Guards Brigade, the Grenadiers had developed another attack on the southern end of the road bridge, this time approaching from the west. All day they fought their way forward literally yard by yard and house by house, until in the late afternoon they captured

Huner Park and the Valkhof, a large, wooded mound which dominates the southern end of the bridge. In the words of the Grenadier Guards regimental history:—

> "Capturing a well-fortified mound like the Valkhof would be an operation fraught with incalculable dangers in any circumstances. It was exceptionally difficult in this case because the Germans had had time to surround it with a network of barbed-wire entanglements, slit trenches and dug-outs, all of which were fully manned, but as one company commander later wrote 'From the first few moments the fighting did not conform in any way to my original plan. But once we got our teeth into the enemy the men's spirit was so terrific—even laughing and joking—that nothing could have stopped us.'"

Of the many battle honours which the Grenadier Guards can claim, none can have been more richly deserved than Nijmegen.

At 7 p.m. it was decided to try and rush the bridgehead, and a troop of tanks commanded by Sergeant Robinson advanced rapidly with guns blazing to the bridge which is approximately 400 yards in width with an embankment of equal length on both sides. While travelling these 1200 yards the tanks were easy targets, not only to the enemy anti-tank guns, but also to those Germans who were firing bazookas from positions in the girders above the bridge. Two tanks were hit, but somehow the troop got over, skidded broadside through a road-block at the far end and knocked out two anti-tank guns on the road. The attack finally came to a halt a mile farther on where the guardsmen met the remnants of their gallant American allies who had crossed the river lower down. Perhaps the bravest of all these brave men was the young sapper officer, Lieutenant Jones, who ran on foot behind the tanks, cutting the wires and removing the demolition charges—though we now know that in spite of Bittrich's protest General Model had refused to allow this bridge to be blown as he wanted to use it for subsequent counter-attacks by the Germans.

Thus, by the evening of the 21st, almost a miracle had been achieved. Thanks to some very hard fighting by British and

American troops, whose co-operation on this occasion should be an object lesson to all allies in the future, these two important bridges had fallen into our hands intact. Another hurdle had been overcome and I went to bed a happy man—almost the last time, incidentally, that I was to do so in this battle.

So far fortune had favoured us, but the sky was darkening. The Germans had been completely surprised by the initial airborne landings, but they had recovered quickly, and their counter-measures were now starting to take effect.

My chief worry lay in the quality of the opposition which we were encountering. Admittedly some of the elderly gentlemen from the " stomach battalions " which had been positioned on the lines of communication were only too glad to surrender, but the bulk of the German troops against us were hard-bitten Nazis from the S.S. and parachute divisions. Young fanatics had even advanced into battle sitting on the outside of their tanks shouting, " I want to die for Hitler."

The 101st U.S. Division guarding our life-line was being subjected daily to increasing pressure from both sides. Hardly a day passed without some fresh German formation making its appearance against us. No wonder, therefore, that on the next day, 21st September, the Guards Armoured Division failed to advance more than two miles to the north. For once, air co-operation was working badly, and though the Typhoons were overhead, the contact-car could not get into touch with them. This was particularly unfortunate because very little artillery support was available.

I had realised, of course, that " The Island " with its dykes, high embankments carrying the roads, and deep ditches on either side was most unsuitable for armoured warfare. It was perfect defensive country in which the anti-tank gun hidden in the orchards was always master of the tank silhouetted against the sky-line. I pinned my hopes, however, on the 43rd Infantry Division, which had been ordered up from the rear. Their move had been much delayed by congestion along our one and only road caused to a large extent by the increasing enemy pressure which was coming in from the flanks.

A heavy enemy attack on the bridge at Son had been beaten

back by the 101st, but on 20th September another German formation had penetrated into the village of St. Oedenrode and halted all traffic on the lines of communication for some hours.

Still, there was no need to despair. Two-thirds of the Polish Parachute Brigade (for this operation under command of the 1st British Airborne Division), had at last been able to take off from England and had dropped that morning (the 21st) just south of the lower Rhine, near the village of Driel.

The 43rd Division were due to arrive that evening and to pass through the Guards the next morning. I hoped that this fresh infantry division would succeed in joining up with the Poles, and that together they would then be able to bring succour to the hard-pressed 1st Airborne.

Up to this time we had received no definite information about the situation north of the lower Rhine, but suddenly the voice of their head gunner was heard on the wireless frequency used by our 64th Medium Regiment. This was our first direct contact with them, and thenceforward we were able to provide considerable artillery support for the airborne bridgehead on the north bank of the lower Rhine.

CHAPTER XVI

ARNHEM 2

NEXT DAY—on the 22nd—the Household Cavalry, taking advantage of the early morning fog, managed to slip some armoured cars right through the German lines. In fact they succeeded in joining up with the Poles, whom they found in position on the south bank of the river near the village of Driel. So from now on we were provided with a reliable source of information about what was happening in this vital area.

Up to this point in the battle no troops could have done more or advanced more rapidly than had 30 Corps, but from now on our rate of progress slowed down and this has been the subject of criticism from several sources, notably by Chester Wilmot in his *Struggle for Europe*. He has suggested that 43rd Division was both slow and sticky. If the leading troops of the Guards Armoured Division were now only six to seven miles short of Arnhem Bridge, why then did a first-class infantry division take so long to get up to the lower Rhine?—particularly as their casualties were comparatively small. That is the general tone of the adverse comments.

I have always strongly deprecated this criticism because I spent the morning of the 22nd with Brigadier Essame, the commander of the 214th Infantry Brigade, which was in the lead, and nobody could have done more. He had tried to launch an attack with his leading battalion on the previous afternoon, but the whole brigade had been delayed by the confusion in Nijmegen and some of his troops were misdirected towards the road bridge, while the remainder crossed to the north bank by the railway bridge. The Welsh Guards were attacking on the sector immediately north of the river, the bridges were being shelled, and movement was difficult along the narrow, twisty roads which ran on the banks with deep dykes on either side.

In my opinion only an experienced brigadier like Essame could have succeeded under these circumstances in concentrating his brigade at all on the night of the 21st, and launching an attack with the leading battalion, the 7th Somerset Light Infantry, early next day.

His orders had been to advance with all speed but, and this is most important, he was told that artillery ammunition must be used with the utmost economy. Owing to enemy pressure on our lines of communication we were forced to economise as much as possible.

The Germans had been thoroughly aroused by the passage of two troops of the Household Cavalry through their lines; in fact the fog lifted just too soon, and the last three armoured cars were knocked out by an enemy tank hidden in an orchard.

The 7th Somerset Light Infantry at once ran into a strong, natural defensive position round the village of Oosterhoot held by approximately a battalion of Germans supported by tanks, some self-propelled guns and mortars.

As the guards had already found to their cost, it was quite impossible for the 43rd Division to deploy armoured vehicles in an attack across this difficult country intersected with high banks and dykes, in which the enemy enjoyed all the advantages of cover and the attacker none. So the Somersets advanced with practically no support at all either from tanks or guns. The first attack failed and the leading company commander, Major Sidney Young, was killed. The C.O., Lieut.-Colonel Borradaile, one of the best C.O.s in the division, now launched another attack round the right flank which seemed to offer the best opportunity of success but this also was held up. The brigadier then decided on a third attack which, in spite of the embargo, he determined to launch with the whole of the divisional artillery in support.

This third effort, which started at 3.20 p.m., was completely successful and by 5 p.m. a gap had been opened in the German position through which Essame slipped a mobile column which he had been holding in readiness. This consisted of one squadron of the 4th/7th Dragoon Guards (Tanks), 5th Duke of Cornwall's Light Infantry, one platoon of machine-guns of the 8th Middlesex and

Talking to a group of soldiers just after the capture of Bremen, April 1945

A wonderful moment. The author receives the surrender of the enemy forces in Northern Germany

The red-letter day of Black Rod's existence, the Garter ceremony at Windsor (1957). The author walks behind the Queen Mother's train-bearer

some D.U.K.W.s. (amphibious lorries) filled with ammunition and much-needed stores for the beleaguered British paratroopers.

George Taylor, the C.O. of the 5th D.C.L.I., divided his force into two; in front, an armoured column with two companies of infantry riding on the outside of the tanks, and behind, the remaining two companies of his battalion in charge of the soft-skinned transport vehicles. They set off from Oosterhoot just before last light and the head of the armoured column covered the ten miles to Driel in thirty minutes, where it joined up with the Poles, but the Germans managed to infiltrate five Tiger tanks and some infantry into a gap which had opened up between the two columns.

Company Sergeant-Major Philp, travelling in a carrier at the tail of the armoured column, rammed the leading enemy tank and killed the German commander as he peered out of his turret before he himself and his driver baled out into the ditch beside the road. Learning that his force had been split into two, Taylor sent back two platoons under Major Parker with extra P.I.A.T.s (infantry anti-tank weapon) and some "75" anti-tank mines to clear up the mess. In a remarkably successful little operation this small force operating in the dark succeeded in stalking and destroying all the Tigers. Private Brown, a young soldier, spotted an enemy tank with its track damaged by some "75" mines, so he left the cover of the ditch where he was lying and, knowing full well the risk he ran, walked to within a few yards before firing his P.I.A.T. The tank was completely destroyed but he himself was blinded by the blast. As he was carried away he was heard to say: "I don't care, I knocked the —— out." After an eventful night drive along narrow by-roads the whole force joined up with the Poles.

I have described this operation in considerable detail in order to remove the slur on the reputation of this first-class west country division. I would suggest that anyone who considers the actions of Brigadier Essame, Lieut.-Colonels Borradaile and Taylor, C.S.M. Philp or Pte. Brown to have been sticky cannot have had much experience of front-line fighting. No one who has not visited this island can have any idea of just how difficult it was to attack over. It is also most unfair to say that because the casualties were low the

43rd Division was not fighting well. If the skill and determination with which an action is fought are to be judged on this basis, then the battle of the Somme during the 1914–18 war must be regarded as one of the greatest of all British victories.

September 22nd was a worrying day for me. When I left the 214th Brigade their second attack had just been halted and during the morning no advance had taken place anywhere on 30 Corps front. As I returned to my corps headquarters, I was met by my chief of staff who told me that reliable information was at last available from north of the lower Rhine. The 1st Airborne had withdrawn west from Arnhem and were now occupying a small perimeter around Oosterbeek which was being attacked furiously from all sides. They were short of ammunition, and unless we could get to them within twenty-four hours they would probably be overrun.

While I was pondering over this unhappy situation, the same staff officer arrived thirty minutes later with the news that a German armoured formation had succeeded in cutting our road to the rear. So in addition to making no progress in front, we were now cut off as well. This was no fault of the 101st U.S. Airborne Division, who had been fighting a series of difficult battles to keep our lines of communication open. But it was no easy matter to defend some twenty-five miles of road with a resolute enemy pressing in on both sides. In fact, many stretches of the road were constantly under shell fire, and at times the banks on either side became the actual front lines facing outwards. As might be expected, this slowed up the traffic moving along the road considerably.

It had been hoped that the 8 and 12 Corps, who were advancing on our right and left respectively, would by now be sufficiently far north to have broadened these lines of communication, but they also were meeting stiff resistance and their progress had been slow. As it was vital to open communications with the rear, I was forced to turn the 32nd Guards Brigade back to start clearing the road from the north, while the 101st U.S. and 50th British Divisions advanced from the south. Though this operation eventually succeeded, for twenty-five fateful hours the road was closed to all traffic.

However, as I have already indicated, the " black 22nd " ended

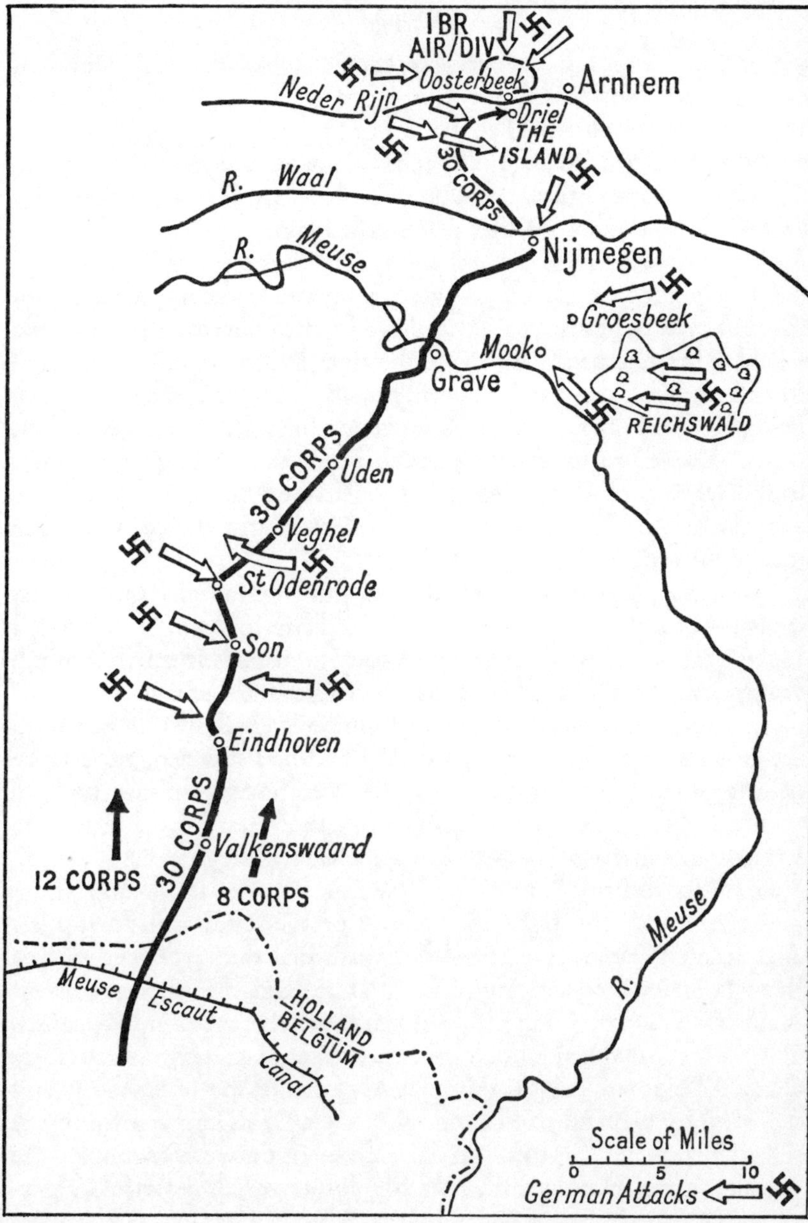

THE BATTLE OF ARNHEM 2

better than might have been expected. Now that the Duke of Cornwall's Light Infantry column had joined up with the Poles there was every chance that the airborne division, replenished with stores and reinforced by Poles and British infantry, might well be able to hold out until we could establish a firm link with them, by driving the Germans off that part of the island.

Our hopes were to be dashed again. Some of the D.U.K.W.s became bogged, while others were destroyed by enemy fire, and in the end only a few Poles succeeded in getting across. The trouble was that the Germans dominated the river by fire from high ground to the west of the airborne bridgehead, and their machine-guns, firing on fixed lines, were taking a heavy toll of our precious assault boats. Elsewhere on the front little progress had been made, and fresh German reinforcements, particularly of tanks, seemed to be arriving on the island almost daily. Well might the communiqué that night report, " The situation is grave."

Looking back I am certain that this was about the blackest moment of my life. I began to find it difficult to sleep. In fact I had to be very firm with myself in order to banish from my mind, during those midnight hours when everything seems at its worst, the picture of the airborne troops fighting their desperate battle on the other side of the river in front. I had had sufficient experience of war to know that any commander who finds it difficult to sleep will soon be unfit to be responsible for other men's lives. And here I was going that way myself—an unpleasant thought.

As this difficult battle progressed I became more and more impressed with the fighting qualities of the 82nd and 101st U.S. Airborne Divisions. I learned afterwards that they were the pick of the whole American Army. What impressed me so much about them was their quickness into action; they were great individualists. They were also commanded by two outstanding men, the 101st by General Maxwell Taylor, subsequently head of the U.S. Army, and the 82nd by General Jim Gavin, until recently in charge of military research and development in America. Both were as unlike the popular cartoon conception of the loud-voiced, boastful, cigar-chewing American as it would be possible to imagine. They were quiet, sensitive-looking men of great charm, with an almost British passion for understatement.

It was a quite normal occurrence for all hell to break out suddenly on the 82nd U.S. Airborne front—shelling, mortaring, machine-gun fire, the lot. Whenever I rang up Jim Gavin to find out what was going on he gave me the same answer: " We're just having a bit of a patrol." I usually discovered that his " bit of a patrol " had consisted of at least a hundred U.S. paratroopers carrying out a large-scale raid on the German positions. Like all first-class troops these two divisions were never content to sit quiet; they were always hitting back at the Germans. And under their deceptively gentle exterior both Maxwell Taylor and Gavin were very tough characters indeed. They had to be, because the men they commanded were some of the toughest troops I have ever come across in my life.

On 24th September I went forward to carry out a personal reconnaissance and met Major-General Sosabosky, the commander of the Polish Parachute Brigade and George Taylor of the 5th Duke of Cornwall's Light Infantry, both of whom luckily were experienced, front-line soldiers, just the men for a difficult operation like this.

I then climbed to the top of Driel church tower from where I was able to study the southern end of the airborne bridgehead on the far side of the river. As there seemed a danger that the airborne troops might be cut off from the river altogether, I told General Thomas, commanding 43rd Division, that in order to relieve pressure on the bridgehead he was to carry out an assault crossing that night with a minimum of one battalion. He was then to pass over stores and finally Polish paratroopers if time permitted. I promised him the support of the complete corps artillery for the operation. I also asked him to carry out a reconnaissance farther to the west, because if things went well that night I hoped to side-slip the 43rd Division, cross the lower Rhine farther to the west and carry out a left hook against the German forces attacking the airborne perimeter. Having given these orders, I then drove back to meet the 2nd Army commander at St. Oedenrode, where we discussed the whole situation thoroughly. This was very necessary because we were approaching a crisis, and I had not seen either Montgomery or Dempsey since the battle started.

When I turned round to return to my headquarters, the Germans had cut the road again just to the north. This was a nasty blow, because not only was it vital that I should get back to my headquarters as soon as possible in view of the critical stage of the battle, but more important still, much needed supplies of ammunition and above all, assault boats, were south of the cut. On this occasion the road was not open again for four days. I was lucky, however. With an escort of armoured carriers from the Durham Light Infantry I was able to get across country and rejoin the road north of the cut.

On arrival at my headquarters at 10 a.m. next morning, the 25th, I found a gloomy gathering awaiting me. The 4th Dorsets had crossed the night before, but all communication with them had now ceased; few assault boats were left, and ammunition was running short. In fact one artillery regiment was down to five rounds per gun.

General Browning and I came to the conclusion that there was nothing for it but to withdraw the 1st British Airborne Division over the river. That night, under a cover of a corps artillery programme, 2323 gallant airborne troops reached our lines. It was a tragic scene. As the exhausted paratroopers swam or were ferried across the river in torrential rain, it seemed that even the gods were weeping at this grievous end to a gallant enterprise.

And so ended the battle of Arnhem. Now for the post-mortem. General Urquhart, the commander of the 1st Airborne Division, has complained that we were very slow in advancing to the relief of his division, and I can well understand his feelings. In fact his criticisms are perfectly reasonable when viewed from the airborne point of view. If I had been in his position, surrounded by the Germans, fighting desperately for eight days and always waiting for the 2nd Army which never arrived, I doubt whether I would have been half so reasonable. But if we were slow then the fault was mine because I was the commander.

I have thought over this battle many times since and wondered whether there was anything more that I could have done. The sense of desperate urgency was there all right. There could be no doubt about that, and it was not for want of trying that we failed to arrive in time. I don't believe that any other troops in the world could possibly have fought better than the Guards and the 82nd U.S. Airborne Division when they captured the bridges at Nijmegen. But, after all we were cut off three times, and it is difficult to fight with one hand tied behind you.

It is always easy to be wise after the event but, knowing what I do now, I think it would have been better to have committed the 43rd Division on a different axis. Instead of passing them through the Guards on the 22nd, I should have ordered General Thomas to carry out a left hook across the lower Rhine much farther to the west and so attack the Germans, who were engaged with the 1st Airborne Division, from behind. This might well have been successful but even then I must emphasise that we should only have been able to establish a bridgehead position on the north bank of the lower Rhine. We could not have advanced any farther as envisaged in our original orders. The failure at Arnhem was primarily due to the astonishing recovery made by the German armed forces after their crippling defeat in Normandy.

Even if the 2nd German S.S. Panzer Corps had not been in a position to intervene so rapidly, and if we had succeeded in getting right through to the Zuider Zee, could we have kept our long lines of communication open? I very much doubt it. In which case instead of 30 Corps fighting to relieve the 1st British Airborne Division, it would then have been a case of the remainder of the 2nd Army struggling desperately to relieve 30 Corps cut off by the Germans north of Arnhem. Maybe in the long run we were lucky.

Now let me turn to the 64,000 dollar question about which military historians will no doubt argue for many years. Was Monty correct in carrying out the Arnhem operation, which meant advancing sixty to seventy miles into Holland? Would it not have been better if, after Brussels, 21st Army Group had turned north-west and cleared both sides of the Scheldt estuary to open the port of Antwerp which could then have been developed into a main base area, thus curing many administrative headaches.

I can only give you the opinion of a corps commander who was on the spot and has since made a study of the problem. Had he adopted this course, as many critics think he should have done, the port of Antwerp would certainly have been open to Allied shipping earlier than it was. But how much earlier it is not easy to say, because the campaign to clear the Scheldt estuary would certainly have been difficult.

The ground could be flooded at will by the Germans, while Walcheren could not be captured until it *was* flooded. Large German forces would have been cornered south of Breskens and could have put up a stubborn resistance in this difficult country where it was almost impossible to deploy large numbers of our troops. If we had devoted all our resources to clearing Antwerp in September it would have been impossible later on to carry out the swift advance up to the lower Rhine at Arnhem, because by then the German defences would have been given time to solidify. We were able to make this deep penetration only because General Student's Parachute Army was still moving down from Germany.

In my opinion Monty was right. We had advanced rapidly up the coastal plain while the Germans were still disorganised. His eyes were focused on the big prize—to bounce a crossing over the Rhine and cut off the industrial heart of Germany, thus finishing the war in 1944. While there was still any chance of this succeeding he would have been wrong to deflect his resources to a subsidiary task.

The clearance of the Scheldt estuary would certainly have eased the administrative situation, but would it have shortened the war by even one day? On the information available, Arnhem was a justifiable gamble. Had the Germans not made one of the most remarkable military recoveries in history, it might well have succeeded. How could we know then that 4th September was the fateful day when victory in 1944 slipped through our fingers?

CHAPTER XVII

BATTLE OF THE ARDENNES

WHEN ON the night of 25th September, the remnants of the 1st British Airborne Division were withdrawn south of the lower Rhine into our lines, all chance of finishing the war in 1944 was over and we were faced with the unpleasant prospect of fighting on throughout the winter. I seem to remember that Hannibal invariably adopted the admirable practice of going into winter quarters, but Eisenhower obviously had no intention of doing so. Quite rightly orders were issued that the Germans were to be given no respite. The first task was to close up to the Rhine, preparatory to forcing a crossing and penetrating deep into the heart of the Reich.

30 Corps became involved in the battle of the Rhineland, as it was called, almost by chance. At the beginning of November we handed over the Nijmegen sectoı to the Canadians and moved down to the extreme right of the British front near Maastricht. Here we found ourselves next door to the 9th U.S. Army, which was preparing, in conjunction with the 1st U.S. Army, to launch a large-scale offensive towards Cologne. The 9th had had little or no battle experience and felt very much a poor relation alongside the experienced 1st U.S. Army. This made them all the more friendly towards their neighbours on the other flank, 30 Corps.

I grew to like General Simpson, their army commander, very much indeed. He was a paternal figure of rather unusual appearance because he always kept a completely bald, shaven head. One day he asked me whether I could help in the forthcoming offensive by capturing the German town of Geilenkirchen. He pointed out that the inclusion of this town as one of his objectives would stretch his front too much. My orders were merely to hold the front and not attack, but I wanted to help if possible, and his request seemed very reasonable. This, however, was an operation for which two divisions were required, and I had only the 43rd (Wessex) Division available. Neither 21st Army Group nor 2nd Army were prepared to give me any additional troops. I was told that the barrel was bare and I was to stay quiet for a change.

A couple of days later I was invited to dinner by Simpson to meet General Eisenhower, who was spending the night at his headquarters. I was delighted to meet Ike again. There was something about his warm, friendly personality which always did me good.

"Well, Jorrocks," he said, "are you going to take on Geilenkirchen for us?" I replied that the spirit was willing, but the flesh, in the shape of one extra division, was weak. Eisenhower then turned to Simpson and said, "Give him one of ours."

It was agreed that the new 84th Division, which had just arrived from the U.S.A., should be placed under my command. This was a great mark of confidence but I didn't altogether like it. I pointed out that the battle in front of us was not going to be an easy operation, because it involved breaching the Siegfried Line, which consisted of concrete emplacements, barbed-wire obstacles and mines. Was it fair, I asked, to launch a U.S. division against all this in their first battle, under command of a Limey general? I felt their morale might have been higher if they had gone in under an American.

No one took the slightest notice of my protest, and by the time we started our meal I was committed to play a subsidiary role in the forthcoming U.S. offensive.

Eisenhower was, I remember, very angry just then with the 82nd and 101st U.S. Airborne Divisions which had been under my command during the Arnhem battle. After being pulled back into reserve they had apparently behaved badly and caused quite a lot of trouble in the rear areas.

"They are a disgrace to the American Army," he said.

This was more than I could stand, because they were both magnificent divisions in battle. I leapt to their defence and suggested that it was a pity the whole American Army did not consist of similar "disgraces." Suddenly I heard a roar of laughter from Bedell Smith, Ike's chief of staff.

"Well, well," he said, "I never thought to hear a Britisher standing up for U.S. troops against an American general!"

The more I saw of the 84th the more impressed I became with the system of training which had been evolved during the war in the U.S.A. It worked on the sausage-machine principle. The different ingredients in the form of men, officers, and material were poured in at one end, and a complete division trained for war came out at the other. Their staff work was naturally rather cumbersome, and they lacked the know how which only battle experience can bring. But they were a good division nevertheless.

I was determined that they should have every possible assistance, so for tank support I gave them my most experienced armoured regiment, the Sherwood Rangers Yeomanry, commanded by Stanley Christopherson, some flails and flame tanks from the 79th Division, and above all the support of my superb corps artillery. The result, in the initial stages, was a complete success. On the first day, 18th November, both the 43rd Wessex and the 84th U.S. captured all their objectives, and by the evening of the 19th Geilenkirchen was in our hands.

Now we began to encounter winter public enemy No. 1—rain. After continuous rain the ground became so sodden that even the tanks were bogged, and the Germans as usual began launching some vicious counter-attacks with their 15th Panzer and 10th S.S. Divisions. We succeeded in holding on to most of our objectives, but all efforts to exploit our initial gains were unsuccessful.

This was warfare at its most beastly, continuous cold driving rain turning the ground into a sea of mud, and constant counter-attacks from experienced German troops. The thing that worried me most was the initial failure of the Americans to get a hot meal through to their forward troops. This is where battle experience counts. It may be necessary to make the most elaborate plans many hours beforehand; but if troops are to go on fighting in winter, somehow or other they must get hot food. Every day my first question to the 84th was, "How many units have had a hot meal during the night?"

The first day the answer was—none. The second day—fifty per

cent, and the third day—100 per cent. The great thing about the Americans was that they were very quick to learn.

Now was the moment, after three days' hard and more-or-less victorious action, for this raw division to have been pulled out of the line. But in war this is not always possible. They just had to stay there, grin and bear it. On 23rd November the 84th reverted to U.S. control as the front had become static. I have deliberately mentioned this small battle in some detail because it was typical of what was going on throughout the winter all along the front.

Early in December I was visited by Field-Marshal Montgomery who explained the next role my corps was to play in this battle of the Rhineland. A large-scale attack was to be launched in a southerly direction from the Nijmegen area, with our right on the Maas and our left on the Rhine, to be followed a few days later by an attack by General Simpson's 9th Army across the Roer in a northerly direction. The German forces west of the Rhine would thus be caught between two prongs.

This was subsequently called the battle of the Reichswald, and on 13th December, 30 Corps was pulled out of the line in great secrecy to prepare for this operation. While the different formations were moving back, I decided to avail myself of the standing invitation from Queen Elizabeth of the Belgians and snatch a brief leave at the Palace of Laeken.

Then the incredible happened. I hadn't been there twenty-four hours when the telephone rang and the voice of a senior staff officer at General Dempsey's 2nd Army headquarters said: "The Germans have smashed through the American front in the Ardennes and the situation is extremely confused. Field-Marshal Montgomery wants your corps, which is our only reserve readily available, to move down and occupy a lay-back position to protect Brussels. Can you return immediately?"

As luck would have it there was a thick pea-souper fog that night, and I couldn't have found my way even through Brussels, let alone get back to my headquarters some seventy-five miles away. So I replied that I would return first thing next morning, and I was quite happy to leave the move of the corps in the hands of my very able chief of staff.

I don't think I have ever been so surprised in my life. Here were the Germans, whom we imagined almost at the end of their tether, and whose air force had been practically shot out of the skies, pulling off the biggest surprise of the war and launching a large-scale counter-attack. It was so uncanny that, sitting there with the fog all round me, I felt very, very uneasy. But then I pulled myself together and began to study the map.

I knew that the Ardennes sector of the American front was very lightly held, with something like four divisions on a frontage of ninety miles. Although it was reputed to be difficult country, wooded and hilly, with narrow roads twisting up the valleys, the Germans knew it well. It was through the Ardennes that they had launched their famour panzer thrust in 1940 which had cut the French armies in two.

Neither the French in 1940 nor the Americans in 1944 had expected an attack in this particular sector, and they were both proved wrong. The Germans had chosen well on both occasions. A further anxiety was that because of Eisenhower's broad front policy almost every formation was in the line all the time, and there were very few reserves available.

Then I began to realise what a fantastic gamble this was. The Germans could not possibly have amassed the resources in men, material and above all in the air to do us any serious damage. In fact they were playing into our hands. Instead of the Allies having to launch their attacks across flooded rivers like the Roer and then stand up to sharp enemy counter-attacks from armoured divisions, the Germans had come to us and stuck their armoured heads into our noose. With any luck we might destroy a large part of their last available armoured divisions.

I heard afterwards that the reactions of that most colourful U.S. General George Patton, had been very similar. When told about the German attack he said: "Fine. We should open up and let them get all the way to Paris. Then we will saw 'em off at the base."

I was feeling quite cheerful by the time I went into dinner, which was just as well, because I found two very anxious women, Queen Elizabeth and la Baronne Carton de Wiart, awaiting me. Brussels had already been occupied twice in their lifetime. Was it to happen again? I did my best to reassure them, and pointed out that as a result of this attack the war might be shortened by several months. Poor Brussels—that cheerful leave centre where the Allied troops enjoyed a short spell out of the line was like a morgue during the next few days.

I have no intention of going into details of this battle, which was largely an American affair. From the moment 30 Corps was in the long-stop position quite close to the battlefield of Waterloo there was no further danger of a German break-through. With three infantry divisions available and some 300 tanks ready to drive in from the flank, I hoped sincerely that the Germans would poke their noses over the Meuse. I had a momentary hope that it might fall to the lot of Horrocks to fight the second battle of Waterloo. In fact I went forward to see General Joe Collins, commanding the U.S. 7 Corps on the other side of the river in front of me and said: "Let them come, we will be delighted to deal with them." He grinned and said, "I can't do that, General, but it is mighty comforting to know you are there!"

The main British interest in the battle centred round the part played by Montgomery. When news of the German offensive was first received, some of the U.S. generals thought that it was only a spoiling attack. But not Monty. Like an old war horse he immediately scented danger. And although to start with the enemy attack was not on his front at all, he immediately moved my corps into position to block any German attempt to break through to Brussels and Antwerp. This was a wise precaution.

Then came General Eisenhower's much-discussed and criticised decision to split the command and place all the troops north of the bulge, including the 1st U.S. Army, under Montgomery, leaving Bradley to command all those in the south. From every military point of view this was a correct decision, but it hurt the Americans badly. They felt that it was a slur on their efficiency. It was a situation which required immense tact—but this is a quality for

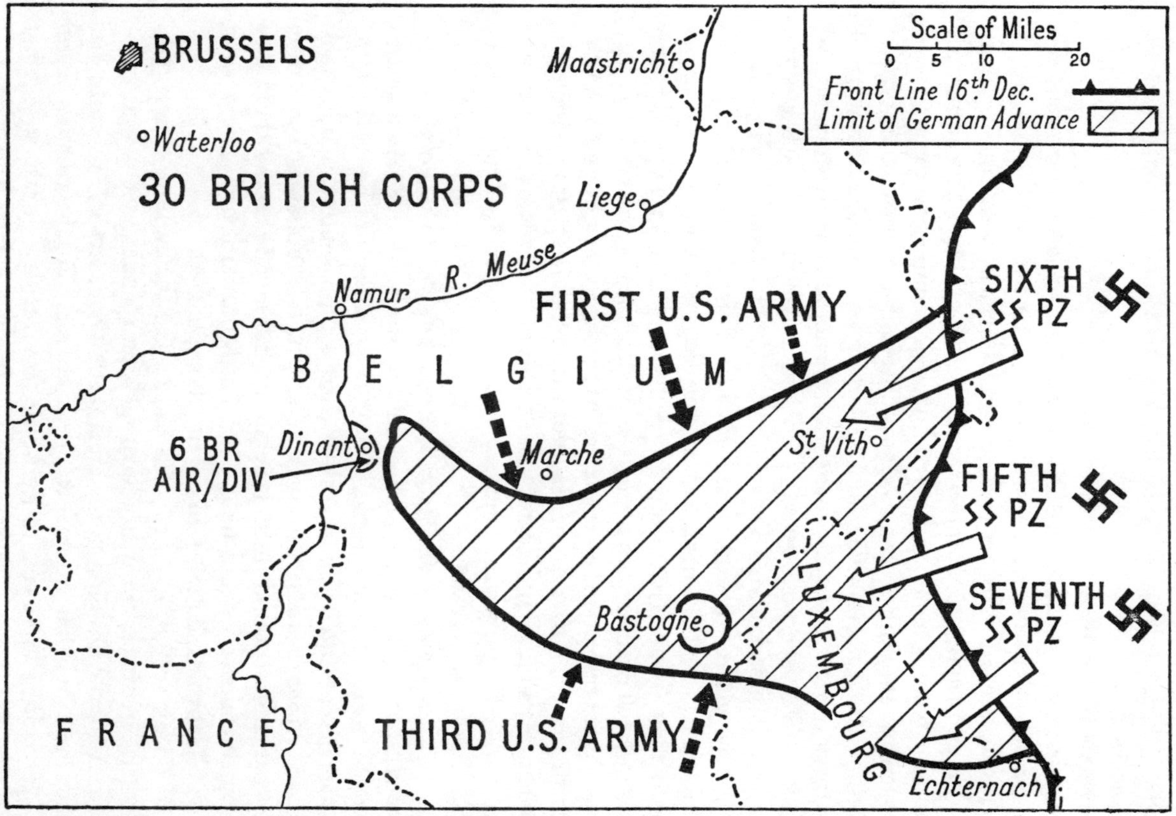

THE BATTLE OF THE ARDENNES

which high-ranking soldiers are not noted, and Monty was no exception.

One of the main difficulties in this battle was to find out what was happening. Rumours multiplied, particularly as regards the activities of the German commandos under Major Otto Skorzeny. These consisted of American-speaking Germans wearing U.S. uniform and riding in captured jeeps. Not more than fifty jeep loads all told were actually employed but their numbers were multiplied at least twenty times. It was almost impossible to move about freely behind the American lines unless one had an intimate knowledge of America, because the U.S. sentries were not satisfied with passes and passwords. Everyone was grilled about America. "What is the second largest town in Texas?" I was once asked. I had no idea.

This was a very confused battle and it was under these circumstances that Monty's liaison officers, or gallopers, really came into their own. They consisted of hand-picked, intelligent, tough young staff officers who lived at his tactical headquarters. Every day they were dispatched to the different formations fighting the battle. In the evening after dinner each in turn would report to Monty on what he had seen and heard. As a result of their reports Monty was probably the only man who had a completely up-to-date picture of the whole battle front.

The only way I could keep in touch with what was going on was to send my intelligence officer daily to study Monty's own operational map. Many people, particularly some of the U.S. commanders, resented the arrival of these liaison officers, whom they called Monty's spies. This was understandable, but at the same time rather silly. I found them very useful indeed. By taking them into my confidence I could be certain that Monty not only knew what was happening but also where the shoe pinched.

I took very little part in this battle. On the evening of the 25th, when I got back to my headquarters after spending the day with the 6th Airborne Division in the Dinant and Givet sector, I was told that the Field-Marshal wanted to speak to me. His first words were, "Jorrocks, I want you to fly home to-morrow." I was somewhat shaken, but when I said: "May I ask why I am being sacked?"

In the B.B.C. Television studios. Above: Showing how Otto Skorzeny rescued Mussolini from a mountain hotel in Italy. Below: Describing the battle of Normandy

Historic pictures showing Black Rod's rôle at the Opening of Parliament, never photograpl before and here reproduced, by permission of the B.B.C., from the telerecording (1958). Abov Black Rod finds himself in a familiar position, advancing before Field-Marshal Montgome carrying the Sword of State. Below : At the bar of the House of Lords after summoning the Commo Behind Black Rod can be seen the Prime Minister, Mr. Harold Macmillan, the Chaplain and Leader of the Opposition, Mr. Hugh Gaitskell

there was an explosion at the other end of the telephone. "Don't be stupid," he said. "You're not being sacked. I want you to go home and have a rest before a big battle I've got in store for you as soon as we've cleared up this mess here."

I pointed out that the German spearhead was far from blunted and this was hardly the time for a commander to leave his corps when we were engaged in a battle which was unquestionably one of the turning points in the war. "This battle is finished," he said. "The Germans have shot their bolt. You fly home to-morrow." And that was that.

I shall never forget the look of horrified astonishment on the face of the Vice-Chief of the General Staff, Archie Nye, when I popped my head round his door in the War Office next day. For a second he obviously thought some frightful disaster had occurred, and that I was the last survivor. His relief when I explained was almost funny. But he kept on muttering doubtfully, "Fancy Monty sending you on leave at a time like this." I could see that he also thought my time had come, and was probably pondering on a suitable decoration with which to grace my military demise.

I mention this personal episode merely to emphasise once more that Monty was always fighting the next battle or the next but one, rather than the current one.

He was quite right. Already on 29th December, Manteuffel, the German commander, was almost beseeching his Higher Command to call the battle off and let him get his troops back behind the Roer before the massive reserves being concentrated north and south of the bulge could strike his flanks. But as usual Hitler refused to give up an inch of ground, and it was not until 3rd January that he reluctantly gave permission for the withdrawal.

By this time it was almost too late. Snow and biting winds added to the misery of the beaten German Armies as powerful thrusts by the 1st and 3rd U.S. Armies struck into their flanks, while the air forces pounded them ceaselessly from above. On 11th January the two armies joined hands at Houffalize, and by the end of the month the Germans were back once more behind their Siegfried Line.

They had failed primarily because they had under-estimated the fighting qualities of the American front-line troops. The American divisions had weathered this unexpected storm most creditably, but their losses had not been light. In five weeks there were 59,000 casualties in the twenty-seven U.S. divisions which were engaged in the battle. The German losses in men and material were, however, much more serious because, unlike the American, they could not be replaced. In the words of Manteuffel himself: "The cost was so great that the offensive failed to show a profit. The last German reserves had suffered such losses that they were no longer capable of affecting the situation either on the western or eastern fronts."

The effect on the morale of the German troops was disastrous. After the Ardennes all hope of winning the war had gone. Disillusionment and bitterness now began to creep in.

CHAPTER XVIII

REICHSWALD BATTLE

On my return from leave we resumed our interrupted preparations for the Reichswald battle. 30 Corps was lent to the 1st Canadian Army for this operation, designed to destroy all German forces between the Rhine and the Meuse. It was to be a two-pronged affair. We, the northern prong, were to attack in great strength on 8th February. Then, when all the German reserves were on the move north to meet this threat, the southern prong, General Simpson's 9th U.S. Army, would cross the River Roer and advance towards us.

The German forces would thus be caught in a vice. If they elected to fight west of the Rhine they would be destroyed and fewer German troops would be available to counter our thrust into the Reich itself. If they decided to withdraw back over the Rhine, 21st Army Group would be right down on the bank poised to make a crossing anywhere along its length, the primary object of the Rhineland battle.

In theory a perfectly straightforward plan, but not quite so easy as it looked. All operations fought by armies are largely influenced by the shape of the ground and also by weather conditions. None more so than this one.

The front line was held by two Canadian divisions and as I studied the country from one of their observation posts I saw in front a gentle valley with small farms rising up on the other side and merging into the sinister blackness of the Reichswald (German forest), intersected by rides but with only one metalled road running through it. North of the forest ran the main road from Nijmegen to Cleve—that is from Holland into Germany. North of this again was the low-lying polder land which had been flooded by the

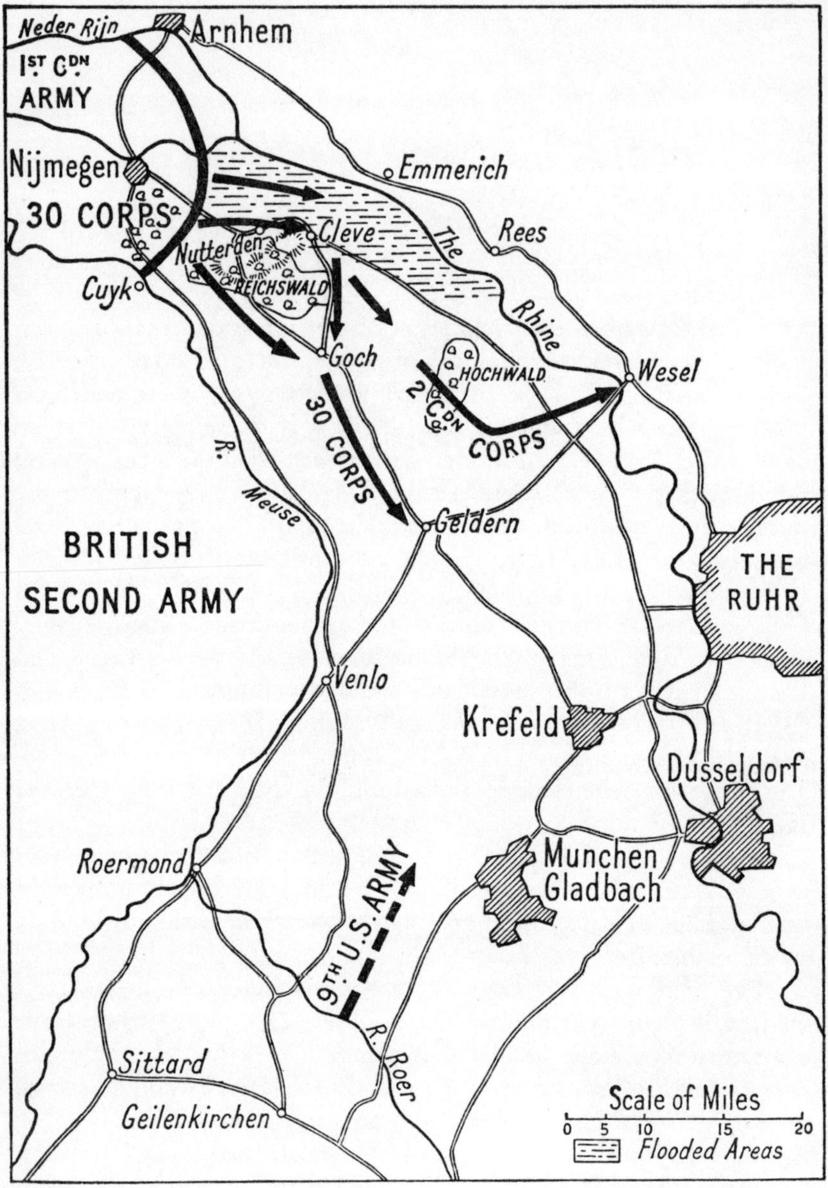

THE BATTLE OF THE REICHSWALD

Germans and looked like a large lake with the villages—built on slightly higher ground—standing out above the water. To the north flowed the broad expanse of the Rhine. The Germans were holding the far bank. South of the Reichswald was more low-lying ground which ran down to the River Meuse. This was completely dominated by the southern edge of the forest. The British 2nd Army held the other side of this river. We were therefore faced with a bottle-neck between the forest and the polder land and this had been heavily fortified in depth by the Germans. Moreover the whole area was lousy with mines.

This was really the outpost position of the Siegfried Line which lay 3,500 yards to the east and consisted of an anti-tank ditch, some concrete emplacements, barbed-wire, mines and so on. Furthermore the small Rhineland towns such as Cleve and Goch had been made into hedgehogs, fortresses prepared for all-round defence. The cellars in the houses of all these German frontier towns had been specially constructed for battle—concrete basements with loopholes and so on, a further example of the careful German preparations for war. Farther east still was one more lay-back position called the Hochwald. So the German defences were in considerable depth.

We had to get through this bottle-neck before we could break out into the German plain beyond and the key to the bottle-neck was the high ground at Nutterden. This was the hinge of the door which led to the open country. The front was held by one German division, the 84th, supported by about 100 guns, but we estimated that there were approximately three infantry and two panzer divisions in reserve which could be brought into the battle pretty quickly.

The first essential was to smash through the 84th as quickly as possible and get the high ground, the hinge, before the Germans could bring up their reserves. It was a race for Nutterden, but at the same time I had to clear the Reichswald itself, otherwise the Germans could have concentrated troops there and struck at my communications. Moreover, I wanted the road running through it because I knew how difficult it would be to supply a large modern army with all its complicated needs along one road. To smash through quickly I determined to use the maximum force possible from the outset and support it with a large amount of artillery. So I decided to attack with five divisions in line, from right to left, 51st Highland, 53rd Welsh, 15th Scottish, 2nd and 3rd Canadian. Behind were the 43rd Wessex and Guards Armoured Divisions ready to pass through and sweep down the Rhineland.

The success of this plan depended on two things. First, obtaining complete surprise, and secondly on the weather. If the Germans got wind of our attack they would move up their reserves before the battle started. But the weather exerted the biggest influence of all, because the ground was frozen hard, and if only the frost would hold until 9th February, our tanks and motor transport would be able to go everywhere across country without any difficulty. I had no doubt at all that under these conditions we should break out very quickly into the plain beyond and I hoped secretly to bounce one of the bridges over the Rhine.

Surprise would not be easy. An enormous concourse of men, tanks, vehicles and guns had to be moved into the outskirts of Nijmegen and the woods nearby unknown to the Germans. This involved the most intricate staff work. By day the roads must remain empty, showing just an occasional vehicle—the normal traffic, in fact. But as soon as it got dark, feverish activity began. Vehicles, almost nose to tail, came out of their hide-outs and started moving up. Thirty-five thousand vehicles were used to bring up the men and their supplies. One million, three hundred thousand gallons of petrol were required. Five special bridges had to be constructed over the Maas. One hundred miles of road must be made or improved. An intricate traffic control system had to be set up involving 1600 military police, and each unit was given the most exact timing.

General Crerar, the Canadian army commander, under whom I was now serving, wisely decided that my assaulting troops should concentrate behind the existing Canadian screen so as not to arouse German suspicions by the sudden arrival of many fresh formations. A great many people had to reconnoitre this forward area, and I was terrified that the presence of hundreds of officers and N.C.O.s walking about with field-glasses and maps might give the show away. So an office was established in the Dutch infantry barracks at Grave from where we controlled the movement of all reconnaissance parties north of the River Meuse. We even made them wear Canadian battle-dress which was slightly different in colour and pattern from ours.

This was the first time I had come into close contact with the Canadians during the war, and as I went round getting to know the 2nd and 3rd Divisions which were to form part of my corps I was more and more impressed. Their long period of training in the U.K. had not been wasted. Moreover, while my corps had been romping gaily up to Brussels, the Canadians had been engaged in some very hard fighting in the coastal areas, so by now they were not only well trained but also seasoned troops. On the whole they seemed larger than our men, but occasionally I arrived suddenly in a unit composed of small alert French-speaking soldiers.

To begin with all the plans went very smoothly. Then we got our first body blow. A sudden thaw set in and the bottom dropped out of some of our vital roads. By now, however, I had a superb staff, all young but very experienced, and somehow the vast concentrations were completed without the Germans suspecting anything.

One thing, during this preparatory stage, caused me almost more worry than anything else; the handling of the immense air resources which were to support us. General Crerar told me that in addition to the whole of the 2nd Tactical Air Force the heavies from Bomber Command were also available. And he put this question to me: " Do you want the town of Cleve taken out? " By " taking out " he meant, of course, totally destroyed.

This is the sort of problem with which a general in war is constantly faced, and from which there is no escape. Cleve was a lovely, historical, Rhineland town. Anne of Cleves, Henry VIII's fifth wife came from there. No doubt a lot of civilians, particularly women and children, were still living there. I hated the thought of its being " taken out." All the same, if we were to break out of this bottle-neck and sweep down into the German plain beyond it was going to be a race between the 15th Scottish Division and the German reserves for the hinge, and all the German reserves would have to pass through Cleve. If I could delay them by bombing, it might make all the difference to the battle. And after all the lives of my own troops must come first. So I said " Yes."

But I can assure you that I did not enjoy the sight of those bombers flying over my head on the night before we attacked. Generals, of course, should not have imagination. I reckon I had a bit too much.

By the evening of 7th February our concentration was complete, and the woods and outskirts of Nijmegen were thick with troops, guns, vehicles, workshops, tanks—all the paraphernalia of modern war. It would have been almost impossible to drop a pea into the area without hitting something. This was probably the last of the old-type set piece attacks because, in face of the threat of tactical atomic missiles, no concentration like this can ever take place again.

Though the difficult and complicated concentration had been achieved secretly, our prospects of a swift success had dwindled since the original plan had been made. The thaw had been a great blow, because in front of us in that low-lying valley the going was certain to be bad. Luckily for my peace of mind I did not realise then just how bad. The second handicap concerned the attack of the American 9th Army. The Germans had wisely blown the dams, and the Roer river had become so flooded that no passage over it would be possible until the flood waters had subsided. How long this would take was anybody's guess. The flood would enable the Germans to concentrate every available reserve against us. We were faced with a battle of extermination, slogging our way forward through the mud. Not a pleasing prospect at all.

With these thoughts in mind I climbed into my command post for the battle in the early hours of 8th February. It was a cold, grey, miserable dawn with low clouds and rain, heralding several days of stormy weather. My command post was a small platform half-way up a tree, and from here I had a wonderful view over most of the battlefield. The noise was appalling, and the sight awe-inspiring.

All across the front shells were exploding. We had arranged for a barrage, a curtain of fire, to move forward at a rate of 300 yards every twelve minutes, or 100 yards every four minutes, in front of the troops. To mark the end of the four-minute period when the guns would increase their range by 300 yards they all fired a round of yellow smoke.

So it was possible to follow roughly the progress of the attack, and down in the valley, behind this wall of shells, I could see small scattered groups of men and tanks all moving slowly forward. I was also able by wireless to keep in accurate touch with what was happening.

This was the biggest operation I had ever handled in war. Thirty Corps was 200,000 strong that day, and we were attacking with five divisions in line supported by 1400 guns. It soon became clear that the enemy was completely bemused as a result of our colossal bombardment; their resistance was slight. The main trouble was mines—and mud, particularly mud. I am certain that this must be the chief memory of everyone who fought in the Reichswald battle. Mud and still more mud. It was so bad that after the first hour every tank going across country was bogged down, and the infantry had to struggle forward on their own. The chief enemy resistance came from the cellars in the villages.

It has been said that no two attacks are ever alike, and that was exemplified in this battle. Every night as soon as it was dusk, the 3rd Canadian Division set out on what were almost maritime operations, each one designed to capture one or more of the villages which, owing to the flooding, looked like small islands jutting out of the sea. Artillery would fire on the village while the Canadians in their buffaloes (amphibious vehicles) sailed off across the intervening lake and carried out their assault.

On their right was an entirely different type of operation carried out by the 44th Brigade of the 15th Scottish. Their task was to breach the northern extension of the Siegfried Line, consisting of anti-tank ditches, mine-fields, concrete emplacements and barbed-wire entanglements. Not one single man was on his feet. The officers controlling the artillery fire were in tanks. The leading wave of the assault consisted of tanks with flails in front beating and exploding the mines to clear passages through the mine-fields. Then came tanks carrying bridges and fascines on their backs to form bridges over the anti-tank ditch. The next echelon was flame-throwing tanks to deal with the concrete pill-boxes, and finally infantry in cut-down tanks, i.e., with the top taken off, called kangaroos.

These proved a great boon in the closing stages of the war. They were, I believe, a Canadian invention emanating from the brain of one of their most famous corps commanders, General Simonds. I once saw a whole brigade of the 51st Highland Division in these vehicles being heavily shelled by the Germans. I thought their casualties were bound to be high, but they had only two men wounded.

That night the Germans breached the banks of the Rhine up-stream, and the floods started to rise, spreading over our one road. Nevertheless the advance was going well, and I was delighted to hear that the 15th Scottish were moving into the outskirts of Cleve. Here was the news for which I had been waiting eagerly and I unleashed my first reserve, the 43rd Wessex Division, which was to pass through the 15th Scottish and burst out into the plain.

This was one of the worst mistakes I made in the war. The 15th Scottish had not got nearly so far as had been reported, and one of their brigades had not yet been employed at all. There was already too much traffic on this one road, and it was impossible to deploy across country owing to the boggy ground. The arrival of this extra division caused one of the worst traffic jams of the whole war, only equalled, I believe, by the scenes in the Liri valley in Italy after the battle of Cassino. The language heard that night has seldom if ever been equalled.

In spite of me, shall we say, the 15th Scottish and then the 43rd Wessex forced their way into the shattered ruins that had once been Cleve and some very hard fighting took place. Meanwhile the 53rd Welsh had disappeared into the Reichswald itself, where they spent one of the most unpleasant weeks of the war, fighting their way steadily forward against increasing German opposition. The

51st Highland were also going well on the right flank, where opposition had been heavier than anywhere else. It was a satisfactory thought that this division which had started at Alamein was now at long last, and after much hard fighting all along North Africa, Sicily, Normandy, Belgium, Holland, in Germany itself.

From now on the battle developed into a slogging match as we inched our way forward through the mud and rain. It became a soldier's battle fought most gallantly by the regimental officers and men under the most ghastly conditions imaginable. It was a slog in which only two things mattered, training and guts, with the key men as always the battalion commanders. The Germans rushed up more guns and more divisions. Eventually we were opposed by more than 1000 guns, 700 mortars and some ten divisions; they were certainly fighting desperately to prevent our getting to their famous Rhine. Slowly and bitterly we advanced through the mud supported by our superb artillery.

Historians may well in the future pass over this battle as dull but it was far from dull for the front-line soldiers. As I went round day after day I marvelled at the stoicism of these youngsters. They were quite unmoved by the fact that they were the cutting edge of a vast military machine stretching right back through bulging lines of communication to war factories in the United Kingdom.

The strain to which the soldier of to-day is subjected is far, far greater than anything experienced by his grandfather or his great-grandfather. This battle was a particularly good example. The 53rd Welsh Division and, farther south, the 51st Highland Division were fighting their way through that sinister black Reichswald Forest. Their forward troops would very often consist of two young men, crouching together in a fox-hole, both of whom had long since come to the conclusion that the glories of war had been much over-written. They were quite alone for they might not be able to see even the other members of their own section and all around them was the menace of hidden mines.

It is this sinister emptiness that depresses them most—no living thing in sight. During training, officers and N.C.O.s had been running round the whole time, but they cannot do it now to anything like the same extent, or they won't live long. Our two young men are almost certainly cold, miserable and hungry, but they are at least reasonably safe as long as they remain in their fox-hole. But they know that soon they will have to emerge into the open to attack. Then the seemingly empty battlefield will erupt into sudden and violent life. When that moment arrives they must force themselves forward with a sickening feeling in the pit of their stomachs, fighting an almost uncontrollable urge to fling themselves down as close to the earth as they can get. Even then they are still alone amidst all the fury; carrying their loneliness with them.

Towards the end of the war I began to feel that in face of modern fire power it is not possible for the human body, unprotected by armour, to move across country at all. That is why we British generals, who had nearly all been through the First World War with its terrible casualties, were always seeking for more ways of helping the infantry forward, more tanks to go with them, clear the way through mine-fields, and give them close fire support in their attacks. More and still more artillery with which to blast the enemy and keep him down at the bottom of his trench, unable to retaliate.

But now let me return to the young soldiers in their empty battlefield, and compare them with their great-great-grandfathers on the battlefield of Waterloo, where the British troops formed up shoulder-to-shoulder, with their officers and N.C.O.s all round them. Every now and then along the ridge in front of them rode their famous commander, Wellington, on his equally famous horse, Copenhagen. Three-quarters of a mile away on the hill of La Belle Alliance they could see their French opponents under Napoleon also forming up. There was shouting, clamour and excitement in the air. It took a brave men to be a coward under those circumstances.

How much worse for our youngsters in their loneliness.

In those days, too, little happened at night. As soon as it got dark the armies of both sides slept round camp-fires, probably warmed with swigs of looted brandy. In the morning when they were all formed up, the generals said, " Let battle commence "—and off they went again.

Now, owing to the power of modern fire, more and more happens at night. In Korea practically all the fighting took place under cover of darkness. And I reckon about the hardest thing you can ask of any man is to form part of a standing patrol in no-man's-land on a winter's night.

Yet nothing in their previous life has prepared our young men for the supreme ordeal of this modern battlefield. The greater proportion of soldiers to-day live in the outskirts of some big town, where they are always surrounded by crowds. At the cinema, the football match, at work in the factory, or in a holiday camp, there are always plenty of people. Quite naturally they don't like being alone. Nor do they like darkness because they are used to the lighted streets. They are also brought up, quite rightly, in an atmosphere of safety first. Going to school there is a man or woman in a white coat to see them safely across the road. I am not suggesting that this is not a good thing. Of course it is, with the state of our modern roads. But what I *do* say is that it is hardly a suitable background for the ordeal of modern war. All the more credit to them then that when properly led they do so well.

The floods rose continuously, and at one stage our one road was covered to a depth of several feet. We attacked every day and every night for five long weeks, and our casualties began to mount. I kept on hearing the sad news that Major, Captain or Sergeant So-and-so who had been with his unit ever since Normandy had been killed.

This was a Canadian battle, and every day I was visited by General Crerar, the army commander. He was always very well-informed because, in spite of the bad weather, he made constant flights over the battlefield in a small observation aircraft. I am afraid he must have found me a rather tiresome subordinate, because this continuous battle in the mud began to take its toll, and I found myself getting very tired and irritable. But Crerar bore with me patiently.

The turning-point came on 16th February, when the 43rd Wessex Division carried out a brilliant 8000 yards advance which brought them to the escarpment overlooking the fortified town of Goch, which was subsequently captured by the Jocks of the 51st

Highland and 15th Scottish Divisions. At this time my right flank was very much a Scottish army. The 52nd (Lowland Division) were on the extreme right and one of the regiments supporting the attack on Goch was that magnificent medium artillery regiment The Scottish Horse.

After the first week the front widened sufficiently for the 2nd Canadian Corps, commanded by General Simonds, to come in on my left, or northern flank. Simonds was a first-class commander with a most original brain and full of initiative. It was his corps which now bore the brunt of the assault on the strongly-held Hochwald position.

They were faced by determined resistance from German paratroopers and it developed into a dour struggle. The Royal Winnipeg Rifles said it was "the heaviest shelling the battalion had ever experienced." The Regina Rifles reported "Just as bad as anything encountered in Normandy." It was during this fighting that two Canadians won the Victoria Cross. Sergeant Aubrey Cosens of the Queen's Own Rifles of Canada almost single-handed beat off numerous German counter-attacks, and then led his platoon, reduced to four men, in an attack against three strongly-defended enemy positions. In the moment of victory he himself was killed by a bullet from a German sniper. The second was won by an officer, Major F. A. Tilston of the Essex Scottish. Though wounded time after time he went on leading his company and eventually, though so seriously wounded that he was barely conscious, he refused to give up until he was satisfied that the position was secure. Only then would he permit himself to be taken back to the aid post.

On the 23rd came the welcome news that the 9th U.S. Army had been able to cross the swollen River Roer. This meant that the southern prong would now start moving northwards, and the German fate was sealed. By 10th March the battle was over and all organised German resistance west of the Rhine had ceased.

During the course of this horrible battle nine British and Canadian divisions supported by a vast array of artillery had been under command of 30 Corps. We had smashed our way through carefully prepared enemy defensive positions under the most unpleasant conditions imaginable. No one in his senses would wish to fight a winter campaign in the flood plains of north-western Europe, but there was no alternative. During the fighting, which had lasted for a month, we had encountered and defeated three panzer, four parachute and four German infantry divisions. We took 16,800 German prisoners and it was estimated that the total enemy casualties was about 75,000 as against 15,634 suffered by us. Our losses seemed very high to me at the time, but this was unquestionably the grimmest battle in which I took part during the last war and I kept on reminding myself that during the battle of the Somme in the 1914-1918 war there were 50,000 casualties during the first morning.

General Eisenhower summed it up in a letter to Crerar in which he wrote, "Probably no assault in this war has been conducted in more appalling conditions of terrain than was that one."

I was very glad to have it behind me. The battle of the Rhineland was over; the western bank was securely in our hands, and the heart of Germany was almost uncovered.

CHAPTER XIX

ACROSS THE RHINE

When the battle of the Rhineland was over I received a message to say that 30 Corps was to revert to the command of the 2nd British Army. Next day General Dempsey arrived to give me his plan for the crossing of the Rhine and the final advance into Germany. We were to attack on a two-corps front between the small towns of Wesel and Emmerich with 12 Corps on the right and my corps, 30, on the left. As the main effort—what the Germans called the *Schwerpunkt*—was to be on the right, the two airborne divisions, 6th British and 17th U.S. were to be employed on 12 Corps front. It was an exciting proposition. The idea of breaching the Rhine of all rivers appealed to me enormously. It wasn't, however, going to be so simple as some people seemed to think, because, whatever might be happening elsewhere on the front, the troops opposed to us were still fighting toughly. According to my intelligence staff, whose information was always astonishingly accurate, we were opposed by the 8th Parachute Division round the small town of Rees with part of the 6th and 7th Parachute Divisions on its flanks. Behind in immediate reserve were our old friends, or enemies, 15th Panzer Grenadier Division and 116th Panzer Division.

A vast concentration of troops, assault boats, buffaloes, bridging material, guns, etc., had to be got into position, and unfortunately the far bank of the broad, swift-running Rhine was slightly higher than ours so that German observers could see all that was going on in the flat ground on our side. To deceive the enemy about our crossing place was a difficult problem involving some intricate staff work under the direction of my B.G.S., Brigadier Jones (subsequently Major-General C. B. Jones, Vice-Adjutant General at the War Office). Once again I had been extremely lucky in my chief staff officer. No one could have wished for a better right-hand man than " Splosh " Jones, and he took the whole thing in his stride. One of his first problems was to control reconnaissance. Before an attack of this sort a large number of people must go forward and reconnoitre the positions they are to occupy. This applies particularly to the gunners who have many mysterious rites of their own to perform before they can bring down accurate concentrations of fire.

We hit on what I thought was rather a bright idea. Nobody was allowed forward on to the flat polder land stretching back from the banks of the Rhine without reporting to a special branch of 30 Corps headquarters where a very large-scale map of the forward area was maintained. This was known as " The Pig Hotel "—30 Corps sign was a wild boar and we were known throughout the army as the old pig. After examining the accommodation which they had been allotted in " the hotel," reconnaissance parties were allowed to go forward a few at a time to see their " rooms." I was particularly angry one day to hear that a certain Major-General who was much too brave to take the normal precautions had walked along the near bank of the Rhine wearing his red hat.

The final move forward on to the flat ground was made under cover of darkness, and from the first night I arranged for a continuous smoke-screen to be put down right along the river bank. This proved most effective, though when the wind blew towards us the smoke was inclined to make everyone feel sick. A river crossing of this nature is a most intricate operation but thanks to " Splosh " and his excellent team of staff officers, by the 23rd March all was ready and at 5 p.m. our artillery opened fire.

This preliminary bombardment was designed to destroy the 150 enemy guns which had been located on our front, or at least to cut their communications and so prevent them firing on our troops forming up for the assault. The 51st Highland Division had been earmarked to carry out the first crossings and just before 9 p.m. I climbed into an observation post on some high ground overlooking the Rhine. All around me were the usual noises of battle, and though I could see very little except the flicker of the guns I had a mental picture of what was going on in front of me in the hazy darkness of that warm spring evening. I could imagine the leading buffaloes carrying infantry of 153rd and 154th Infantry Brigades lumbering along their routes, which had been taped out and lit beforehand, and then lurching down into the dark waters of the Rhine.

Upstream at Wesel I could hear the aircraft of Bomber Command preparing the way for 12 Corps which was to assault later that night. Then at four minutes past nine precisely I received the message for which I had been waiting—in its way a historical message because it was from the first British troops to cross the Rhine—" The Black Watch has landed safely on the far bank." The initial crossings went very smoothly, opposition was not as heavy as might have been expected and our casualties were comparatively light.

But the enemy was quick to recover and very soon reports came in that Rees was proving troublesome. As the night wore on enemy resistance stiffened and some very bitter fighting took place. Within twenty-four hours of the assault the 15th Panzer Grenadier Division hit back at us with a vicious counter-attack. I will give just one example of what was going on. Soon after the village of Speldrop had been captured by " C " Company of the 1st Black Watch it was violently counter-attacked by German infantry supported by self-propelled guns. The situation became very confused and, as one platoon could not be located, nineteen-years-old Lieutenant J. R. Henderson volunteered to take out a patrol to try and find how far the Germans had penetrated.

After going a few hundred yards he came under intense fire, so ordering the rest of the men to take cover he went forward accompanied by only one man carrying a bren gun. Almost immediately an enemy machine-gun opened fire at very close range. The bren gunner was killed and Henderson's revolver was knocked out of his hand. Undaunted he charged the machine-gun position alone and killed the gunner with his shovel.

He then went back to the patrol, and although the only building at hand was in flames he decided to occupy it. By this time he and his patrol were cut off from the rest of the battalion. Realising that it would be difficult to hold out without a machine-gun, Henderson crawled back several hundred yards under very heavy fire to the place where the bren gunner had been killed, collected the gun and with great difficulty made his way back to his men.

By now the house was blazing so he led his men across the open into another one where they established themselves in a defensive position. During the next twelve hours enemy attacks against the house never relaxed and it was not until the following evening that the Highland Light Infantry of Canada, attacking with considerable artillery support, cleared the village after stiff fighting and so relieved Henderson and his men who were still holding out most gallantly.

Reports were coming in of Germans surrendering in large numbers to the British and American forces on our flanks but there was no sign of any collapse on our front. In fact the 51st Highland Division reported that the enemy was fighting harder than at any time since Normandy. It says a lot for the morale of those German parachute and panzer troops that with chaos, disorganisation and disillusionment all round them they should still be resisting so stubbornly. Their casualties during the last nine months had been very heavy, and the reinforcements arriving from Germany had not been of the old calibre at all, yet somehow the tough, experienced officers and N.C.O.s who were such a feature of these parachute and panzer formations managed to turn the callow youths into good soldiers.

It was a slow business widening the bridgehead and Rees proved a particularly hard nut to crack. It took the 1st Battalion The Gordons forty-eight hours, dour fighting before the whole place was in their hands. During the morning of the 24th as I was driving round in my jeep I received a wireless message which caused me great grief, to the effect that Thomas Rennie, the commander of the 51st Highland Division, had been killed by a mortar bomb when visiting one of his brigades on the far side of the river.

I have always felt that Rennie had some foreboding about this battle. He and I had fought many times together but I had never seen him so worried as he was over this Rhine project. He hated everything about it and I couldn't understand why, because the actual crossing was fairly plain sailing compared with other operations which he had undertaken quite cheerfully. Like so many Highlanders I believe he was " fey."

Something had to be done quickly as all the three brigades of this division were involved in heavy fighting, so I crossed the Rhine in a buffalo and summoned the three brigadiers to a conference. They were very upset by the death of their popular commander, and no wonder, because Rennie was a great leader and it was thanks largely to him that the division had recovered after a somewhat inauspicious start in Normandy. After discussing the situation and co-ordinating their future movements I appointed James Oliver, commander of the 154th Brigade, to take over the division temporarily until a new commander arrived. Rennie's successor was Macmillan of the Argylls, a most able and popular officer, known throughout the army as " Babe." It was a fortunate choice because as commander of 152nd Brigade in Sicily he was a familiar figure to all the Jocks.

With the Rhine behind us the drive into the heart of Germany began—9th U.S. Army, 8, 12 and 30 British, and 2 Canadian Corps from right to left. Due to the stubborn resistance of the German parachute troops we found ourselves echeloned back behind 8 and 12 Corps, a somewhat unusual experience for the old pig because up to now we had usually led the hunt through north-west Europe. Not only were these German rearguards well handled but their demolitions delayed us a lot. All bridges were blown and many cross-roads cratered, usually by large aerial bombs. A considerable delay on the River Ems was avoided thanks to a particularly gallant action carried out by the Guards. This was such a brilliant little operation that I propose to describe it in some detail.

On 3rd April the armoured cars of the Household Cavalry reported that one bridge over the River Ems was still intact; but it was prepared for demolition and strongly defended. The Coldstream Guards infantry and tanks (1st and 5th Battalions) working together were ordered to capture this bridge intact. From a wooded hill some 400 yards from the river Lieutenant-Colonel Gooch was able to study the German defences. The road leading up to the bridge was on an embankment and the actual approach was barred by a solid timber road-block. Six 500-lb. aerial bombs were wired together on the bridge ready to blow it up; on the far side were numerous trenches and at least three 88 mm. guns could be seen.

If the bridge was to be captured before it was destroyed split-second timing was required. The attack opened with a sudden, intense, artillery concentration on the German positions while the tanks moved up into firing positions on the wooded hill. When the artillery fire lifted the tanks opened up on the German positions with every weapon they possessed. Under cover of this No. 3 (Infantry) Company led by the company commander, Captain Liddell, moved forward on either side of the embankment. As Liddell didn't want to risk his company being blown up on the bridge, he halted them just short of it and going forward by himself climbed over the road-block. He then ran on to the bridge in full view of the enemy, all of whom were firing at him, and cut the wires leading to the bombs. He climbed back on to the top of the road-block, waved his company on and charged over the bridge at their head followed by a troop of tanks which smashed the road-block.

The German positions were overrun, forty were killed, ten wounded and forty-two taken prisoner, and the bridge was captured intact. Thanks to the speed and courage displayed, only one guardsman was killed and four wounded. The slightest hesitation or mistiming and the bridge would unquestionably have been destroyed. A captured German sapper said afterwards that he was the man responsible for blowing the bridge but when he pressed the plunger nothing happened.

I was delighted at this success and next day visited the site where Liddell took me round and explained how the battle developed. He was killed eighteen days later by a stray bullet before he knew that he had won the Victoria Cross for his very gallant action on the River Ems. It was a great tragedy but it is always the best who die in war. How much we have missed the Liddells of this world in the post-war years.

Slowly—too slowly for my liking—we penetrated deeper into Germany. The Guards Armoured, 3rd Division, 43rd (Wessex) and

51st (Highland) Divisions all took a hand. We heard rumours of underground resistance movements being organised behind our lines but this was never taken very seriously because even though the German Army might be still fighting the civilian population had had more than enough of the war. As soon as our advanced guards entered a village, white sheets fluttered from all the windows.

Not for the first time I marvelled at the curious mentality of the German people who one moment are fighting hard and the next are surrendering by the thousand. Somehow or other I couldn't see the British housewives in Kent, Sussex and Surrey welcoming German invaders with white sheets—more likely with coal hammers and picks.

Towards the middle of April it became clear that I should be forced to capture Bremen. I had been doing my best to sell this task to Neil Ritchie, commanding 12 Corps. No commander likes having to take on a large city which eats up troops in the most exasperating way. But by now his corps was on the Elbe so there was nothing for it. The more I studied the problem the less I liked it. We were not properly balanced for the task. While I was trying to find the best way out the telephone rang and a staff officer informed me that Field-Marshal Montgomery was on his way down to see me.

A few minutes later he arrived and entering the map lorry which served as my mobile office he said, "Jorrocks, I am not happy about Bremen." "Nor am I, sir," I replied. "Tell me about it," he said, sitting down in front of a large-scale map. He listened carefully without saying a word while I explained my difficulties. There was a short pause while he pondered on what he had heard. Then, stabbing the map with his finger he said, "We will do A, B, C and D." The four decisions which he then took cleared up the situation completely, and as far as I was concerned Bremen was finished.

To my mind this was a very good example of higher command in war. At his headquarters many miles away Monty was in sufficient touch with the feel of the battle to appreciate beforehand where difficulties were likely to occur. He then went forward to see the man on the spot, in this case me, and having listened to my tale

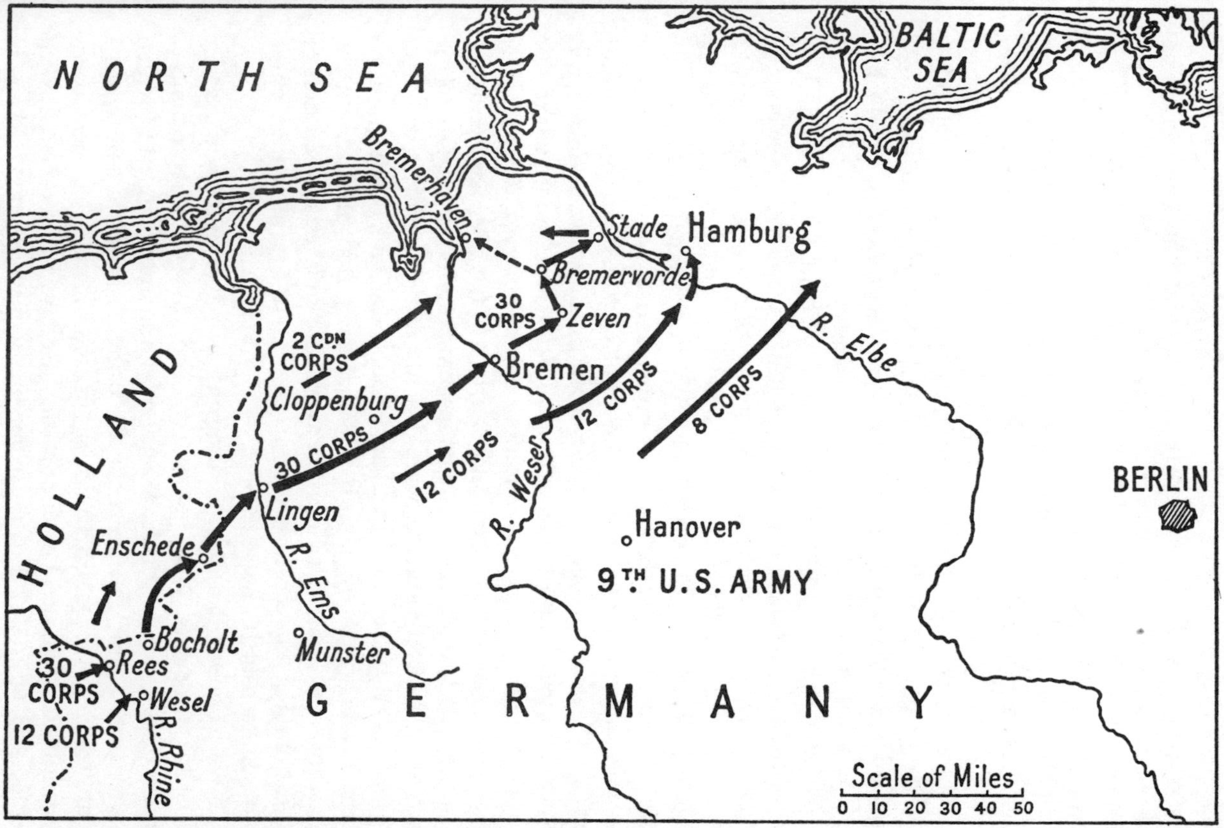

THE ADVANCE FROM THE RHINE TO THE ELBE

he made up his mind instantly about what should be done. From his point of view, also, Bremen was finished and, as I knew very well, he would now relegate it to the back of his mind, while he went on to consider the next problem.

The main assault started on the 24th April with 52nd (Lowland) Division north of the Weser and the 3rd Division converging from the south. At this stage of the war the 52nd was one of the best divisions in the 2nd British Army because it still retained a number of the original personnel. It had been specially trained for a long period as a mountain division but its first important battle had taken place below sea-level at Walcheren—such is fate.

While roaming round the Bremen battlefield, I stopped my jeep and went up into an attic where I had a wonderful view of the first objective which the 3rd Division was then attacking across a flooded airfield. The attic was already occupied by two young gunner-observation officers who were busily engaged in bringing the fire of their regiment on to some German anti-tank guns which were holding up our tanks. They had no idea I was the corps commander; in fact they hardly glanced at me at all, so for a few minutes I was able to forget the problems of a corps battle and lose myself in this front-line duel which was unfolding before my eyes. Our artillery concentrations got nearer and nearer to the German position. Suddenly it was all over. The guns were pointing drunkenly in the air, and the young gunners were dancing round the loft crying out, " Got them, direct hit," and sure enough our tanks could now be seen advancing once again. It was in Bremen that I realised for the first time just what the Germans must have suffered as the result of our bombing. It was a shambles; there didn't seem to be a single house intact in this huge seaport.

Up to now I had been fighting this war without any particular hatred for the enemy but just short of Bremen we uncovered one of those horror camps which are now common knowledge, but which at that time came as a great shock. I saw a ghastly picture when I entered with General Allan Adair, the commander of the Guards Armoured Division. The floor of the first large hut was strewn with emaciated figures clad in most horrible striped pyjamas. Many of them were too weak to walk but they managed to heave themselves up and gave us a pathetic cheer. Most of them had some form of chronic dysentery and the stench was so frightful that I disgraced myself by being sick in a corner. It was difficult to believe that most of these hardly human creatures had once been educated, civilised people.

I was so angry that I ordered the burgomasters of all the surrounding towns and villages each to supply a quota of German women to clean up the camp and look after these unfortunate prisoners, who were dying daily at an alarming rate. When the women arrived we expected some indication of horror or remorse when they saw what their fellow-countrymen had been doing. Not a bit of it. I never saw a tear or heard one expression of pity from any of them. I also brought one of our own hospitals into the camp and when I found some of our sisters looking very distressed I apologised for having given them such an unpleasant task. "Goodness me," they said, "it's not that. We are only worried because we can do so little for the poor things—many of them have gone too far." A somewhat different approach to the problem by the women of two countries.

But to turn to a more pleasant subject. We discovered a collection of sailing yachts of all sizes tucked away in odd creeks and on hards along the River Weser near Bremen. As the war was nearly over I thought these would come in handy for our troops in the army of occupation so I ordered a couple of soldiers to be placed on each, just to make certain they didn't disappear. A few weeks later I received a signal from the senior British Admiral in the area asking for these boats to be handed over forthwith to the Royal Navy. I flatly refused, and added in my message, "Who captured Bremen, the army or the navy?" Back came a terse message, "Everything that floats belongs to the navy," to which I replied "Rather than hand them over I'll sink the lot." The quarrel ended peacefully when we shared the spoils between us. And when the war was over many soldiers spent profitable hours learning to sail. Bremen produced 6000 prisoners including two generals and one admiral.

Our final task now was to clear the Cuxhaven peninsula which lies between the estuaries of the Rivers Elbe and Weser. On 3rd May I was told confidentially the Germans were negotiating for surrender, but that this was not to be communicated to anyone else. I was particularly anxious to avoid even a single casualty with the war practically over, so instead of urging on the divisional commanders I went round inventing excuses to slow them down. I could see them looking at me with astonishment and they were no doubt saying to themselves, " The old man has lost his nerve at last."

I had often wondered how the war would end. When it came it could hardly have been more of an anti-climax. I happened to be sitting in the military equivalent of the smallest room when I heard a voice on the wireless saying " All hostilities will cease at 0800 hours tomorrow morning 5th May."

It was a wonderful moment—the sense of relief was extraordinary; for the first time for five years I would no longer be responsible for other men's lives. The surrender on our front took place at 1430 hours on 5th May when the German general commanding the Corps Ems and his chief of staff arrived at our headquarters. Elaborate arrangements had been made for their reception. Our military police, looking very smart escorted them to a table in the centre of the room; all round the outside was a ring of interested staff officers and other ranks of 30 Corps.

When all was ready I came in and seated myself all alone opposite the two Germans. After issuing my orders for the surrender I finished with these words, " These orders must be obeyed scrupulously. I warn you we shall have no mercy if they are not. Having seen one of your horror camps my whole attitude towards Germany has changed."

The chief of staff jumped up and said, " The army had nothing to do with those camps." " Sit down," I replied, " there were German soldiers on sentry duty outside and you cannot escape responsibility. The world will never forgive Germany for those camps."

The German forces who were concentrated in the north-west corner of the Cuxhaven peninsula were ordered to stack all their weapons at certain points. A couple of days later I drove round the area to see how the disarmament was proceeding and found the remnants of the parachute army concentrated on an aerodrome. When I saw the miserable equipment—just a few, old, patched up self-propelled guns and tanks—with which they had managed to delay our advance for so long I turned to their divisional commander and said, " I must congratulate you on the fighting qualities of your division," but then I added, " Your officers and N.C.O.s will be placed in a concentration camp for the time being under our guards. This is really a compliment. They look much too tough and dangerous to have them knocking about just at the present moment."

We celebrated the final victory by holding a parade in Bremen where I took the salute and all the formations in 30 Corps marched past. As I saw these smart men, well-polished tanks, guns and vehicles passing by, it was incredible to think that only a week before they had been covered with the grime of battle. So ended the active war of 30 Corps. It had been a long journey through many lands; starting in the Western Desert some three years before, it had now ended deep in the heart of Germany.

I was very anxious to visit Heligoland but as our navy had not yet taken over Cuxhaven it was arranged that I should go with a British naval sub-lieutenant in a German E-boat, and as no one could raise even one White Ensign we flew the German flag. So, escorted by four other E-boats we set off. Half-way across I told the British sub-lieutenant to complain to the German captain that the escorts were keeping very bad station. I thought the latter would die of apoplexy; that a general, and a British general at that, should complain about the seamanship of the German Navy was almost more than he could bear.

Heligoland was well worth a visit. Although everything above ground had been destroyed by our fearsome bombing, the underground galleries were more or less intact. On the return journey the E-boats kept station meticulously.

CHAPTER XX

POST WAR GERMANY

DURING THOSE first few days after the German capitulation we all felt as though an immense weight had been lifted from our shoulders; but this wonderful, carefree atmosphere did not last for long. We were faced by the many intricate problems involved in the resuscitation of a stricken Germany. Having spent the last six years doing our best to destroy the German Reich, almost overnight we had to go into reverse gear and start building her up again. This required a considerable mental switch.

The British zone of occupation, containing some twenty million Germans, was divided up among the corps for administrative purposes, and I found myself responsible for the Hanover Corps District. There is something terribly depressing about a country defeated in war, even though that country has been your enemy, and the utter destruction of Germany was almost awesome. It didn't seem possible that towns like Hanover and Bremen could ever rise again from the shambles in which the bulk of the hollow-eyed and shabby population eked out a troglodyte existence underneath the ruins of their houses.

Things were better in the country districts, but what struck me most was the complete absence of able-bodied men or even of youths—there were just a few old men, some cripples, and that was all. The farms were almost entirely run by women. How appalling were the casualties suffered by the Germans was brought home to me forcibly when I first attended morning service in the small village church of Eystrop where I lived. The Germans commemorate their war dead by means of evergreen wreaths; and the whole wall was covered with wreaths—dozens and dozens of them. In a similar church in the United Kingdom I would not expect to see more than eight to ten names on the local war memorial. The Germans certainly started the last war, but only those who saw the conditions during the first few months immediately after the war ended can know how much they suffered.

Monty laid down the priorities as (1) food and (2) housing; he then, as always, gave us a free hand to look after our own districts until such time as proper military government could take over from us. It was a fascinating task. I found myself to all intents and purposes the benevolent (I hope) dictator of an area about the size of Wales. At my morning conference, instead of considering fire plans and laying down military objectives, we discussed such problems as food, coal, communications, press and so on. I soon discovered the merits of a dictatorship. I could really get things done quickly. One day in the late autumn a staff officer reported that the output of coal was dropping every week in our corps district. This was very serious with winter approaching. The reason, I was informed, was that the miners lacked clothes. I immediately ordered a levy to be carried out in certain nearby towns to provide adequate clothing for the miners, and sure enough a few weeks later the graph showing coal production began to rise. I smiled when I thought of what would happen in dear old democratic Britain if the Cabinet ordered clothes to be removed compulsorily from Cardiff, shall we say, to clothe the miners in the Welsh valleys.

Luckily I had some extremely able young men on my staff. 30 Corps had been one of the original corps to be formed and had therefore many years of operational experience behind it. In time of war it is a case of the survival of the fittest; officers don't last for long on a corps staff unless they are highly efficient. I doubt if ever there has been collected together in one place a more able group of young men than those serving in 30 Corps headquarters at the end of the war. The resuscitation of Germany was just up their street. The vital thing was to open up communications, so that food and goods could be moved freely from one area to another. The bridges and railways had been widely destroyed and even crossroads had been cratered by the retreating Germany Army.

To start with a great deal of this work had to be carried out by British troops and quite naturally this caused resentment. I remember being asked by an intelligent sapper corporal, " Why should I now have to work hard and repair bridges for the so-and-so Germans who have caused so much misery to the world ? " As he was obviously voicing the doubts of many others, I collected the company together and explained to the best of my ability that the war was now over, so Germany must take her place again as a European state. Many of the people were on the verge of starvation and if food couldn't be moved freely into the towns they would die that winter. And this would cause great bitterness. Furthermore, it was essential for our own British economy to start trading again with Germany and we would never be able to do this until communications had been repaired. Whether I convinced them or not I have no idea, but they went back to work at once without any further questions. I mention this small incident because it is typical of the modern soldier. He always wants to know why. And he will only give of his best if he understands the reason for what he is doing.

The British soldier has often been described as our best ambassador and this is particularly so if he forms part of an army of occupation because one of the most difficult things in the world is to occupy a foreign country and yet remain friendly with its people. If left to himself the British soldier will soon be on the best of terms with the local population. Unfortunately this time he was not left to himself and all sorts of regulations about non-fraternisation with the German population were issued. No doubt there were good reasons for this policy but it caused endless trouble at our level. What happened was that our troops were prevented from getting to know the ordinary, decent families in an open and normal way, and were driven to consorting on the sly with the lowest types of German women.

In spite of the non-fraternisation rule I was determined somehow or other to make our occupation as palatable as possible for the local inhabitants. This may sound sloppy, but I had experienced the difficulties of occupying Germany after the First World War. I knew very well that nobody will ever keep the Germans down for long because they belong to a very rare species which actually *likes work*. I also understood the menace of Communism better than most—thanks to my time in Russia. So, without claiming any particularly brilliant foresight, it seemed to me that the Germans were the sort of people whom it would be better to have on our side than against us. I therefore ordered all units in my corps to do everything they could to help the German children. Nobody could blame them for the last war, and they had obviously had a bad time. Some of the children had never even seen chocolates in their lives. Units were told to open special youth clubs, and camps in the summer, and organise sports, etc.

The British soldier loves children and he entered into all this with great zest. It became common in the villages to see a khaki-clad figure hand in hand with a small flaxen-haired child on either side. Parents began to come up to the men and thank them for being so kind to their children. Then I gave a tea-party at my tactical headquarters which was attended by some 150 German children. The cooks had done marvels with the ordinary rations, and we were all looking forward to a pleasant afternoon, but unfortunately the party was also attended by some reporters from the British Press. Not the famous war correspondents whom we knew so well and who would unquestionably have understood the wider implications of what we were trying to do. The war was now over in Europe, and Germany had ceased to be front-line news, so the first eleven had left, and their places had been taken by inexperienced, callow, young men who were concerned mainly with getting an angle to their stories.

It soon became obvious that they were hostile. They went round saying to the soldiers who were helping as waiters, " What about the British children? Are they having a party like this? " Their attitude from the short-term point of view was perfectly understandable and next day headlines appeared in the British Press, " British General Gives Tea Party for German Children." The fat was now in the fire. I received an enormous number of letters in which the kindest comment was " that I had obviously gone mad."

These were of little consequence, but unfortunately owing to all the adverse criticism I was ordered to cease my activities with the German children at once. Orders had to be obeyed but I still feel that this was a serious mistake. Instead of mixing with the civilian population on a friendly basis we were driven back into ourselves and when I returned to Germany some three years later to take over the appointment of commander-in-chief, I found that the B.A.O.R. was an army of occupation in the true sense of the word, living quite apart from the German people.

Although the resuscitation of Germany loomed large on our horizon I still felt that my first responsibility lay towards the British troops in 30 Corps district, consisting of three divisions and one armoured brigade. It was difficult to know how to keep them occupied, and idle hands could get into a lot of trouble in the Germany of those days. With the exception of certain guard duties on stores, vulnerable points, and internment camps, there were no military duties with which to occupy the men. It is astonishing, however, how even when engaged on that most dreary of pastimes, sentry duty, the British soldier is sustained by his greatest asset, his sense of humour.

One of our sentries was posted on a bridge spanning a river which, for security reasons, was closed to all civilians from 9 p.m. to dawn. One evening at 9.30 p.m. the sentry was faced by a party of German girls who wished to cross. After some discussion he allowed them to do so, "But only on this occasion," he emphasised. "If you are late to-morrow night you will have to stay where you are." Next night the girls appeared again at exactly the same time. This time, however, the sentry remained unmoved by their story that they had been kept late at work, they lived on the other side of the river, and so on. Eventually they were reduced to tears but the sentry remained adamant. Then one of them said, "If we undress and swim across, will you bring our clothes over to the other side for us?" This was a brilliant solution. The girls would not be crossing the forbidden bridge, honour was satisfied, and the sentry agreed at once. When telling me this story, the sentry's commanding officer remarked, "Private —— obviously has an eye to the main chance."

Demobilisation had started promptly and was working smoothly, but even so, some time must elapse before the bulk of the men could get home. It was ridiculous to carry out military training with men who had fought through the war and would shortly be returning to civilian life. So it seemed to me there were only two ways in which to keep them occupied. First, to prepare them for their return to civilian life and, secondly to provide first-class recreational facilities. Both these measures were completely successful. We formed training centres, using captured German machinery, where men could undergo courses to regain their old skill, and be brought up-to-date or their civilian trades, before returning home. There was no difficulty about finding instructors. It was most inspiring to visit these centres and see the enthusiasm shown by the trainees. The men were so happy to handle the tools of their particular trade again that in many cases they would not even stop for meals, let alone for the, by now, almost sacrosanct tea intervals. Such enthusiasm, it seemed to me, augured well for British industry in the post-war years.

The scope of the welfare arrangements organised by my staff became almost frightening. Bad Harzburg, a holiday resort in the Harz mountains was taken over completely as a leave centre, and this proved very popular with all ranks. We were told by the local authorities that this lovely part of Germany had been earmarked by the Nazis as an S.S. stud farm, where physically perfect S.S. types were to be mated with specially selected German women of pure descent. How much truth there was in this, I have no idea, but it was widely believed throughout the Harz mountains.

In addition clubs, canteens and special gift shops stocked with toys which came from all over Europe, specially for 30 Corps, sprang up everywhere. I realised that I was the head of a vast chain of holiday and recreational centres, all of which, in spite of minimum charges, were coining money. I therefore set up a board of five chartered accountants to examine the whole concern. After some five weeks of hard work they reported that everything was in order: in fact that it was brilliantly organised, but they added a rider to the effect that when the existing welfare staff was demobilised it might be difficult to find replacements sufficiently capable to handle what amounted to a huge business concern.

There was a third problem which took up much of our time—the Russians. Immediately after the war we occupied an area which stretched as far east as Magdeburg on the Elbe, but in accordance with Allied agreements about the partitioning of Germany we were due to withdraw back to the Harz mountains and hand over the territory in the east to the Russians. This involved countless conferences, which were less wearisome for me than for the others because I had once been a Russian interpreter, and although my knowledge of the language was rusty I could still understand enough to follow what was going on. This gave me a big advantage because I was able to think out my answer while the interpreter was translating what the Russian general had said. The main difficulty was that while I, in accordance with normal British practice, was allowed to decide all minor details myself, the Russians could give no decision on anything at all without reference to Zhukov in Berlin.

This was understandable because the majority of their corps and divisional commanders were uneducated by western standards. They were very brave men who led their formations personally into battle and most of them had been wounded two or three times. I had always liked the Russians whom I had met in their country in 1919-20. These men were quite different. They were so suspicious that they hardly dared open their mouths. They were particularly suspicious of me when they found that I spoke Russian. The young men were the most frightening, because as a result of the intensive indoctrination to which they had been subjected almost from birth their brains worked quite differently from any with which I had previously come in contact. They talked in clichés, and it was impossible to discuss anything with them at all.

When I inquired whether my old friends the Tzigane (gipsies) were still flourishing in Russia I was told, " No, they do not exist any more; they were bad for the morale of the Russian people." Poor Tzigane, they were so gay with their camp-fires and haunting gipsy music. The most I ever got out of the Russians was at a luncheon party when one general actually dared to discuss the Russian High Command. "Zhukov was the Iron Man," he said, "but Rokossovsky! ah he was the clever one." The only time I ever saw the former was during the victory parade in Berlin. I was standing on the platform beside that famous character, the United States General George Patton, waiting for the great man to arrive. Suddenly Patton started growling like an angry bear, "Look at the bastard," he said, and out of an immense car there emerged a small, squat figure whose chest and stomach were almost entirely covered with decorations. He looked like a well-fed, mobile advertisement for an ironmonger's shop.

At our meetings the generals did not count at all. There were usually one or two sinister-looking individuals at whom the others kept glancing surreptitiously. These conferences were most exasperating. We made such very, very slow progress, and here, if I had only realised it, was the pattern of all the conferences that have taken place between east and west ever since. The only pleasant Russian I met was the young general who was attached to my headquarters as liaison officer. I can see him now, dining in my mess and, together with the Bishop of Dover, who was paying us a visit, singing "Lilli Marlene" lustily to the accompaniment of a small German orchestra. He was too friendly. One day he disappeared behind the Iron Curtain and we never saw him again.

The discipline of these Russian troops was very strict indeed and they always saluted their officers. They had come a long way from the Red Army I first saw at Krasnoyarsk, in Siberia, in 1919 when everything was run on the "friend—*tovarish*" principle and no order could be issued unless it was passed by the political commissar.

The Russian Army of May, 1945, may have been young, may have been uneducated, may have been uncouth, but it was a truly formidable fighting machine.

Somehow or other we reached agreement about the method of handing over the eastern strip of Germany to the Russians and the day came for our withdrawal back to the Harz mountains. As I had never seen their army in bulk I positioned myself on a small hill to watch them enter the zone which we had evacuated. It was an astonishing sight—rivers and rivers of men, most of them very young, for even Russia with her almost inexhaustible supply of man-power had had to scrape the barrel in order to replace her enormous casualties. They looked very menacing, those hordes of dirty, tough Slavs, each with an automatic weapon and a sack over his shoulder. But the thing that interested me most of all was the almost complete absence of motor transport, just an occasional car, that was all. I felt how simple war must have been for my Russian opposite number, relieved of that perennial problem—transport, and still more transport.

One of my staff who happened to be standing beside a wounded German officer pointed to the Russians and said, "How was the great German Army beaten by those half-savage peasants?"

"I can tell you," the German replied, "because I was on the eastern front most of the war. They are the toughest soldiers I have ever met; they have an almost Asiatic disregard of death. In those sacks are a few raw vegetables, perhaps crusts of bread, and they can live on those for weeks; very often each infantryman carries as well a couple of shells to help out the gunners. In mid-winter, with temperatures many degrees below zero, I have seen them lying motionless in the snow all day when their attack has been halted, and then in the evening suddenly leaping to their feet and charging with great spirit. We shot and we shot; we killed and we killed; but still they came on until we ran out of ammunition and were overrun. We were beaten by solid masses of tough, extremely brave troops."

I doubt if there is a word in the Russian language for welfare. I reflected on the contrast with the armies of the western world with their mobile laundries, mobile dental centres, bakeries, N.A.A.F.I.s, gift shops, and so on. It is not surprising that in the United States Army out of every 100,000 men only 23,000 went into battle while in the Soviet Army 80,000 out of every 100,000 were front-line troops. An army is, in many ways, a mirror of the standard of civilisation which exists in its country, and in the west the bulk of the population leads soft lives compared with the spartan existence of the Russian peasants who form a high proportion of the armies behind the Iron Curtain. They live in small villages of wooden huts surrounded by miles and miles of bleak steppes, forests and swamps. Many of them are hunters who can melt into the ground, and move across country silently by day or by night, and their climate is so hard that only the fittest survive. To these men army life is almost a luxury.

Our problem is much more difficult. During the last war, in order to maintain morale, the western Allies did their utmost to bring as many of the amenities of civil life as possible right up to the soldier on the battlefield. Hence the masses of transport. I do not believe, however, that this is the correct approach to the problem. From the moment a man is enlisted he must be taught toughness—how to look after himself under all sorts of conditions of climate and terrain without endless comforts. It is a fact that troops prefer this sort of training to constant square bashing.

In the late autumn my time in Germany came to an end and I returned home to take over the Western Command with headquarters at Chester. A few days before my departure I went to dine with my old friend the 51st Highland Division. We had come a long way together since our first meeting on the ridge at Alam Halfa in the Western Desert, and I was very moved when they drank my health with Highland honours. My final departure was not without incident. On the last night I was sitting down to a farewell dinner with my staff when an orderly rushed in to say that the house was on fire. Fire engines arrived from all over the place but owing to lack of water they fought a losing battle with the flames, and we had to evacuate the house. My last night with 30 Corps was therefore spent in my caravan and when I flew off next day the house was still burning merrily. The fire was started in my study by a smouldering beam under the floor, but no one has ever believed this. I shall go down to history as the commander who burned down his house during some fantastic orgy on the night before he left.

CHAPTER XXI

G.O.C. WESTERN COMMAND

At the beginning of 1946 I found myself responsible for one of the four commands into which the British Isles, exclusive of Northern Ireland, was divided.

My home was just outside that attractive old town of Chester with its cathedral, city walls and, above all the famous rows, but my headquarters bore little resemblance to those which I had just left in Germany. Here I found the real peace-time set-up, when every decision was hedged round by regulations and finance. It soon became obvious that the real commander was not me at all but the command secretary, the direct representative of the civilian and therefore financial branch of the War Office. Luckily, he was a very understanding man because I must have proved a great trial to him. I have always been bad at regulations and am too impetuous to be a success in peace-time soldiering where every decision has to be approached by a circuitous route. The successful peace-time commander can only achieve his objective by the principle of " Softly, softly, catchee monkey." I am afraid that during my two years in Western Command I caught very few monkeys.

Before the war Western Command had always been regarded as a backwater: very much a poor relation of Aldershot, which contained the spearhead of the British Expeditionary Force, and of Southern with its better training facilities including Salisbury Plain: in fact the sort of place where an ancient general browsed sleepily before being finally put out to grass. But that had been in the pre-war days; now national service had altered everything. We were responsible for a vast area stretching from the Scottish border in the north to the south coast of Wales, and including Warwick, Birmingham and Manchester in the east, with the Isle of Man thrown in for good measure in the west. It was a fascinating command because it contained a little bit of everything—the beautiful Lake District—industrial Lancashire—the vast port of Liverpool—north and south Wales as different from each other as chalk from cheese—Worcester with its orchards—Birmingham where they claim to have constructed some part of every single item of equipment which was used in the last war—and finally Manchester where the lord mayor holds a position second only to his elder brother in the mansion house.

From the military point of view the primary importance of this command lay in the fact that it contained many centres to which the young national serviceman reported on first call-up. In France conscription is part of the "*tradition militaire*," and every regular officer has grown up surrounded by conscripts. But for us the problem of training national servicemen in peace-time was something quite fresh. An added complication was the fact that I was far from clear about what we should train them for. My mind was still full of the last war and I had not had time to shake myself clear of it, as I obviously must. It is all too easy to fall a victim to the virus of complacency which always attacks victorious nations in the immediate post-war period. From the military point of view nothing is more dangerous than winning a great war. But even in 1946 it was obvious that we had reached a cross-roads in military development, for the atomic bomb on Hiroshima had blown most of the accepted military doctrines sky-high. The difficulty was to know down which road we should now go. One thing was quite clear. The battlefield of the future was bound to be a very empty place. In face of the atomic threat, concentration of troops would be too dangerous; dispersion and still more dispersion would certainly be called for. This meant small bodies of men prepared to live hard on their own for long periods at a time; the days of mass transport bringing up amenities and working from bulging lines of communication had gone for ever.

So there was the problem. How to turn these young national servicemen, most of whom had been thoroughly spoilt by Mum, into tough, self-reliant soldiers with a gleam of battle in their eye and plenty of initiative. I couldn't help thinking of that old Arabic proverb which should be carved in large letters over the entrance to every school in the country, " In the eyes of its mother every black beetle is a gazelle."

The first thing to do was to go down and have a look at the gazelles arriving straight from the arms of their mothers to undergo their period of national service.

It was a sobering sight, for in army parlance most of them were thoroughly " browned off." They looked sulky, disgruntled and fed-up with having their civilian lives interrupted by military service. The war was over, so why should they be messed about by the army? No doubt their elder brothers had also painted a gloomy picture of sergeant-majors spitting fire and brimstone, of red-faced Colonel Blimps but, above all, of the deadly monotony of the barrack square. Whenever I asked a young soldier what he hated most of all in the army I always got the same answer, " Square bashing." It seemed to me that shock tactics were required right from the start. So I insisted that on the first day after their arrival all these boys should be taken out into the mountains for a twenty-four-hour exercise where they could fire all their different weapons. They had no idea, of course, how the weapons worked, but there is something exciting about the feel of an automatic. In training I am a great believer in running before you can walk, because by finding out how difficult it is to run, men take greater interest in the problem of learning to walk. All training must be done through the brain; the bored man absorbs nothing.

When it got dark the recruits were assembled and told that some prisoners had escaped into the mountains and it was their job to round them up during the night. They were also told to choose their own leaders—it was interesting to see whom they selected in those early days. All night they would be on the go. Next morning they were issued with food which they had to cook for themselves or go hungry. At the end of this gruelling twenty-four hours in the mountains they were then marched eight to ten miles back to barracks, tired, wet, footsore but—and this is the point—with their heads up. The army was tough, not just messing about on the barrack square. From that moment there was a different look in their eyes and the whole atmosphere changed. What the planners will not realise is that there is nothing wrong with the young people of to-day, they take to toughness as a duck takes to water; what they cannot abide is boredom and all too much army training is dull beyond measure.

I soon found myself with another battle on my hands—the battle of accommodation. I was horrified at the conditions under which the troops and, above all, the married families were required to live. I got into trouble for supporting Monty to the hilt (he was C.I.G.S. at the time) in his plan for more comfortable barrack-rooms, including bedside lamps—" What did we think we were doing; mollycoddling the soldier like this?"—and so on and so on. Our critics did not seem to appreciate the effect of bright, comfortable living quarters on the mentality of the modern soldier; there is nothing more deadening and stultifying than the normal, grim, barrack block. The toughest possible training allied to comfortable living conditions has always been my object. The married quarters made me shudder every time I even passed them. So I decided on a somewhat grandiose programme of modernisation, new construction and the conversion of existing huts into comfortable bungalow accommodation.

Not unnaturally I at once ran into trouble. Everything was scarce, including labour, and the War Office forbade me to do anything until their experts had produced plans for the future quarters. But as month after month went by without any plans, I decided to launch my own offensive. My right-hand man in all this was my major-general in charge of administration, Joe Holland, a man with a brilliant and unorthodox brain. Somehow or other, out of nothing at all, he conjured up baths, bricks, in fact everything. Like so many people with original minds he paid no attention at all to dress. It always amused me to see the horror on the face of some distinguished army councillor when Joe appeared with all the buttons of his tunic undone, his tie flowing, glasses on the point of his nose and his uniform cap well on one side. He was a perfect joy to work with and I have never known him to be defeated, even on the question of labour.

As no British labour was available, I suggested employing German prisoners among whom were men skilled in every trade. This was greeted with a howl of anguish from the War Office. "The British trade unions would never allow it under any circumstances." I didn't believe this for a moment as I have always found the trade unions to be very reasonable people, so I invited our local representatives to lunch, and then took them round some of our existing quarters. Their reaction was what I expected. "Go ahead," they said, "but for goodness' sake don't let our bosses in London know what you are doing." So we went ahead and achieved quite a lot but protests got stronger and stronger from the quartermaster-general's branch of the War Office until eventually the great man himself, Monty, was brought into the struggle and I received a letter in his own hand. "You must remember, Jorrocks, that this is peace-time and you cannot go on as though we were still at war. The quartermaster-general never stops complaining about your nefarious activities." I replied that it was quite like old times to get a letter in this strain written by the field-marshal himself. Anyhow, rightly or wrongly, quite a number of married families obtained better accommodation and that was what really mattered.

Almost my first official engagement after taking over Western Command was to attend a parade of the British Legion in Blackpool, so I set off with my wife in our large, black, official saloon car with an army commander's pennant flying on the front of the bonnet. As we entered the town the car stopped at a traffic crossing and a face peered in. I then heard a voice saying, in an unmistakable Lancashire accent, "We don't want no bloody generals up 'ere." This was positively my first introduction to the realities of the civilian world, and my wife sat up looking rather startled. As usual it was raining steadily and as we stopped once more at a crossing I heard another disgusted onlooker say, "Frightened to get his bloody feet wet, he is." I explained hurriedly to my wife that the Lancashire people really had hearts of gold. She replied that they certainly had an odd way of showing it. As I am half-Lancashire myself I wasn't unduly disturbed.

The warmth of our welcome when we arrived on the parade more than made up for our somewhat rough passage in transit. Blackpool is one of the most remarkable towns I have ever seen in my life; it fascinated me—wet or fine there is always somewhere to go and some form of entertainment awaiting the visitors. And the local authorities could give all of us a lesson in the astonishing way they handle their vast, week-end traffic problem.

As petrol rationing was still in force I felt it behoved me to set a good example by not applying for extra vouchers so I decided to ride a bicycle instead. I borrowed one from my batman—a good old army model built more for strength than for speed. When the moment came for our first outing—my wife was coming too—the bicycle, looking very spick-and-span, was positioned at the mounting block in the drive. Our official residence, which was in Eccleston Park, had in the years gone by been inhabited by one of the Duke of Westminster's agents. How he would have shuddered if he could have seen the lowly use to which his mounting block was now being put. We set off in fine style and all went well for the first few miles, then there was an ominous noise in the rear wheel which indicated that the worst had happened. I had a puncture. To repair the damage was quite beyond my capabilities, so I pushed the bike into the nearest farm and telephoned to my A.D.C. Within a few minutes he arrived in my large, official, Humber car followed by a truck for the bike. And I returned home ignominiously, feeling that my first effort at saving petrol could hardly be called a complete success. My wife returned on her bicycle alone.

We naturally had a stream of visitors, mainly from the War Office. The first was Emanuel Shinwell, who had become the Secretary of State for War a few days before. I had not previously met many ministers, and as he had only just taken office I was somewhat apprehensive about what would happen. I needn't have worried. We took to him at once, and I soon realised that here was a man who, once he was convinced of the justice of a cause, was prepared to stand up for the army through thick and thin. He was a shrewd politician and a great fighter.

The highlight was a visit from Monty. I had not realised until then how popular he was with all and sundry. It was almost like a Royal tour, with people lining the route—and he loved every minute of it. Just before his departure for Liverpool, where he was to catch his train back to London, the mayor of Birkenhead rang me up to say that over 1000 people were waiting for him on the near side of the Mersey tunnel. A small platform had been erected and he hoped that the field-marshal would be prepared to say a few words to the crowd. This was quite unexpected so, as we drove along, I did my best to brief him on the role which Birkenhead had played during the war. I spoke most of the time to his back as he was continuously leaning out of the window and waving to the crowds while he murmured "Yes, yes, Jorrocks—three battleships constructed—I have got that. Yes, go on." We arrived, and he then made a sparkling speech which delighted everybody without mentioning one single word of what I had told him during the journey.

At the time of this visit we were about to go away for a short period of leave and the house was in the usual state of hectic packing which is always an inevitable prelude to any move of the Horrocks family. Monty was most scornful. "I always do my own," he said. He then gave us a short lecture on packing, in which he described how he took everything out of the drawers and laid it on the bed so that nothing was ever overlooked. An hour after his departure an A.D.C. arrived to say that the field-marshal had unfortunately left all his shirts behind.

It was during this visit that Monty told me I was to become commander-in-chief of the British Army of the Rhine. I was delighted because this was almost the only active command, with troops available, in the post-war army.

Unfortunately my time at Chester, which should have been the pleasantest period of my whole career, was marred by illness. I kept on getting attacks of fever accompanied by pain and sickness. Eventually my senior medical officer insisted on my going into Manchester Infirmary where I was operated on by that fine surgeon and very charming man, Professor Morley. When I came round from the anæsthetic he was standing by my bedside holding up a curious looking object which he assured me was a piece of my shirt which had been lurking in my bile duct ever since I was wounded at Bizerta. As this was my seventh operation, my stomach was beginning to resemble an abstract picture, with scars running in every direction.

Very unwisely I went out to Germany before I had completely recovered and then followed the most unhappy period of my life. I arrived to command B.A.O.R. just when things were getting more and more difficult with the Russians. It was a time when vigorous action was required to prepare our extremely modest resources in men and material in case trouble should break out. It would have been a worrying period even if I had been fit, but in my state of health it soon became impossible. Somehow or other my brain would not work, and I found that when my able chief of staff, Bill Stratton, tried to brief me about the current situation I couldn't take it in. The final straw came when I addressed all the senior officers who had been collected from all over Germany for the purpose. I managed to get through my speech just in time before being violently sick, and I then retired to bed with yet another temperature.

It was a difficult decision to take, because, after a long career in the army, I hated having to give up at this final hurdle. But I knew instinctively that I was not fit enough to give the troops the leadership which the precarious situation demanded. I was beginning to worry unnecessarily, and I knew only too well that a commander who worries is no good in moments of crisis. So I sent for my head doctor and asked him for his opinion. He shook his head sadly and said, "I have been expecting this ever since you arrived. I didn't think you could possibly make it." Fortunately for me he was an old friend with whom I had served before. It is nicer to be given your military death sentence by someone whom you like. Within two days I was flown back to Millbank Hospital, and my active career in the army was over.

CHAPTER XXII

GENTLEMAN USHER OF THE BLACK ROD

THE AUTHORITIES treated me with great consideration but, even after a year of sick leave, a medical board would not pass me fit for service, so I was invalided out. This produced a remarkable contrast in my way of life. In Germany we had been forced to live in considerable state. Government House was large and ugly but filled with a number of servants—mostly Germans. We had horses, several cars, an aeroplane, a large motor launch and the use of a private train. From this we went straight to our lovely, little, old thatched cottage at Compton, near Winchester, staffed by a daily who came in at odd intervals during the week, and our only means of transport were a small, rather old, Hillman Minx and two bicycles. Yet we were much happier. I was very sorry, of course, to leave the army in which I had spent thirty-five eventful, happy years, but my main reaction was one of intense relief. I was now out of it all and there was no longer any need to put on an act. If I felt ill, I could be ill, and no harm would be done to anyone. I would not be letting anybody down and no elaborate programme would have to be altered. Furthermore, I knew instinctively that I was far too impatient to be a success in the higher ranks of the army during peace-time. In the war we had lived a simple life at a small headquarters and had been able to get on with the job. In peace it all became rather pompous and complicated—visitors, entertaining, large staff and so on. It would be a relief, I felt, to settle down and pass the rest of my days in this pleasant backwater.

My quiet life in an English village lasted for exactly fourteen days.

One morning the postman delivered a large, imposing-looking envelope. As we were just setting off in our car I put it in the small locker under the dashboard and forgot all about it. Later that day my wife suddenly said, " By the way, what was in that official-looking letter which came for you this morning ? " I ferreted it out and saw it was from the Lord Chamberlain at St. James's Palace. Still quite unsuspecting, I opened it, and then, to my amazement, read : " You are offered the appointment of Gentleman Usher of the Black Rod in the House of Lords." I had no idea what this meant because I had never been in either of the Houses of Parliament and had not even heard of Black Rod. But it sounded rather exciting. In my heart of hearts I was delighted, because, to be honest, the rustic retreat idea was already, after only a fortnight, beginning to pall. Fortunately, my predecessor, Admiral Sir Geoffrey Blake, who was giving up owing to deafness, had done a considerable amount of research into the history of this ancient and honourable office, and the more I read the more it appealed to me.

The appointment goes back to 1348 when Edward III founded the Order of the Garter. The first holder of this office was a certain William Whitehorse who received the not inconsiderable salary of twelve pence per day for life. He walked in front of the Sovereign carrying on his shoulder the Black Rod. It is made of ebony, three-and-a-half feet long with a golden sovereign fixed in the bottom. If anyone offended against the Order of the Garter it was the duty of the Gentleman Usher to tap him on the shoulder with the Black Rod, whereupon the offender was expelled and William White-horse received £5. Unfortunately there is no such monetary reward today.

In addition to his " Garter " duties he was also " The principal Usher of the Realm." His job was largely to call for order on Royal occasions, which in ancient times were apparently very noisy affairs. On the sovereign's command he would attempt to still the tumult by calling out loudly " Order—or hush." He was in fact "The Husher" from which apparently, the word "Usher" is derived.

The original charter laid it down that the holder of this office had to be " a gentleman of Blood and Arms born within the Sovereign's Dominions " and that is why nowadays it is held in turn by a sailor, a soldier and an airman. I took over from an admiral and handed over to an air-marshal. The final selection is made by the reigning

Sovereign from a list of names submitted by the service ministry concerned. I have never ceased to thank my lucky stars that King George VI's choice fell on me.

Such is the continuity of things in this country that the Gentleman Usher of the Black Rod still walks in front of the Sovereign during the Garter ceremonies which are held annually at Windsor. This is unquestionably the red-letter day for Black Rod. In the morning the Sovereign invests any new knights who may have been appointed during the year with the insignia of the Order. King George VI took a deep personal interest in the Garter ceremony and always held a rehearsal at Buckingham Palace beforehand. In spite of this, things could and did go wrong in the elaborate ceremonial which had to be carried out.

I remember one particular episode all too well. The Ceremony takes place in the Throne Room of Windsor Castle. At one end sits the Sovereign on a special chair or throne, while on his left and right sit the existing Garter Knights, facing inwards, with a wide space in the middle; some chairs are left vacant, awaiting the arrival of the new Knights standing outside the room on the far side of a closed door, each with a supporting Knight on either side. At the end of the room sit the wives of the Knights and members of the Royal Family and Court.

When all was ready, the Sovereign would say " Garter and Black Rod, summon the Knights." Garter King of Arms, Sir George Bellew and I would then bow to the Throne, turn about and, on reaching the door, I would knock once with the Black Rod. It was then flung open. We would bow, turn and lead the new Knights to their seats, from where they would be summoned in turn to go through the Investiture Ceremony.

On this memorable occasion there were three Knights, headed by the King of Denmark, waiting outside the door: we went through the ceremony but, on our return, as we approached the King I saw that he was looking very angry and in a loud whisper he hissed, " Where are the Knights? Bring in the Knights!" I looked over my shoulder and saw that we were being followed only by the King of Denmark. Somebody had closed the door behind him, and the other two Knights were still outside.

Together again. On the occasion of President Eisenhower's visit to Britain, September 1959, his war-time associates foregather at a dinner at the U.S. Embassy. Left to right, standing: Montgomery, John Hay Witney, the American Ambassador, Portal, Tedder, the author, Ismay. In front: Alanbrooke, Churchill, Eisenhower, Alexander, Macmillan

With my wife and Maxie outside our cottage at Emsworth

" Do it again very slowly, and no-one will notice " I whispered to Garter. So once more we bowed to the Sovereign and returned slowly to the door, on which I knocked once more—outside were the two remaining Knights, headed by the Duke of Wellington with their supporters, looking very uneasy. So we bowed, turned, led them in, and all was well. In fact, I heard people saying afterwards, " The old drill is so correct—how right it was to bring the King in first on his own . . . " The spectators may have thought this, but King George certainly did not!

This ceremony is followed by lunch, at which all the Royal Family, members of the Court, Knights and their wives, plus Garter and myself, were always present. In the afternoon we moved in procession down to St. George's Chapel where the new knights were led to their stalls by Garter, the senior officer of the Order, and by Black Rod.

This procession is one of the most colourful pieces of pageantry in the country as it winds its way slowly down the hill from the castle along the route lined by the Household Cavalry and the Brigade of Guards, against the background of the old castle walls. It is led by the Military Knights of Windsor; then come the Heralds in their gold tabards, followed by the Knights in their Garter blue robes, walking two by two, all of them men who have distinguished themselves in the service of this country; the Officers of the Order in their scarlet cloaks come next, then the Sovereign followed by pages, and finally the Gentlemen at Arms.

After the service we all returned to the castle by car. I used to go with Field-Marshal Montgomery in his Rolls-Royce, driven by the famous Sergeant Parker. One year we suddenly came face to face with the Guards marching back, and Parker was forced to reverse rapidly down the hill, much to the delight of the crowd, one of whom called out " Look, there's Monty in full retreat for a change."

The Gentleman Usher of the Black Rod ceased to be an active member of the Court when Henry VIII moved from Westminster to the Palace of Whitehall. The peers of the day declared that they didn't require anyone to be in charge of their debates ; they were perfectly capable of running them themselves. They were prepared, however, as far as discipline in the House was concerned to submit to the King's representative. Henry VIII nominated the Gentleman Usher of the Black Rod for this task and he was then excused from all his other duties at Court (except attendance at the Garter ceremonies) in order to undertake these additional Parliamentary responsibilities.

In those early days Black Rod had wide responsibilities in the Palace of Westminster, where he lived in considerable state and received a large salary. He travelled to and fro mainly by barge and Black Rod's steps leading down to the Thames still exist, but their only link with their past glories was when Black Rod and his staff embarked in a river-steamer for their annual outing. The office was, however, held by one man for many, many years and towards the end of his long reign certain malpractices crept in. It was therefore decided to hand over the responsibilities for the whole Palace of Westminster, except when the House was actually sitting, to the Lord Great Chamberlain.

Therefore, during the time that their Lordships are in session, Black Rod is responsible to the reigning Sovereign for everything, except the actual business of the House, which takes place on the floor of the House of Lords.

Black Rod and his nineteen doorkeepers, all of whom are retired petty officers or warrant officers from the services, admit all visitors, control the heating, lighting, etc., and handle the actual mechanics of a division—the ringing of the division bell, the locking of the doors and so on, though the responsibility for checking the peers through the division lobbies rests with the Clerks of Parliament. The doorkeepers' main duty, however, is to maintain order both in the strangers' galleries and on the floor of the House itself. During my period of service as Black Rod the only serious interruption came from the late Miss Vivien Leigh, who suddenly jumped up from her seat beside me and protested against the destruction of the St. James's Theatre. She is reputed to have said afterwards that it was the worst audience to which she had ever played, as no one took the slightest notice.

Somewhat surprised, and to be honest a little hurt, as I had taken considerable trouble to find a good seat for this most distinguished lady, I took her by the arm, and led her out of the chamber saying,

" Now you will have to go." A few days afterwards I received a cutting from an American paper. Under the headline " Chief Usher throws out Famous Actress " I read, " When the last Lord sat down Sir Brian turned to Miss Leigh and said, ' Now you have a go ! ' " Surprising what a difference the omission of two words can make.

In the unlikely event of a peer causing a disturbance, it would have been my duty to escort him from the chamber. But before this could happen the Leader of the House would move " That the Noble Lord be no longer heard," on which the House would be required to express an opinion. If the answer was " Content " and the peer still persisted, only then would I be called upon to enter the House with a couple of doorkeepers and remove the offender.

On every Tuesday, Wednesday and Thursday, and sometimes on other days as well if business was heavy, when Parliament was in session, I was to be found clad in court dress, which meant knee-breeches and silk stockings, seated in Black Rod's box, on the west side of the House, just below the bar—therefore, outside the actual House itself. Although I naturally regarded myself as a servant of the House and always complied with the requirements of the House of Lords offices' committee, strictly speaking, as the Sovereign's representative, I came directly under the Lord Chamberlain at St. James's Palace.

From the number of peers, M.P.s, and doorkeepers who approached my box during the course of the afternoon, visitors might well have thought that I wielded some sort of hidden influence on the affairs of their Lordship's House. But things are not always what they seem. Most of them merely required seats for their guests, and there were other reasons quite unconnected with the business of the House. When " Plum " Warner was sitting beside me the latest Test match scores were brought to us every fifteen minutes. The principal door-keeper during my first few years as Black Rod was a keen student of horse racing and as many of their lordships were owners he used to approach me with that particularly knowing look which only the racing fraternity adopt and say, " His Lordship thinks, sir, that so-and-so is a certainty in the 3 p.m. race." Not realising, as I do now, that the worst possible tips always come from owners I used to risk a modest sum each way. At 3.10 p.m. precisely a stately figure in tail-coat and white tie would approach my box, bow, and murmur mournfully, " Not in the first three, sir." He never, as far as I can remember, said anything else.

The standard of debate naturally varied considerably, but some of their Lordships were very witty. During a Debate on Pornographic Literature *Lady Chatterley's Lover* came in for considerable censure. One peer who defended it most gallantly, was asked by a Member of the Opposition whether he would encourage his wife to read it. " Certainly," he replied, " But not my gamekeeper."

On one particular occasion, the Upper House was required to move out in procession, in order of precedence, i.e. Archbishops, Dukes, Marquises, Earls, Viscounts, Bishops and Barons. An old and extremely amusing Liberal peer approached me and said, " Are you responsible for forming us up, Black Rod ? " When I replied, " Yes," he shook his head and said, " You will have to look out for the Barons—they always barge in." Fortunately for me, the Order of Precedence was not attempted, as it was realised in time that the Peers of the Upper House did not take readily to discipline.

What brought me most into prominence, however, were certain quaint, ceremonial duties which have their roots deep in British history, and the most famous of these, I suppose, was in connection with the Royal Commission which is summoned by the Sovereign to signify her Royal Assent to Acts passed by Parliament. Before an Act can become law three things must happen ; it must be passed by the House of Commons ; passed by the House of Lords—though in case of disagreement the Upper Chamber can only delay a bill for one year ; and thirdly it must receive the Royal Assent. Obviously the reigning Sovereigns would not have time to attend in person to give their Assent, so this power is delegated to a commission which usually consists of the Lord Chancellor and two peers who must be privy councillors. The three, clad in their robes, enter the chamber and seat themselves on a bench just behind the woolsack. Meanwhile Black Rod is standing below bar, wearing his chain of office and holding the Black Rod on his shoulder. He wears black gloves. As soon as the commission is ready he advances into the chamber until he is a few feet from the woolsack.

The Lord Chancellor then tells him to summon the Commons to hear the Royal Commission read. After bowing, he withdraws and makes his way down to the House of Commons. In front of him walks the inspector of police and the principal doorkeeper in the House of Lords, who call out at intervals, as they have done no doubt for many years, " Hats off, strangers." In the members' lobby he passes through the House of Commons doorkeepers lined up on either side.

The door to the actual chamber is ajar and peering through a small grille he can see the face of the Serjeant-at-Arms. As he approaches, the Serjeant slams the door in his face. This dates back to 1642 when Charles I tried to arrest five members of Parliament—Hampden, Pym, Holles, Haselrig and Strode. Since then no reigning Sovereign has ever been permitted to enter the House of Commons. On this occasion Black Rod is the Sovereign's representative. He therefore knocks three times with the end of the Black Rod and the door is flung open. The senior doorkeeper of the House of Commons announces, " Black Rod "—who walks up to the table bowing three times. He then most politely summons " This honourable House to attend the House of Peers to hear the Royal Commission read."

The Speaker descends from his chair and, led by the Serjeant-at-Arms carrying the mace, they walk in procession, with the members following two by two behind, up to the bar of the House of Lords. The Royal Assent is still given in Norman French. After the titles of the Bills have been read the Clerk of the Parliaments turns towards the Commons and says " *La Reine le veult* " or, if it is a money bill " *La Reine remercie ses bon Sujets, accepte leur benevolance, et ainsi le veult.*" Until these words have been pronounced it is not a lawful Act. The ceremony of knocking on the door is therefore the outward and visible sign that the House of Commons has the right of freedom of speech and uninterrupted debate.

I carried out these summons for fourteen years but they were always an ordeal. There was a build-up in tension as I walked through the Palace of Westminster until I entered the Chamber of the House of Commons where whoever happened to be speaking at the time sat down. Normally a hush descended. But I never knew quite what to expect. On one occasion when I arrived in the middle of a particularly lively debate I was told, " Go away and come back tomorrow," of which, of course, I took no notice. Another time one of the Bills which was about to receive the Royal Assent happened to be extremely unpopular with the Opposition and my summons was greeted with vociferous cries of, " No, no, no."

The most interesting occasion of all, particularly from a historical point of view, came at the beginning of a new Parliament, when the Speaker standing at the bar of the House of Lords made the historic claim for the " undoubted rights and privileges " of the House of Commons, " freedom of speech in debate, freedom from arrest and free access to Her Majesty whenever the occasion shall require."

This petition dates back to at least 1400 though the form of words has varied ; in fact some Speakers have spoken for upwards of two hours at the bar. In the reign of James I the Commons made it quite clear that this application was a gesture " only of manners "—in fact that the Sovereign was powerless to withhold their rights.

Two or three days later the new session is opened by the Sovereign in person. As this has been described on television I will not attempt to do so now. From my point of view the chief interest lay in the wording of the summons. Once more I was dispatched to fetch the Commons but this time by the Lord Great Chamberlain who had been instructed to do so by the Sovereign seated on the Throne, so the summons was rather more abrupt. It was, in fact, a Royal Command :

> " Mr. Speaker, the Queen commands this honourable House to attend Her Majesty immediately in the House of Peers."

There was one other interesting bit of ceremonial with which I was concerned, namely the introduction of a new peer into the House of Lords. The master of ceremonies on this occasion was Garter King of Arms acting in the name of the Earl Marshal, the Duke of Norfolk, and the new peer was led into the House in the following order : Black Rod, the Earl Marshal, the Lord Great

Chamberlain, Garter King of Arms, the peer himself with a fellow peer as supporter in front and behind. The peers were robed and Garter wore his gold tabard ; so it was a colourful little procession. The ceremony itself was quite complicated because the new peer had to kneel to the Lord Chancellor, bow a number of times, take the oath, sign the roll, and finally, with his two supporters, take off his hat and bow three times running to the Lord Chancellor. Nobody knew why it was three bows. Various explanations have been offered : " the Trinity " or " the union of England, Scotland and Wales ". These were two suggestions, but the real origin is hidden somewhere in the dim past. This introduction ceremony was always rehearsed beforehand and when life peers were first introduced, seven peers and peeresses went through the ceremony in two days. Garter King of Arms and I worked out afterwards that in the course of the proceedings we had bowed no fewer than 395 times.

I was often asked whether the introduction of life peeresses had altered the Upper House, once regarded as the last male stronghold in the kingdom. The answer is ' not at all '. The only difference was that during the introduction ceremony peeresses did not remove their very becoming tricorne hats.

Sitting in my box in the House of Lords I often felt rather like a referee at a boxing match, though fortunately the contest there was waged by words and not by blows. I once heard a newly-created peer who had previously been a member of the House of Commons complaining about the undue politeness of our debates : " This place needs pepping up," he said. Wherepon an elderly baron looked at him quizzically and replied : " You must remember that you come from a place where they use the bludgeon. Up here we prefer to use the rapier, but it kills just the same." And in the hands of the really skilled debater it most certainly did kill. There was one very distinguished member of the House of whom it was said that you had no idea at all how devastatingly rude he had been until you read what he said in *Hansard* next day.

In 1949, when I first took up my appointment, the situation in the Upper House was particularly interesting. The Labour Government was busy introducing a programme consisting mainly of nationalisation bills. Yet the House of Lords contained a large Conservative majority to whom all these bills were anathema. Each could in turn have been thrown out without any difficulty at all, thus imposing at least a year's delay on the Government legislation. But to do this would have been fatal. It is precisely because of this overwhelming Conservative majority that very naturally the Labour party has always viewed the Upper House with grave suspicion, and it would obviously have been quite wrong for a chamber composed mainly of hereditary peers to try and impose its will on the Government elected by the people. Luckily there were very wise and experienced politicians in charge—Lord Addison, Labour, on the Government side, Lord Salisbury, the leader of the Opposition, and Lord Samuel, the head of the small Liberal party. Salisbury and Addison were bitter opponents across the floor of the House, yet behind the scenes they had a great respect for each other's point of view. And this I found was the atmosphere which permeated the whole place. I was once lunching with some Labour peers before the introduction into the Lords of a distinguished member of their party from the Commons. His daughter opened the proceedings by saying brightly, " Of course I don't approve of the House of Lords at all ". The two Labour peers turned and smote her hip and thigh. They ended by saying : " When you know a little more about it, young lady, you will realise how small a part party politics plays up here. We are concerned entirely with doing the best we can for the country."

CHAPTER XXIII

I STRAY FROM THE STRAIGHT AND NARROW PATH

THROUGHOUT HIS life my father had been fond of games and the open air as his chief relaxation from unremitting work, and he looked forward to his retired life, continuing as editor of the R.A.M.C. *Journal*, writing, reading and working with his microscope. In 1923 he became seriously ill and was taken into Millbank Hospital for a major operation from which he never really recovered, being left with an internal infection which caused him a lot of trouble. During the last eighteen years of his life the things he loved were taken from him, one by one. His outdoor activities were reduced gradually to a minimum ; even bending over his microscope gave him a good deal of pain and had to be given up. But he never uttered one word of complaint. When something had to go, he looked for something else to take its place. He was an immense reader and edited the R.A.M.C. *Journal* to the day of his death. In fact he never allowed his physical condition to beat him. Unfortunately my father died during the war when I was a brigadier. If only he could have lived a little longer until I was a corps commander he would have realised that all his self-sacrifices and unstinting devotion to his most unsatisfactory son had not been in vain.

This example was his final gesture to me. Almost precisely the same thing has happened in my life. Owing to the after-effects of the wound which I sustained in North Africa I have also been forced to give up practically all those outdoor activities which had filled so much of my life. I can no longer ride, play golf or even go for long walks, but like him I have been fortunate to find an outlet for my surplus energy in other and more sedentary occupations.

I was extremely fortunate to be appointed Black Rod and for the first year or two I was completely absorbed by this strange new world of politics which I could now observe from a ring-side seat, but gradually my innate restlessness began to reassert itself. The truth of the matter was that I had too good a staff to help me. They were men of great experience, who did not require constant supervision from their boss. Their task was not so easy as it might sound because they had to know when and how to break the rules. A too rigid adherence to the myriad regulations which controlled the activities of the Upper House could be very irritating for the peers and their guests. With such an expert team to help me, once I had learned the ropes, my day-to-day duties became less and less arduous.

My first tentative steps away from the straight and narrow path trod by my many distinguished predecessors came as a result of a visit made to the battlefields of N.W. Europe in 1950 with the rather vague idea of one day writing a book. By the kindness of the British Embassy in The Hague my wife and I were able to hire cheaply a motor launch in which to explore the waterways of Holland. The boat was in the care of a very nice and extremely expert young Dutchman. We set off from Rotterdam and each night we moored to the bank in the vicinity of some village. The Red Ensign seemed to be immensely popular in those days and we were always being invited on board some barge or other for a glass of schnapps or bols. I had never before seen one of those large continental barges, which form the permanent home of the bargee, his wife and numerous family, and I was staggered at the comfort in which they lived. Staircases with carpets, electric light, running water, push and pull lavatories, large, comfortable beds and so on. I have been in many a house which wasn't nearly so roomy and well furnished. Nor so clean ; they were always spotless and gaily painted.

As I wanted to revisit Rees, which had caused us so much trouble during the Rhine crossing, we tried to penetrate a few miles over the Dutch frontier into Germany. Although my wife and I both had passports with the correct visa our Dutch skipper only had his identity card. I explained patiently to a young and insufferably conceited British official of the Control Commission that we should certainly not spend more than three hours inside Germany and on no account would the Dutchman land anywhere, but it was all useless.

I was once more up against officialdom at its most dense. " My deah General," he said, " you must remember that the war has now been over for some time." I was so angry that we almost capsized as I swung round at full speed in too tight a circle and set off back into Holland again.

On approaching Nijmegen we saw crowds manning the river banks. Then into view steamed majestically a large, white yacht. On the bridge was standing a small figure reminiscent of the pictures of Napoleon. At a respectful distance in rear stood a group of senior and much be-ribboned staff officers from the three services. Suddenly I realised that it was Monty, and the crowd were there to welcome the man who had been responsible for liberating their town. What a curious coincidence ! The last time that I had seen Monty in Nijmegen was just after the unhappy battle of Arnhem.

When the yacht tied up I saw the burgomaster and councillors going aboard. As I was wearing a dark-blue sweater, a pair of dirty grey flannel trousers, no socks and an old pair of rubber-soled shoes, I was improperly clad for this high level party. So I waited until the introductions were over and then, pushing my way past an understandably suspicious Dutch sentry, I confronted my late commander on the bridge. His astonishment at this unexpected appearance of his erstwhile corps commander, looking like a scruffy tramp, was not unnatural ! It appeared that he had been carrying out a personal reconnaissance of our frontier with the Russians. It was as a result of this incident that I wrote my first newspaper article which was published by the *Daily Dispatch*, Manchester; and so started a long, and from my point of view, very happy association with Kemsley (now Thomson) Newspapers. But the *Daily Dispatch* is no more, neither is another paper for which I wrote several articles, *Picture Post*.

I have thoroughly enjoyed my amateurish attempts at journalism, though writing is probably more difficult for me than it is for most people owing to my extremely inadequate education. It is an exciting world and though all journalists are prone to duodenal ulcers and die young, I have never met one who would be anything else. They have always been very helpful and kind to me, an elderly General whose intrusion into their highly specialized world they might easily have resented. I was lucky of course to be guided by that remarkable man, C. D. Hamilton, now Chairman and Editor-in-Chief, Times Newspapers Ltd., who on one occasion, when I was tearing my hair over some article for the *Sunday Times* which simply would not come right, looked at me sadly and said: "Whatever you do, General, don't try and write English." I have never had the slightest difficulty in following this excellent advice. Thanks to this connection with the Press I managed to keep much more up-to-date than would have been possible as a retired general-cum-Black Rod. I spent several weeks with the French and Spanish Armies, visited the Canal Zone of Egypt at the height of the troubles, saw the Israeli Army at work and paid many visits to the British Army of the Rhine and S.H.A.P.E.

The most interesting trip of all, however, was a visit to Cyprus where I stayed with Field-Marshal Sir John Harding at the time when he was holding a series of discussions with Archbishop Makarios. This, however, very nearly proved my undoing. I found it quite impossible to write about Cyprus without also commenting on the political background. The article which I cabled to London included two-thirds military material and one-third political, but owing to the inevitable shortage of space it had to be drastically cut. The final result which appeared on the front page of the *Sunday Times*, "from our special correspondent in Cyprus, Lieut.-General Sir Brian Horrocks," was two-thirds political and one-third military. When I first saw it at the airport near Rome, on my way home, I realised that I was in for trouble, because at all costs Black Rod must avoid becoming involved in political controversy. My worst fears were realised and quite naturally certain peers took grave exception to what I had written. After this I tried hard to avoid anything which faintly bordered on politics.

I never imagined that at one time I would become a fairly regular contributor to that pillar of British journalism, the *Sunday Times*. How astounded my teachers would have been if they could have seen London plastered with posters bearing my face and adjuring the British public to read a series of articles which I was then writing for that paper. Their astonishment, however, would not have been greater than my own. I had no idea that an advertising campaign of this magnitude had been launched so it came as a shock on my return to London from our holiday to be faced suddenly in Victoria Street by a huge poster of myself. I have never felt so embarrassed in my life.

One day a young woman arrived in my office. Her name was Therese Denny and she worked for the Australian Broadcasting Corporation. Almost before I realised what was happening I found myself sitting in the cellar of a B.B.C. building in Oxford Street prepared to broadcast to Australia on the historical background of the office of Black Rod. This was my first introduction to that peculiar instrument of torture, the microphone, which was to play such an important part in my life from then on. When we had finished our fifteen minute broadcast, Miss Denny, apparently deeply moved, said : " That is the best broadcast we have ever recorded ". I was delighted ; but my feeling of complacency was quickly dispelled when I compared notes with some of her other victims who had also broadcast to Australia. We had all succumbed to precisely the same treatment. As far as I can remember Miss Denny had no appointment—yet she arrived in my office. I had no intention of broadcasting—yet I was very soon confronted with a live mike. And what is more I thoroughly enjoyed the whole proceeding.

Since those early days when I was her victim I have benefited considerably from her astonishing ability to get things done, as with Huw Wheldon she produced my " Men of Action " series on television.

B.B.C. sound studios are always divided into two. In one half sits the victim who is to make the broadcast, gazing uneasily at a microphone perched in the middle of the table in front of him, and trying to watch out of the corner of his eye a series of green and red light signals which indicate the timings, when to start, if he is going too slowly, when he is approaching the end and so on—which is all very frightening. These are controlled by the producer who is in the other half of the room separated from his victim by a soundproof glass panel. With the producer are usually several other people ; an engineer who controls the volume, secretaries with stopwatches to check the timings with the script, and any other members of the B.B.C. staff who happen to be interested in the programme.

During my first broadcast in this country on the Home Service I found myself to start with in the second compartment watching and listening to Wynford Vaughan Thomas interviewing a distinguished member of the Farmers' Union on the thorny subject of the military acquiring too much land for training purposes in Wales. I was to put the army point of view during the next interview. The farmer had prepared a long script which he had obviously tried out on his wife and had every intention of delivering in toto. Not by the flicker of an eyelid did Vaughan Thomas show that he was bored stiff, but the producer in our compartment was showing signs of approaching apoplexy. " My God ! Cut, cut, cut," he kept on saying. Listening to the unsuspecting farmer I thus learned two important lessons of broadcasting :

1. The subject matter must be tailored to the time available, and the more it is tightened the better it will sound over the air.

2. Broadcasting, and lecturing to an audience, require entirely different techniques. It's no good attempting to deliver an oration into a mike in Broadcasting House because the recipient is one person sitting in a chair in his or her room. Wynford treated the mike as though it were his wife with whom he was having a quiet, pleasant discussion. The farmer was rallying an immense audience to do battle with the hated military. There was no doubt who carried the most conviction on the air.

Thanks to the B.B.C. I have been privileged to broadcast the unveiling of war memorials in many countries, and have thus had the opportunity to appreciate the remarkable work which has been carried out since the war by the Imperial War Graves Commission. No future generation will ever be able to point a finger at *us* and say that we neglected to care for the dead of the last two world wars. The cemeteries where they lie are not grim burial grounds but places of beauty, bright with flowers and carefully tended green lawns, very often with trees around them. The atmosphere of peace and tranquillity which pervades all the war cemeteries must surely have brought comfort to the thousands and thousands of parents and relations who have visited them all over the world.

I have been to many. Each has its special niche in history.

Cassino in Italy with the famous monastery towering above it. Bayeux, the first French town to be liberated. Groesbeck in Holland, gazing across the valley to Germany and the sinister Reichswald, where so much bitter fighting took place. Dunkirk, which was unveiled by Queen Elizabeth the Queen Mother, and afterwards, from the deck of a destroyer, she laid a wreath on the sea in memory of the little ships which evacuated our army from Dunkirk and its neighbouring beaches. And finally Brookwood in the heart of the United Kingdom where the whole Royal Family were present for the unveiling. The British Commonwealth may now rest content in the knowledge that these men, and women too, who died in our defence lie in honoured graves.

Though sound broadcasting is intensely interesting, television now began to fascinate me more and more. So, greatly daring, I penetrated the inner keep of that immense television centre which was rising slowly and majestically in Wood Lane, and had a talk to Cecil McGivern and Leonard Miall. The former was the presiding genius of all B.B.C. television, the corps commander who fought the tactical battle on the TV Front, and Leonard Miall was one of his subordinate commanders, the controller of TV talks. I used to think that the last war was a pretty merciless affair but I soon found that it was child's play compared to the ferocious conflict waged day in and day out between the B.B.C. and the independent television companies. I have deliberately used military terms in connection with TV because the whole business with its split-second timings, accuracy, team work and discipline, is the nearest approach to battle which I have met since retiring from the army. The only major difference is that appearing on the TV screen is much more frightening than commanding a corps in any battle.

All this, however, is going much too fast. I came down to the television centre to try and persuade the presiding genius that many ex-servicemen and their wives would be interested in an account on TV of some of the more important battles which were fought during the last war. I did not realise then that, at the age of sixty, I was venturing into something which would have a major effect on my whole life. After a most hilarious interview—I cannot understand why we laughed so much, but we did—they decided to take a chance, and I was booked to do a series of fifteen-minute programmes called " Men in Battle." Initially these were put on at 10.45 p.m. when most sensible people are on their way to bed, the object being perhaps to hurry them up. Though nobody said so I was left in no doubt that unless I convinced my expert critics that these programmes were really worthwhile, their duration would be short. I shall always be indebted to these two men for having the courage to allow an ancient general to try and sell the craft of war on the screen.

I very soon found that this TV business which I had entered into so light-heartedly was a far more difficult medium than sound. The people who handled it, producers, cameramen, artists, studio managers, make-up girls, were all very different too. They were younger and very enthusiastic. It was impossible to enter that funny old rabbit warren, Lime Grove, without becoming aware that the whole place was full of atmosphere and teeming with energy. My first shock was to find that it takes forty people full-time to put one person on the air.

What makes TV so difficult is the sinister influence of the camera, and that awful feeling of being absolutely alone in a huge, bare studio filled with nothing but machinery. I found it difficult to get used to the brilliance of the arc lamps directed on me alone while all round were cameras and microphones mounted on things called dollys which enabled them to move about in every direction. During a performance they were rarely still. I have already likened TV to a battle, but I soon found that I was no longer the general but the front-line soldier who had to go over the top. The commander was the producer—originally Huw Wheldon and then Therese Denny—sitting somewhere out of my sight, in a room full of monitor television sets and surrounded by the chief staff officers concerned with sound, light, and cameras, to mention the three most important. All the men who were operating the dollys on the floor of the studio were wearing ear-phones and from her box Therese controlled their movements like a commander on a battle-field. This must be a nerve-racking job because the producer can make or mar the programme ; no theatrical producer exerts such a personal minute to minute control of the performance as does his confrère in the TV studio.

Baron, successor to Maxie

The end of the lane. Emsworth harbour at low tide

The camera is the lynchpin of the whole performance because ultimately success or failure depends on what appears on the screens in millions of homes all over the country. It is all too easy to become mesmerised by the camera. Some people lecture it, some are frightened of it, others hate it, but the wise man treats it as a friend—just a friendly old camera—and talks to it accordingly. There are many pitfalls for the unwary, as I found to my cost, and the unforgiveable sin is to talk to the wrong camera. When sitting at the table I had to talk to camera A ; if I went to the map, to camera B, or if I was explaining something on the model, camera C would take over, and woe betide me if I didn't always move my hands the same way from left to right, or vice versa, so that the camera could follow them. One added difficulty was the use of film. Very often I used pieces of film to illustrate some part of the talk and these had to be " cued " into the programme at exactly the right moment.

Because of all these complications it might be thought that there were many hours of rehearsal but this was not so. Studios are always scarce and when in use they cost a lot of money, so rehearsals are cut to the minimum. If I were due to appear at 9.30 p.m. I probably arrived at Lime Grove at 7 p.m., by which time the cameras had been lined up and the lighting, maps and model, etc. adjusted in accordance with the producer's instructions. I was lucky if I got more than two runs through before zero hour. I have heard that while on the stage an opera singer must surrender herself entirely to the conductor. The performer on TV does the same but in this case the camera is the master ; no performer is a free agent. I realised very soon that, the whole business being so complicated, if I wished to give a smooth, relaxed performance I must be clear in my mind about what I was going to say and do. Otherwise it is only too easy to be thrown out of your stride by the myriad distractions of the studio. I also felt that, if from the remoteness of the studio, I was to establish personal contact with the unseen audience in their homes I must be able to talk to them the whole time, which ruled out the use of a script. Every time a performer looks down from the camera, even for a split second, he breaks that personal contact with the viewers which is so difficult to establish. Their automatic reaction is " Oh, he's looking at his notes," which distracts their minds from the story which he is trying to tell. So I always made it a rule to do without notes though I kept a few headings by me just in case I got a black-out.

The preparation of a programme involved much hard work. After hours and hours of research I started by writing out everything I wanted to say, and then timed myself. As a rule the first script lasted for anything up to an hour or more ; then started the process of ruthless cutting in order to reduce it to approximately twenty-five minutes. I used to hate doing this ; now I know that the tighter the script the better it is. Then came the conference with McWatt who was an expert at maps ; followed by numerous visits with the producer to small cinema theatres in order to view the existing film, and select the bits which we wished to use. These were then cut and tailored by the film editor who worked in the Ealing studios.

When this had been completed I tried the programme out on the most non-military minds I could find, to ensure that, in the extremely unlikely event of Mum wanting to watch the programme, she would understand what I was talking about. Some unsuspecting B.B.C. secretaries were usually selected as guinea pigs, and if there was some military detail which they did not understand I altered it until they did. The next problem was to rehearse the wretched thing in my mind. Most of this was done while walking round the parks with my boxer dog Maxie. He was the only person in the world who heard every word of every programme. I regarded it as highly significant if at any stage in my recital he lay down and went to sleep.

By now the two producers, Huw and Therese, would have approved the general pattern and we all met at Ealing or at some small studio in Soho. Everyone who had anything to do with the production was present and I tried a complete run through. I always enjoyed these trial trips because after a time the others managed to forget that I was an old general and accepted me as one of themselves. In the middle of the day we had a break and if at Ealing we all lunched together in the canteen, surrounded as like as not by a large number of people in period costume from some play which was being shot in a neighbouring studio. Ultimately the great day approached and the first jerk to my self-confidence was the arrival of the *Radio Times*. My programme looked so professional in black-and-white surrounded by all those well-known television personalities who were also appearing that night. I became acutely aware of my amateur status. The worst time of all was when I appeared on the cover of the *Radio Times*. Nobody had told me that this was going to happen and the first I knew of it was when I looked down on a bookstall and to my horror found I was looking at myself. I returned home a chastened man.

On the previous day I carefully avoided watching TV in case I should run into my own trailer. On the actual day I always woke up with a pleasant feeling of excitement. It was all rather fun, but this soon disappeared and from breakfast onwards my spirits sank rapidly until by the evening I wished that the bottom would drop out of the floor. I was acutely nervous, far more so than before any battle. I arrived at Lime Grove to be met with an atmosphere of forced heartiness. Everyone looked at me as though I was about to undergo a surgical operation, which indeed I was. How I envied all those sensible, old, retired generals who were slowly digging themselves to death all over the country. I found no consolation in the fact that it was entirely my own fault.

I was introduced to the studio manager who controlled all the operations on the floor of the studio ; from then on he or she was my only contact with the outside world and I looked anxiously to see if he or she had a kind face. Like everyone else they wore ear-phones through which they received the producer's instructions, often, I suspected, highly explosive. As I sat in my brightly illuminated corner all the rest of the studio seemed relatively dark and the cameras became more and more like Quatermass's fearful insects.

" General, Therese would like a complete rehearsal, please "—and off we went. At the end I gazed rather anxiously at the shapes behind the cameras and wondered whether they had liked it or not, because by now, having been through the script so often, the whole thing seemed complete nonsense to me. I then heard a clatter above and saw Huw, the chief consultant, descending from his box to have a few words with the victim on the operating table. The hospital atmosphere was heightened still further by the fact that he had now assumed his best bedside manner. " General, it won't hurt nearly as much as you think." He was accompanied by a young woman who looked suspiciously like a nursing sister, but who turned out to be the make-up queen on duty for my programme, faced with the impossible task of making me look like a successful general. The more she could make me resemble the Iron Duke the better the audience would be pleased, at least that was the theory. I was only once really coated with make-up and that was when I was suffering from 'flu and looked ghastly. After the programme I received many letters from friends saying how glad they were to see me looking so well.

One more rehearsal and zero hour approached. By then I could not remember a single word of my script, except for the opening sentences which, from experience, I knew must come out absolutely automatically. There were murmurs from the outside world. The previous programme was early, late, or on time. I heard the studio manager's voice saying "Silence in studio." Curious light signals appeared on the walls. "Sound on," "Vision on," an unseen band struck up the signature tune, a camera was shooting the title on my right, but I was watching the studio manager like a hypnotised rabbit. He dropped his arm—and I was on the air. Nobody could help me then ; it had become a personal matter between me and several million viewers. I have been told that my peak figure was eight and a half million viewers, but I found it difficult to visualise what even one million people looked like and anyhow what were a few million more or less ? After the first few sentences I forgot the viewers altogether ; my world was limited to one camera.

And then almost before I knew it all was over. The tension in the studio dropped. Huw and Therese had returned to normal. "Bang on, General," meant a reasonable performance. A brief word of thanks to the studio manager, cameramen and technicians on the floor, without whom the programme could not have been produced at all, and then a much needed whisky and soda. I felt exactly like a deflated balloon with no sense of achievement at all. On the night after the programme I found it difficult to sleep and it took twenty-four hours to unwind.

I have already said that television began to alter my life. This was not because of the programmes themselves but because of the aftermath. First of all there were the letters. I never ceased to be astonished by the number of people who took the trouble to write, and I tried to answer them all myself because the great majority came from men who served with me in the war, or their wives, and I enjoyed their letters very much. The tone, of course, varied considerably. The most complimentary I ever had came in a short newspaper article from Canada where my "Epic Battle" programmes had recently appeared. It was quite brief. "Let us hope the commercials (Canadian equivalent) do not get hold of this old boy. I reckon he could sell a collar to a giraffe."

At the other end of the scale I must quote two, both from women. The first said, "You annoy me so much that every time you appear I throw an orange at the television set." I thought this was a healthy reaction, much better than switching off. The second writer was more personal. "Dear General, you are a thug, waiting for the next war in order to increase the salad bowl (medals) on your chest. I suppose you spend your time licking the shoes of old Granny Churchill. Wait till we get in and you will both be out on your necks." I regarded it as highly complimentary even to be considered alongside that old warrior-statesman.

The sad thing about these letters is that a few came from people who were obviously mentally ill. Some were so filthy that even after years of barrack-room language I felt sick when I read them. Others consisted of pages and pages with no logical meaning at all.

The second and most disturbing effect of television was the personal approach. I appeared on TV only from time to time, say every month or six weeks. I have a theory that it is fatal to be seen on the screen too often, particularly in specialised programmes like mine. But even so, after a time many people recognized me in the street, in buses, in the tube and, above all, in shops. This was extremely flattering, and I don't pretend that I didn't enjoy it, but it can also be embarrassing. Presumably because I, so to speak, appeared inside people's homes they all felt they knew me personally and did not hesitate to come up and talk about the programme. Everyone liked or disliked something different. At one time I could not travel in the tube between Sloane Square and Westminster without at least two people speaking to me. I cannot imagine what life must be like for the popular television personalities who appear regularly. I have heard it said that it is almost impossible for them to travel by public transport at all and I can well believe it.

My best moment came when my car was held up in a traffic jam at Reading. A man with a brief case emerged from a house and set off down the road. Before he had gone more than a few yards, a boy ran out of the same house and called after him, " Don't be late tonight, Dad, Horrocks is on ! "

So I had really gone astray from the straight and narrow Black Rod path; amateur journalist, sound broadcaster and TV performer. It says much for the broadmindedness of their lordships that they bore with me at all.

CHAPTER XXIV

ANOTHER WORLD

IN THE early part of 1963 I suddenly realised that I was getting very stale, which was not surprising, as I had held the office of Black Rod for 14 years. I could hardly bear the thought of having to put on fancy dress—knee breeches, silk stockings, etc., at least three times a week. Somehow, in this nuclear age, dressing up for duty seemed all wrong. So I began to contemplate retirement. Then, once again the Goddess of Good Fortune took a hand in my life. Looking back, it is astonishing how often this has happened. The troops have a saying, "If you wish to succeed in the Army you must be at the right place at the right time and your face must fit." I cannot think of anyone to whom this has applied more often than to me.

It so happened that, in the spring of 1963, I was returning from one of my trips abroad, where I had gone for the *Sunday Times*, when a friend of ours, Neville Vincent, a barrister and a most charming man, offered to drive my wife to London Airport to meet me. This drive, though of course I did not know anything about it at the time, marked a further milestone in my life. Neville asked Nancy whether I would like to become a director in a largish group of building contractors called Bovis, of which his brother, Harry Vincent, was Chairman.

"Why don't you ask him?" she said, "I know that he is getting bored with being Black Rod." The idea of course fascinated me, but before accepting, I wanted to find out something about this completely strange tough building and property world. So I engaged the services of an architect and then of a quantity surveyor, and asked them to tell me about their professions, and describe a little how a building site functioned. No mention was made of Bovis, but I had found an advertisement with the name BOVIS in large letters at the top, and as casually as possible I pulled this out and asked each of them in turn whether they knew anything about this company, as the name was new to me. It appeared that Bovis was a largish group of companies, playing in the top half of the second division of the construction league. But both my instructors thought highly of them, and each used the word for which I had been seeking—" Integrity". All the Bovis Companies were apparently noted for this ; so I made up my mind. Having met and liked the other directors, I gratefully accepted their offer, and resigned my appointment as Black Rod.

My first introduction to the Group en masse before I actually joined them was the Annual Dinner of the " Guv'nors' Club," at which most of the directors, site agents, foremen (in building circles the foreman is always known as " The Guv'nor ") and some important clients were present. It was a most impressive gathering and the Chairman, Harry Vincent, seemed to know personally each of the several hundred foremen who were present. I soon discovered that this was really the hub of the whole Group. Directors become Associate Members automatically, but the real Guv'nors are the site agents and foremen who have to be elected by their fellows, and must have had at least ten years' experience of work on the site. As might be imagined, they were a remarkable body of men, with a great pride in their Company. The atmosphere reminded me of the Sergeants' Mess in a first-class regiment. Fortunately, a high proportion had served with me during the last war, and, as I was to find out later on, this, plus the fact that I had appeared fairly often on what is commonly known as " the lunatic box," proved an invaluable link between us when I visited their sites.

The Group at that time consisted of four main companies: Bovis, Gilbert-Ash, Yeomans and Constructional Units. I also realised, even before I had joined, them that Bovis was very much a family firm and that this was one of the main reasons why the Group was so successful. The longer I have been with them the more I have realised that the Top Brass really cares about their subordinates. Let me give just two examples: when the Conservatives were in opposition, Sir Keith Joseph, whose father was an ex-Lord Mayor of London, and one of the original founders of

Everyone involved in my Television series The Peace Keepers, *the last programme made by T.W.W. in their Bristol studios before Harlech took over*

Editor and Publisher: Leo Cooper, the originator and now the publisher of the Famous Regiments *series*

With Frank Sanderson, the then Chairman and Managing Director of Bovis Ltd

Presenting the Eisenhower Papers to the British Museum. Sir John Wolfenden is on my left

On a visit to the M3 motor way near Bagshot, built by Bovis Construction

Launching the Texaco "Free Badges" commercial

Bovis, became Vice Chairman of the Group. He was no novice at building as, like his cousin Harry, he had worked in his youth on building sites, and knew quite a lot about the different trades involved. Everyone was delighted to get him back, and it was astonishing how quickly his influence was felt throughout the whole Group. In addition to his technical knowledge, he is an expert on finance, a very nice man of complete integrity, and works harder than anybody I have ever met. I have even seen him dictating letters while going down in the lift.

One day after a Board Meeting, he drove me down to Whitehall. I was on the way to the Ministry of Defence in connection with one of my television programmes. He, I presumed, was going to the House of Commons, but when I asked him, he looked rather embarrassed and said " no "—that he was driving down to Kent. Further questioning, which on looking back I now realise was most impertinent on my part, elucidated the fact that he was going to have tea with a Mrs. X—the widow of a foreman who had just died. " I am not happy about her financial position," he said, " So I want to see what we can do to help her." To my mind this is what makes the business tick.

Far too many chairmen and directors spend most of their time in centrally heated offices, tended by highly efficient secretaries and, I am afraid, completely out of touch with their employees working on the factory floor or on the building sites, but not so in Bovis.

Just one more example will suffice. A couple of years ago, a very well-known foreman decided to build a bungalow for himself in Somerset not far from where I live, to which he would ultimately retire, but he died before it was completed. Within 48 hours his widow was visited by the Company Secretary and a financial expert, to advise her about her pension, and how best to invest her capital, etc. The Company—Gilbert-Ash, for whom the foreman had worked for many years—was instructed to complete the bungalow without any cost to her. A little later I visited her, and found that she was very lonely, which is not surprising, in an isolated country village : she wanted to go to a little house she had heard of in a London suburb near her friends. I rang up the nearest branch of our Housing Division, which was in Gloucester. They handled the sale, etc., without it costing her a penny, and she is now happily settled in her new home. A plaque, commemorating her husband, was erected in the precinct of Bath University, the last job on which he had been engaged.

So one day in August, 1963, I found myself in a modern office on the tenth floor of a large building in London, containing the headquarters of the Bovis Construction Companies operating throughout the British Isles. I had just been appointed a Director on the Holdings Board, the summit of the whole Group.

From my window I could see for many miles right over London, and around me was all the panoply of the modern business world—external and internal telephones, cabinets for holding secret documents, and a large, somewhat awe-inspiring desk on which was a bell-push to summon my highly competent secretary from her room just down the corridor.

This was my first experience of the business world and it was all very different from the dark Victorian-type rooms which I had inhabited on the ground floor of the Palace of Westminster, or indeed, from the many headquarters I had occupied in war and peace during my time in the Army. The only familiar and comforting sight was my wife's abstract paintings hanging on the wall in front of me.

Had I been very stupid to retire from my previous historic position and enter the tough, competitive, business world, particularly this type of business, compared to which, I had been told, jungle warfare was a parlour game?

I could just imagine the caustic comments coming from the able, hardworking young men in the corridors below, " Relative to General Blimp," " Bull," " Barrack Squares," " Jobs for the Boys," and " What does he know about building ? " And of course they were quite right.

This was the problem. Had I, as a result of my previous experience, any contribution to make towards this thriving company ? Because if not, having a lively conscience about these things, then at the end of twelve months I would be off, and I made this perfectly clear when I was appointed.

I felt strange and rather lonely on that August morning but

luckily my military training came to my aid. I had been through this sort of experience—new job, critical subordinates, and so on—many times before and particularly during the war. After all, I had been faced by a far worse situation than this when in August, 1942, I had been sent for by Montgomery, who had just assumed command of the VIIIth Army in the Middle East, to fly out to the desert and take over XIII Corps.

Then again in April, 1943, when I was despatched from the VIIIth Army to take over command of IX Corps in the Ist Army in North Africa for the attack on Tunis. My reception was anything but cordial. There was intense rivalry between the Ist and VIIIth Armies and the mere sight of my desert camouflaged car was enough to make those Ist Army warriors spit with rage.

So I was quite used to unpopularity. On both these occasions I had assembled my staff, explained the reason for my arrival, " Anyhow," I went on, " I am probably not as bad as I look ; here I am and you had better make the best of me."

Then of course I had been the commander. Now, as I was only a director, I obviously could not employ such drastic steps as those but I could at least do my best to get to know as many as possible of those working in the headquarters and learn something about their jobs. So the first week of business life was spent going round the offices and talking to their occupants. Whether or not they took a better or worse view of me after my visit I do not know.

Remembering my Army experience I had always been brought up on the principle that when faced with any problem the first thing to get clear is always, " What is our object ? " As I went round I put this question to many people and got a variety of answers. " To increase dividends ", " Construct better buildings ", " To build on time", and so on.

None of these quite satisfied me and then suddenly it became clear, " Our object, surely, was to enable the man on the site to give the best possible service to the client." This was obviously an over-simplification, but it proved a more-than-useful peg on which to hang decisions. Anything which did not contribute to this object must be regarded with considerable suspicion. Another simple question which in the past I had been taught to ask myself in relation to tactical training was, " If we were not doing this now, would we start it tomorrow ? " I don't believe that directors ask themselves this question sufficiently often in the business world.

During the war it had been my practice to spend at least 90 per cent of my time visiting front line units—smelling the battlefield, I used to call it. In the Construction Industry, the front line is the building site, so I made a practice of visiting as many of these as possible every week. In this way, I got to know the lynch pins of the building business, those remarkable people, the site agents or general foremen. Woe betide anyone who walks round a site without first calling on " The Guv'nor ". It was quite extraordinary how many of them, and of the key personnel who worked under them, had served with me during the last war.

I shall never forget a visit which we paid to a new store which the Company was building in the West Country. On arrival, the Contract Manager told me that the foreman had served under me in the War and he had twelve other men on the site who had done likewise. He had collected them, and would I have a word with them, which I did. Then I saw in the background a man whose face I thought I knew so I went up to him, shook him by the hand and said, " I think we have met somewhere." He looked at me piercingly, and replied, " Yes, Guv'nor, you used to work for Marks and Spencer." I was delighted, because it was really a great compliment ; if he had only known, my shirt and underclothes all came from this famous store.

Marks & Spencer have had a great influence on Bovis, and oddly enough I got to know the Company fairly well. When Sir Simon Marks was made a peer he came into my room in the House of Lords, sat down in the armchair and said, " Now, you have been here for some time. Can you give me any advice about speaking in the House of Lords ? " I looked at him with considerable admiration. No other peer had ever asked me this, but obviously I was fairly experienced, having been there for such a long time. So I said, " Yes, may I give you three rules ? 1, If you intend to speak, get here early and place yourself under a microphone, because otherwise nobody will hear what you say. 2. Don't speak for longer than ten minutes, because that is about the limit for anyone to hold their attention. 3. Know your subject, because there are bound to be a number of people present who have spent their lives doing what you are talking about, and you will certainly be cross-examined expertly afterwards." "Thank you very much," he said, and departed. During his first speech, he complied with all three points. I had previously got seats for all his fellow directors of Marks & Spencer and it was a very successful initial debut in the House of Lords. I got to know him fairly well, and found that Bovis had built or enlarged practically every Marks & Spencer store in the country, and there is no doubt that this has had a profound effect on the Company. Lord Marks always insisted that his staff should be able to leave the shop and go straight to a dance. I was staggered at the first-class arrangements which were made for all the Marks & Spencer employees—rest rooms, canteens, spotlessly clean hairdressing saloons for the girls, and so on. He insisted that similar facilities should be made available for everyone working in a Marks & Spencer building, and this applied also to the builder. The normal building site, to my mind, is a disgrace to the latter half of the twentieth century. On all too many, practically nothing is done for the men at all. Bovis, on the other hand, influenced by Marks & Spencer, have good offices, lavatories, canteens and, above all, drying rooms for all the men. There is no doubt that this has had a profound effect thoughout the group. I was visiting a Marks & Spencer store in the Midlands, and the foreman told me that on arrival he was informed that there was no skilled labour available in the neighbourhood at all. Within a week he had all he wanted because the conditions were far better than on any normal building site. Moreover, the standard of work required from the men was very high and skilled men appreciate this. Marks & Spencer give a wonderful service to the public, but they can only do this if all the people who supply them and build for them are equally skilful. So this relationship which has existed for many years now has been of great benefit to the Bovis Group.

I think I can say that, as far as the people in the industy were concerned, my previous military experience probably helped me considerably, but my confidence suffered a severe setback at the first board meeting when the vast financial implications were being discussed. Compared to most of the other directors I was a child groping in the dark, because this is something which the Army does not teach its commanders—in fact, in war it is rather the reverse, because the military dividend is victory in battle won with the minimum loss of life. This was particularly so in the Second World War as many of us generals had experienced the appalling losses of 1914–18.

I was always prepared to use a hammer to crack a nut—in fact, to expend tons of ammunition to save one human life. Looked at from the strictly business point of view " my overheads were often far too high."

Although I was supposed to be retired, having been invalided out of the army, I found myself extremely busy, because, in addition to Bovis, I accepted an invitation to become President of the Electronic Rentals Association (now renamed National Television Rental Association). This consists of all the major firms which rent television sets; in addition to monthly meetings, it was our responsibility to protect the interests of the different companies, which involved heading deputations to Ministers or their senior Civil Servants, and keeping Members of Parliament informed about the effect of legislation on our rental activities. In the early days I was probably of some assistance, because, having been Black Rod for so long, I knew most of the M.Ps fairly well but many new faces have appeared in Parliament during the past ten years, and any influence which I might have had has now become so small that my active conscience has, as usual, come into play, and I regretfully resigned the Presidency early in 1973. I was sad to go because, over the years, I had got to know and admire these able, hard-working men: we had fought successfully many battles together, on behalf of rental, which I am convinced is the only sensible way to watch television.

At this time, I was also involved with a number of Service Charities, such as St Dunstan's, The Forces Help Society, The Stoll Foundation and, above all, the Queen Alexandra Hospital Home for Disabled Sailors, Soldiers and Airmen at Gifford House, near Worthing, where many paralysed men have been on their backs since they were young soldiers in the 1914-18 war. I have come to the conclusion that suffering brings out the best in people. Gifford House is the happiest place I have ever been to, and I always came away a very humble man.

St Dunstan's is the same. On one occasion, when I was Black Rod Lord Fraser asked me to take a party of blind and deaf St Dunstaners round the Palace of Westminster. " There is no need to worry," he said, " They will each have a companion who will pass on to them what you say by deaf and dumb language on their hands. All you have to do is to speak more slowly than usual." I had taken many parties round the Lords and Commons, but this was something special and I gave it considerable thought. The actual Chamber of the Upper House in which the Debates take place is, of course, sacrosanct when the House was not sitting; visitors walked through under the eagle eyes of the law, but that was all which was permitted. When I arrived there with my St Dunstaners I went up to the policeman who of course I knew well and said, " Please lock the doors and don't let anyone come in until I say so, as things are going to happen here which you must not see." He did as I asked and the stream of visitors stopped.

Then I turned to my party and said, " Now we will have a Debate. You sit on the woolsack as the Lord Chancellor. You are the Leader of the Government and opposite you will be the Leader of the Opposition." Then I started a Debate. They were splendid and needed very little encouragement. I knew, of course, that all the time visitors were building up like a flood tide outside the door, so after about five minutes I collected them, and said, " Today you have done something which, as far as I know, has never been done before." They were delighted and turned out to be one of the cheeriest and most interested groups I have ever had the privilege of taking round the House of Lords.

As I was still at intervals producing television programmes on battles, Commanders, Castles, etc., almost the first task I was given was to make a short film about Bovis—the original Company in the Group. Without going into technical details, this Company is quite unique in that it never tenders for work, but is paid a fee depending on the size of the contract, and thus becomes the client's own building firm for the duration of the job, with all the advantages which accrue from such a personal relationship. This Fee System has become almost a religion with many of the young men who work in Bovis, and I have been told over and over again that, if the Directors ever decide to do away with The Fee System they will leave the Company.

A firm called Derrick Stewart Productions was engaged. They almost lived with Bovis and went round numerous sites. Eventually they produced for me a highly imaginative and clever script, backed by some excellent coloured cartoons. It was called *The Right Knight* and the story was based on a King of olden times who always lost his battles because he employed the wrong Knights to fight for him—presumably other Building Companies. Eventually, a friendly monarch introduced him to "The Right Knight" who curiously enough fought his battles in the Bovis Fee manner and was always successful.

This film became rather an agony for me because I cannot bear to watch myself on the screen or TV set. It was shown first in London, and then travelled round most of the big towns. A distinguished audience was always invited, and the film was followed as a rule by a cocktail party and discussion. While the audience was watching it, I used to sit morosely in the next room, consuming the strongest drink I could lay my hands on. It must, however, have spread the Bovis gospel more than I thought possible, because their profits have risen steadily over the years.

Although I had changed my job, we still lived in a small house in Caroline Terrace near Sloane Square, and went down to our cottage at Emsworth for the weekend. During the week I travelled a lot because, curiously enough, I was repeating almost exactly what I had been doing as a Corps Commander during the last War, i.e. smelling the battlefield, the only difference being that these battlefields were building sites scattered all over the British Isles. Though I knew very little about the technical side of building I have, in the course of a fairly long life, met many people, and I very soon learned to get the " feel " of a site. Moreover, after a glass of beer and some sandwiches with the foreman in the nearest pub, I came away knowing if and where the shoe pinched.

Now let me turn to my efforts as an author. I remember so well arriving at Collins, the publishers of the original book, to hear whether or not they were prepared to go ahead with *A Full Life*. I was escorted to a room where I found the directors sitting in a portentous circle. It was a somewhat alarming experience, as Generals do not, as a rule, move in the higher intellectual circles. They were, however, very kind, and quickly put me out of my agony. I then said, " May I ask you a question?" They looked surprised, but agreed at once. Whereupon I said, " You have the reputation of selling more copies of a book than any other publisher, if you decide to go to town over it, but you don't go to town over every book. What I would like to know is whether you will go to town over mine, because if not, I might do better with a smaller publisher." There was a roar of laughter and they said, " Yes, General, we *are* going to town over *A Full Life*!" and they most certainly kept their word.

Copies of the book appeared on all the station bookstalls, and in most of the big stores all over England. On the opening day of the Campaign I was standing with the Collins representative in Truslove & Hanson, that famous bookshop in Sloane Street. One counter was completely covered by copies of *A Full Life*, and a huge photograph of my boxer dog, Maxie, adorned the window, but nobody took any notice at all. I became more and more pessimistic. Then suddenly a man strode over, picked up one copy, and took it to an assistant. I then heard, for the first time, the sweetest music in the world, " the tinkle of the cash register."

Most of the big stores agreed to devote an entire window to the book, provided I would go there at a certain time and sign copies. This is a terribly embarrassing performance, because beforehand I always felt certain that no-one would appear, but somehow they always did.

One day, I was sitting at a desk in Bentalls of Kingston, when a woman with a shawl over her head, who had obviously come from cleaning out some office, appeared in front of me with three copies for signature. " This is very flattering," I said, " But why three?" " I want one for my husband, one for my son, and one for myself," she replied. " It is very nice of you " I said, " But I still don't understand."

"We like you on the telly," she replied—such is the power of the lunatic box. I don't suppose they read a single word of any of them.

Unquestionably, the most terrifying performance of all was when I was asked to attend a "Meet the Author" tea at Harrods. I then began to wonder whether I had been wise to encourage Collins to "go to town" over my book. A window in Harrods, however, offers publicity which no author could possibly afford to lose, so one day an extremely anxious General found himself on a platform in the restaurant, confronted by some 150 women, all having tea, and to whom I was expected to give a scintillating account of my life. I couldn't see any men present at all; they obviously had better things to do. I asked the Manager how much he was charging for the tea. He replied that it was a very special tea that day, including Devonshire cream, and it would cost them 5/- a head. "How much would you have charged if I hadn't been speaking?" I asked. "Four and six a head," he replied, which gave me some idea of my true value.

After I had spoken and the Devonshire cream had disappeared I was asked to sign copies. It was certainly an ordeal, but I was consoled by the thought that they sold over 300 copies.

CHAPTER XXV

CONCLUSION

AFTER a couple of years in my new job, life in London began to pall, mainly owing to the noise and the difficulty of parking, so we started looking for a house in the country—if possible, near Bristol, where Bovis and Gilbert-Ash had regional offices. After much searching, we found just what we wanted in Manor Farm, East Compton, one and a half miles south of Shepton Mallet, a typical small, friendly, west country town of considerable antiquity. Shepton Mallet claims to be the second oldest town in Somerset, but its exact origin is uncertain. In Roman times it was probably occupied by the Belgae who had come over from the Continent to raid the south of England. Caesar considered them the bravest people among the Gauls. Subsequently, in about the 6th Century they were displaced by the Anglo-Saxons. Initially, Shepton was a sort of suburb to Pilton and for 400 years it belonged to successive Abbots. Its name was derived from two Saxon words, Scep—a sheep, and Ton—a town. It was chiefly known for its wool which came from large flocks of sheep reared on the downs, then called the Forest of Mendip. Subsequently, the Manor of Shepton passed into the hands of the Malet or Mallet family who, as was customary in those days, added their name to that of the town and it has been called Shepton Mallet ever since. In the Doomsday Book Pilton and Shepton Mallet were valued at £9. In the fifteenth Century many skilled artisans who were driven from France, Belgium and Holland owing to bitter religious persecution, settled in the neighbourhood and taught the local inhabitants their skills as weavers. Soon, West of England cloth, weaved in mills along the Sheppy, became famous throughout Britain but this lucrative trade lasted only until the Industrial Revolution when, alas, it moved to the Midlands.

Shepton is now famous for two things—its prison, and Babycham—the discovery of the Showering family, who have been connected with the town for 300 years. Memories are long in the west country; some four years ago I was invited by Ralph Showering to be the principal Guest at the Annual Dinner of the Shepton Mallet Grammar School. Some 60 people from all over Britain were present, yet this school closed down 30 years ago—truly a remarkable record.

Manor Farm was a small, rather broken down farmhouse, some 300 years old, with plenty of out-buildings and six acres of land. A great deal of work had to be done before we could move in. In fact, a representative of Bovis was so horrified when he saw it first that we were advised to pull it down and start again. Needless to say, we had no intention of doing this. So we sold our house in London, and handed over our cottage at Emsworth to my daughter. Our grandchildren have sailed there happily ever since. A local builder called Scourse was engaged to do the rebuilding. He employed about 20 men, most of whom were highly skilled craftsmen. Bovis, as usual, were very helpful and lent us a Contract Manager called Bob Wooldridge, to keep an eye on the job. We were lucky enough to rent a flat nearby, so that we could keep in touch with what was happening. Bob is now the Head of the Bristol office of Bovis Fee Construction. He has often told me since of his horror when he first heard that he had to hold the hand of a General who was also a member of the Bovis Holdings Board of Directors. As it turned out, we all got on very well together and have remained friends ever since. Whilst Scourse and his men did the actual building under the watchful eye of Bob, my wife, who has a very special eye for houses, was entirely responsible for the design and layout of the building. We used to hold what were called site meetings; Nancy was always placed at the head of the table, and became known as "The Working Foreman." My contribution was to back her up in the things she wanted done. The result is that we now have a house exactly as we want it and the last six years have been among the happiest of my life. We really have the best of both worlds because we live in the depths of the country yet are within five minutes drive of the town.

One of the main reasons for settling in the west was the admiration and affection which I had developed during the war for the 43rd Wessex Division. It had been in my Corps for most of the fighting in Europe, and sure enough since settling in Somerset I have met many of my old wartime friends.

I had imagined that life would be more restful in Somerset than in London, but the reverse was the case; somehow or other I always seem to get myself heavily involved.

East Compton is not a village in the true sense of the word. It has no shop or post office, and consists of six farms only. So very soon I became involved in the farming community. I found my neighbours very friendly people, and it was pointed out to me that two empty grass paddocks were a disgrace. The first year I sold the keep, and then I became the smallest farmer in Somerset. Aided by Austin and Gordon Sims, two of the best known and most successful farmers in the west country, I became the proud owner of four Hereford cross steers. I went with Gordon to purchase them at Gloucester market. This was the first time I had seen a large market in operation, and I was filled with admiration for the highly-skilled organization shown by everyone. Nearly 1,000 cattle were disposed of in approximately four hours. They were weighed, entered the sales arena, were sold by auction, then into a different pen and finally into their new owner's lorry, and off to his farm. There was no confusion and no waste of time. Many a business that I have come across could take a lesson from our farmers.

It gave me a very pleasant feeling to look out of my window and see my own steers grazing in my own fields.

Farmers' Dinners are great occasions. The first which I attended (not in Somerset) had been preceded during the morning by a Farming Conference, at which apparently the man who had been detailed to propose our health had not been able to get his chief grouse off his chest. He was, however, determined to do so at the Dinner. When the moment came he leapt to his feet and said, " It is my privilege to propose the toast of the Guests, which will enable me to say a few words about the feeding of pigs!"—roars of laughter from his audience and from us pigs as well.

The Glastonbury Fat Stock Dinner is probably one of the most famous in South-West England. The Fat Stock prizes are judged beforehand and announced at the Dinner in the evening. We guests and officials sat at a long table which ran the length of the hall, and from this, at right angles, ran a series of tables each occupied by a different farming community. There must have been upwards of 200 farmers present. Suddenly, at a given signal, a man at the end of each of these tables rose to his feet, put on a white coat and left the hall. When I asked what was happening I was told that these men were butchers who had presented a joint to the Dinner and their own joints were then being cooked on a series of stoves in a room outside the hall. Sure enough, in a few minutes they returned, carrying the most enormous joints I have ever seen. Each butcher then carved his own joint for his own table, and this consisted of huge portions with the meat piled high on plates, but this meant nothing to the farmers. Soon, the piles had disappeared and empty plates were being passed down for second helpings. It was a really rural setting, and I came to understand why most of my farmer friends were built more for comfort than for speed. The modern farmer hardly walks a step as the Land-Rover has replaced his horse.

In a way, it was a very romantic setting because, of course, Glastonbury is the very heart and shrine of Somerset. It is dominated by the famous Tor, which can be seen for miles around. The town lies at its foot, and at Chalice Hill nearby St Joseph of Arimathea is said to have buried the Holy Grail of the Last Supper. The Abbey, though now in ruins, is very impressive, as it was here that St Joseph built the little wattled Church which is reputed to have been the first place of Christian worship, not only in England, but in all the world. In the cemetery lies a large, flat stone, which marks the burial place of King Arthur—in Avalon Island, as it was then called. As I gazed round the hall, I felt that many of the farmers present were descended from families who had tended the land round these holy places for hundreds of years.

Since retiring, I had lost almost all contact with the Army, though I had done a series on Television about some of the great Commanders, and this had been produced by three men, Tony Hoyland, Peter Lilley and Ken Morris, who, although independent, worked almost continuously with Television West and Wales, (T.W.W.) in their Bristol studios. Hearing that I now lived in the west country, within 30 to 40 minutes drive from Bristol, they suggested that, under their management, I should do 13 programmes dealing with the operations carried out by our Armed Forces in a Peace Keeping role, since the end of the last War. To my intense astonishment, I found that the Army had been employed in an internal security role on no fewer than fifty separate occasions. The number of troops employed varied between one platoon and the equivalent of a corps.

We called the series, " The Peace Keepers ", and included Campaigns which had been fought in Muscat and Oman, Aden, Malaysia, Borneo and so on. The programme was directed by Ned Kelly, whose chief hobby is climbing the highest mountains he can find. In order to get the real feel of the different operations, I had to interview numerous officers, N.C.Os and men who had taken part and were now stationed in the south of England in Strategic Command. It was thought that these programmes might encourage recruiting, so everything possible was done to help. Fortunately, the Helicopter Training School is located near Farley Wallop. Very often I would travel to and from some camp or headquarters by helicopter, which used to land in one of my fields, pick me up in the morning, much to the interest of my neighbours and then return me in the evening, when my wife had the unenviable task of ensuring that the landing space was clear of cows. It was hard work but great fun, and I was very impressed by the army units which I visited. In my time, nearly all the officers came from the public school class. Some were excellent but others, I am afraid, did not take their profession too seriously. I was delighted to find that this rather stupid snobbery had now disappeared, and all that really counted was efficiency. For instance, the father of one of the best officers I met is a plumber in the Rhondda Valley.

Unfortunately, half way through the Series, T.W.W. lost their contract to Harlech Television, who naturally hated any programme which had been made by their predecessors, so mine, which had appeared at the reasonable hour of 6 p.m. was swiftly relegated to around midnight, when everybody had gone to bed. The final programme in the Series was the last to be made by T.W.W. in the Bristol Studio. When I had finished, I heard Ned Kelly's voice over the air, saying, " Everyone to do with 'The Peace Keepers' in the studio please!" I had forgotten how many people are involved in each programme, and was astonished to see some forty people appear. Numerous photos were then taken, and we all went up to the canteen for a last drink to mark the end of T.W.W. Next day, Harlech had taken their place.

It was about this time that Leo Cooper, then working for the publisher Hamish Hamilton, started producing the "Famous Regiments" Series of books: subsequently, he became a publisher in his own right, and continued the series. I was asked to act as Editor, and write an Introduction to each book, which I gladly agreed to do, because all the Regiments in the British Army were losing their individual identity and were being merged with others. We felt that, as these Regiments disappeared from the Army List, they deserved a better fate than just to be forgotten. Very few people, to my knowledge, have ever read a Regimental History from cover to cover, because they are as a rule monumentally dull. The poor author has been obliged to mention as many names as possible and to include every action carried out by the Regiment, however small. The normal reaction of someone receiving his Regimental History is to look in the Index and then read what has been written about him and his friends before placing the book in some remote corner of his study, where it has remained, covered with dust ever since. Yet these Histories, in the hands of a skilled author, can make fascinating reading.

Leo Cooper has not only found the authors, but has also produced the books very well, and most economically. We have now completed some fifty, and I am proud to have been associated with this unique historical Series, and, what is more, I have learnt a lot about the fascinating role played by the different units of the British Army in the development of our vast Empire.

There were two other minor sideshows which might be of interest. In 1970 I was invited to lunch by Lord Brooke, heir to the Earl of Warwick, who now lives abroad. He asked me to be responsible for the " spoken word " of the Son et Lumiere which he proposed to stage at Warwick Castle during the summer of 1971. I accepted with alacrity, as I had already done a TV Programme about the Castle, entitled "The King Makers" and as the narrator does not appear in person, all I had to do was to read the script out of camera, so very little strain was involved. He invited me to stay for the first night, but fortunately I was otherwise engaged. I say fortunately as I cannot bear the sound of my own voice.

The Second Sideshow was of rather a different nature. From time to time Publicity Firms have approached me with a view to doing Commercials in order to advertise particular products. One, indeed, offered a vast sum, or so it seemed to me, for 50 seconds advertising of a product connected with food. I will say no more, but I will not pretend that this was not a very tempting offer, and a battle now developed inside Horrocks. Financial greed, versus my conscience. I could not help feeling that many of the old soldiers who had served under me in the War might feel rather let down, if the man who had been responsible for their lives for so long suddenly started trying to sell things on television. Had I been in almost any other profession, I would not have hesitated, but as their Leader in battle, I felt that I could not do it. But of course the figure mentioned was not to be sneezed at. Then something happened which helped me to make up my mind. One day, on my way to a meeting of the Television Rental Association, I travelled in a taxi from Paddington to the City where their Headquarters were then located. When I asked the driver how much was the fare, he replied, "Nothing. I could not possibly charge my old Corps Commander." I was, of course, immensely touched, and this finally decided me against the Commercial, so I refused the offer.

So much for the sideshows. My main interest, of course, was Bovis, and I watched happily as our shares steadily increased in value year by year, and a number of additional firms were gradually acquired by the Bovis Group. Then suddenly, our growth accelerated with a bang, and there is no doubt that this was due largely to the influence of certain people at the top. The first was Neville Vincent, whom I mentioned earlier. He agreed, after considerable pressure, to join his brother, Harry, our Chairman, on the Board of Directors. I had not realised till then that he had one of the most brilliant brains of any man I have ever met. His step-daughter once said to me, "It is no good lying to Neville. After I have said one sentence, he knows not only that I am lying, but also why." In addition, he is a man who cares deeply about his fellows, and is an active member of *Amnesty* and *After Care for Prisoners*, to mention only a couple of his activities.

If anyone in the business is worried, or has a problem, however private it may be he will always take it to Neville, who is prepared to spend hours and hours of his precious time, helping others out of their difficulties.

I have always felt that business in this complicated world in which we live depends very largely on the skill of top management. It would be difficult to find three men more capable than Harry Vincent, who was then Chairman—an out-of-doors man who was very welcome on any of our Group sites, and thus kept in touch with the grass roots—Keith Joseph, his cousin, with a brain like lightning, and an expert on Finance, plus Neville Vincent, under whose skilful handling the Bovis Property Division started flourishing exceedingly.

Thanks to Neville, Frank Sanderson joined the Group when Bovis bought his very successful housing business in 1967. Frank Sanderson has since ceased to be Chief Executive of Bovis as a result of disagreements with the Board over management, but in the immensely capable hands of Neville Vincent, the new Chairman, supported by the splendid management of the operating Companies there is no doubt in my mind that Bovis will continue to go from strength to strength.

So much for work, but today any man who leads a well filled life should have a private lane down which he can escape to his other world—preferably as far removed as possible in feeling and tempo from his everyday existence.

For some, the lane leads to a garden, or shelves of books, or a workshop in which absorbed hours can be spent, with wood, tools, glue, nails and screws. The essential thing, I think, is that the lane should lead away from ever ringing telephones, radio, TV, pavements filled with hurrying, elbowing crowds, and roads congested with impatient, hastening drivers. For many years, my lane led down to a quiet water's edge, where a small boat lay at her moorings.

At the age of 61, I attended with my wife a course in Small Boat Sailing, first of all at Bosham, then at Emsworth Sailing School. Thus we found something which occupied all our spare time most happily. I only wished that I had taken it up many years before.

During the lovely summer of 1959, day after day, I sat at the window of our cottage in Emsworth writing the first edition of this book, while the sun shone down outside and in front of me lay the wide expanse of Chichester Harbour, stretching away to Hayling Island, covered with white, blue and yellow sails. I could see my own boat, a 16-ft. Emsworth one design, bobbing about at her moorings. In the early morning, when there was nobody about except the odd cruising boat, taking advantage of the favourable tide, my wife would go off alone in her Gull dinghy for a sail, at what she always said was by far the best time of the day. Eventually, I could stand it no more. I stepped on board, cocked an eye at the weather, felt the wind and cast off.

My little craft turned and headed out into the wider waters of the Harbour. The irritations and frustrations slipped away. The only things that mattered were the pulse of the restless sea coming to me through the tiller, and the chuckle and talk of the water against the sides of the boat.

The enchantment lasted until the westering sun sent me reluctantly, in golden twilight or stormy sunset, back to the shore and the seaward end of the lane which leads to every day.

We gradually acquired a larger keel boat which we named *Ilona*, after our grand-daughter. It was paid for by the proceeds of the first edition of this book, and in it we were able to go further afield.

On moving to Somerset we transferred our aquatic activities to Poole Harbour. For eleven years this sailing enchantment has lasted, but now, alas, I am getting too old, and my last boat was sold in 1972.

My Television career has also ended, as I am beginning to feel it is too much of a strain. But my last appearance on the lunatic box gave me great satisfaction. Curiously enough, it was a Commercial. Two aspects of this particular promotion appealed to me. Texaco decided to give a nicely made regimental badge to everyone buying four gallons of petrol, thus creating another link with the past for those infantry regiments which have lost their identity through amalgamation with others. But more important still, they also offered to present a large sum of money to Army Charities, and I was able to ensure that Gifford House, which I have mentioned before, received a healthy proportion of this sum. It was nice to feel that I could bow out of the television world knowing that the Army, in which I had spent so many happy years, would benefit from my last performance.

However, in spite of my advancing years, life is still full of incident and enjoyment. Who knows, there may yet be a third edition of this book.

INDEX